ELLA
BAKER

ELLA BAKER
Freedom Bound

Joanne Grant

Foreword by Julian Bond

John Wiley & Sons, Inc.

New York • Chichester • Weinheim • Brisbane • Singapore • Toronto

Published by John Wiley & Sons, Inc.
Published simultaneously in Canada.

Library of Congress Cataloging-in-Publication Data:

Grant, Joanne
    Ella Baker : freedom bound / Joanne Grant : foreword by Julian
Bond.
      p.   cm.
    Includes bibliographical references and index.
    ISBN 0-471-02020-6 (cloth : alk. paper)
    1. Baker, Ella, 1903–1986. 2. Afro-Americans—Biography. 3. Afro-
Americans—Civil rights. 4. Civil rights workers—United States—
Biography. 5. Civil rights movements—United States—History—20th
century. I. Title.
E185.97.B214G72   1998
323'.092—dc21
[B]   97-33034

Printed in the United States of America.

10 9 8 7 6 5 4 3 2 1

*To all of her children, too numerous
to name, but you all know who you are,
and especially to Reginald Robinson,
to Ella's grandniece, Carolyn,
and to my son, Mark Rabinowitz*

"Ella's Song"

We who believe in freedom cannot rest
We who believe in freedom cannot rest
      until it comes

Until the killing of Black men,
      Black mothers' sons
Is as important as the killing of White men,
      White mothers' sons

That which touches me most is that I had a
      chance to work with people
Passing on to others, that which was
      passed on to me

To me young people come first, they have
      the courage where we fail
And if I can but shed some light, as they
      carry us through the gate

The older I get the better I know that the
      secret of my going on
Is when the reins are in the hand of the
      young, who dare to run against the storm

Not needing to clutch for power, not needing
      the light just to shine on me
I need to be one in the number, as we stand
      against tyranny

Struggling myself don't mean a whole lot,
      I've come to realize
That teaching others to stand up and fight is
      the only way my struggle survives

I'm a woman who speaks in a voice and I
      must be heard
At times I can be quite difficult, I'll bow
      to no man's word

Composed and performed by Bernice Johnson Reagon for the film *Fundi: The Story of Ella Baker,* © Songtalk Publishing Company.

Contents

Acknowledgments

There are many, many people who should be thanked for their perseverance, their help, their willingness to put up with my persistent phone calls and queries. I am particularly grateful to those who granted me interviews. I know that all who participated in the creation of this book did so to honor Ella Baker, and I honor them. I especially thank Jacqueline Brockington, Ella Baker's niece, for her friendship and for her helpfulness, above and beyond the call of duty. Jackie, when speaking to me, always referred to her Aunt Ella as "your girlfriend." I liked that. Jackie has contributed more than one could ever hope for in the creation of this book. She has always been there for me and for Aunt Ella and has helped to the extent of her resources to make this biography as accurate as possible.

Ella Baker's close friend, Lenora Taitt Magubane, has been most helpful in recalling high points of Baker's life, as have other friends: Lee Simpson, Frances Johnson, Estelle Noble, Jack O'Dell, the Reverend Fred L. Shuttlesworth, Percy Sutton, Anne Braden, and a host of SNCC people. Among those are Julian Bond, Judy Richardson, Courtlandt Cox, Doris Derby, Ivanhoe Donaldson, Marion Barry, Eleanor Holmes Norton, Charles "Chuck" McDew, Dion Diamond, Robert Moses, Janet Jamott, Vincent Harding, Joyce Ladner, Dorie Ladner, Rep. John Lewis, Reginald Robinson, Avon Rollins, James Forman, William Strickland, Michael Thelwell, Dorothy Zellner—some of whom have not been quoted in this book, but all of whom have enriched it.

I wish also to thank the many archivists and librarians who have been there when needed: the staff at the Mugar Library at Boston

University, at the Yale University Library, and at the National Archives. Particularly I thank the librarians at the Library of Congress, with special thanks to archivist Joe Sullivan for his help in ferreting out the relevant NAACP files on Ella Baker. I also wish to acknowledge the help I received from Dr. John Bracey, NAACP scholar extraordinaire.

I am most grateful to the Schomburg Center for Research in Black Culture, the New York Public Library for bestowing on me a one-year term as scholar-in-residence, and wish to especially thank Diana Lachatanere and Aisha Al-Adawiya, both of whom responded to calls for help long after my tenure. I am also indebted to Howard Dodson, the chief of the Schomburg Center, for his deep interest in the project. Special thanks are due to Dr. Hyman Lewis and Dr. Arnold Rampersad, the guiding lights of the resident scholars program.

I am unfailingly astonished at the helpfulness of librarians. They seem to be, in the Ella Baker tradition, dedicated to a "life of service." They enjoy helping. I found helpful shortcuts when I talked with several librarians, especially Peggy A. Haile of the Sargeant Memorial Room, Norfolk Public Library. Dr. John Fleming, and Robena Bradley and Brian Cumberbatch of Shaw University, were most helpful in providing records of Ella Baker's time in college.

Ella Baker's relatives and friends in Littleton, North Carolina, gave glimpses of small-town Southern life. Dempsey Faulcon, the caretaker of Baker's Littleton house, was a gracious host and guide. My thanks to my researchers: Bess Rattray, Peter Hobbs, Renah Feldman, Betsy Esch, Yonni Chapman, Faye Goodman, and David Maynard, who produced last-minute miracles, and to Ana Ramos, Susan Ruddick, and my sister, Jean Hubbard, who transcribed taped interviews. I am most grateful to Elaine Delott Baker, Jewell Gresham, Casey Hayden, and Mary King for combing their files for documents, and special thanks to Betty Garman Robinson and Constance Curry for putting me up and putting up with me, and copying needed documents. And thanks to Judy Richardson for transcribing her shorthand minutes, to Lynn Lane for sharing her expertise, to Kathryn Dobkin for her keen ear, and to Charles and Barbara Foxx, who helped find the old streets of Norfolk.

Recognition of the important role which artists' colonies have played in the completion of this book is of prime importance. I wish to thank the Virginia Center for the Creative Arts for its steadfast support of my work. The VCCA has been a haven for me. Not least among the positive attributes of a stay at VCCA is the sharing of works-in-progress with others in the process of beginning or completing a work. I wish also to thank the Berkshire Forum and Blue Mountain Center.

For encouragement and critical readings of parts or all of the manuscript and providing helpful comments, I owe a debt of gratitude to: Nora Chase, Mary Clemmy, Blanche Wiesen Cooke, Christopher Cory, Clare Coss, Hyman Lewis, Claire Reed, Helen Rattray, Patricia Sullivan, and John J. Simon, who, well known for his grasp of history and his phenomenal memory, was consistently available to answer factual questions. But let me add here that neither he nor anyone else herein named is responsible for any errors of fact or mistaken judgments. The author takes full responsibility.

The input of the biography seminar of which I am a member, Women Writing Women's Lives, co-sponsored by the Center for the Humanities and the Women's Studies Center of the City University of New York, has been of inestimable value. The support and expertise conveyed have been of no mean aid and encouragement. My thanks to Charles Payne, the sociologist, and Howard Zinn, the historian, for careful reading and valuable comments. My profound thanks to my husband, Victor Rabinowitz, who read and reread, made incisive critiques, and suffered the intrusion into our living room of papers, files, and books. Thanks also to our son, Mark, for his support and willingness to adjust to my distraction.

Finally, I extend my deep gratitude to my agent, Carol Mann, and my sincere admiration to my editor, Hana Umlauf Lane, whose patience has been enduring and whose pencil, unerringly wondrous.

Foreword

I first met Miss Ella Baker in 1960. I was 20; she was in her late fifties. She worked for Martin Luther King, Jr. I was active in Atlanta's sit-in movement against segregated lunch counters.

I used "Miss" advisedly then and now; properly, it should have been "Mrs.," and later, for others, it became "Ella," but her demeanor always seemed to demand the formal "Miss" from me. There was about her something pleasingly prim and benignly schoolmarmish, formal but not rigid, proper but not proud or arrogant. This propriety was coupled with warmth and an inviting openness. She was approachable. She challenged my ideas without assuming the superiority of hers. My ideas could be as worthwhile as hers, but—an important but—I would have to prove I could think mine through.

She was what she appeared to be—a middle-aged black woman about whom we knew nothing but who had an amazing store of experiences and contacts to guide the young militants of the Student Nonviolent Coordinating Committee (SNCC).

Except for those students of civil rights history, most have not heard more of Ella Baker. She is both one of thousands of anonymous women and men who made the twentieth-century movement for expanded democracy work, and among the most extraordinary members of that group. It is time for a larger audience to meet her, and thanks to Joanne Grant, they will.

This book is part of a welcome new trend in civil rights historiography: history written from the bottom up rather than the top down; history that's about the people who made the movements that made great men, rather than simply about great men themselves. These new histories focus on the movement for civil rights with a magnifying glass and bring its personalities and events into sharper focus.

Ella Baker's career intersected with the major figures of the modern-day labor, civil rights, and peace and economic justice crusades. Her image isn't seen in photographs leading celebrated marches, but rather recalled as the behind-the-scenes organizer of the demonstration. Newspaper clippings from the mainstream press didn't record her speeches; you read Ella Baker's words in the *Southern Patriot,* the *Amsterdam News,* the *Atlanta World,* and the *Birmingham News.*

Grant's diligent search through the archives of major civil rights organizations—the National Association for the Advancement of Colored People (NAACP), the Southern Christian Leadership Conference (SCLC), and SNCC—reveals that Baker helped create SCLC and SNCC and tried to democratize the NAACP.

But Baker also created or worked with uncelebrated groups, most of them small, which provided financial and political support or the intellectual underpinning for the larger, more familiar movements or organizations. Her circle of collaborators was enormous, a virtual who's who of civil rights history and progressive politics.

Through it all, as Joanne Grant reminds us, Baker sought to help ordinary people rise to extraordinary heights and to make their own decisions.

She had mixed success.

Inside the NAACP, Baker was never able to convince the New York headquarters to listen to the voices of members in the field. In SNCC, by contrast, our unofficial slogan—"do what the people say do"—could have been written by Ella Baker. Her deep suspicion of the personality cult that grew around King was sadly validated when his organization neared collapse after his death.

But she did manage to touch the lives of thousands, ingraining her suspicion of hierarchies and her faith in democracy—always with a lower-case "d."

For my generation, she was mentor and model—she set a high standard for commitment to the movement.

In these pages, Joanne Grant sets a high standard for exploring the life and contributions of a remarkable figure of twentieth-century American history.

—Julian Bond

Julian Bond is a Distinguished Visiting Professor in the School of Government at American University and a lecturer in history at the University of Virginia.

The Life of Ella J. Baker: A Chronology

December 13, 1903: Born in Norfolk, Virginia

1911: Moves from Norfolk to Littleton, North Carolina

1918–27: Attends secondary school and college at Shaw University, Raleigh, North Carolina

1927: Moves to New York City and works as a waitress.

1929–31: Works on the editorial staff of the *American West Indian News* and *Negro National News*

1931: Serves as executive director of the Young Negroes' Cooperative League (YNCL) and is active in the consumer cooperative movement

1934: Joins staff of the 135th Street Branch of the New York Public Library

1935: Serves as publicity director of the Sponsoring Committee of the National Negro Congress (NNC)

1936: Works as a teacher with the Works Progress Administration (WPA)

1937: Becomes assistant project supervisor of the WPA

1941: Joins the National Association for the Advancement of Colored People (NAACP) as Field Secretary

1943: Becomes Director of Branches, NAACP

1946: Joins staff of the New York Urban League

1947: Joins staff of the New York Cancer Society

1955: Helps found In Friendship, a support group for Southern school desegregation and the Montgomery, Alabama, bus boycott

1957: Helps establish the Southern Christian Leadership Conference (SCLC)

1958: Moves to Atlanta, Georgia, to set up the SCLC

1960: Is a prime mover in founding the Student Nonviolent Coordinating Committee (SNCC), and serves as Human Relations Consultant to the National Student YWCA

1963: Becomes consultant to the Southern Conference Educational Fund (SCEF)

1964: Heads Washington, DC, and Atlantic City, New Jersey, offices of the Mississippi Freedom Democratic Party (MFDP)

1965–68: Acts as consultant to the executive council of the Episcopal Church

1971: Becomes associate director of the Coalition of Concerned Black Americans

1972: Elected vice-chair of the Mass Party Organizing Committee and board member of the Puerto Rican Solidarity Committee

1974: Gives major speech for Puerto Rican Solidarity Committee, Madison Square Garden, New York City

1979: Is honored with 75th birthday celebration at the Carnegie Endowment for Peace, New York City

1981: Attends premiere of *Fundi: The Story of Ella Baker,* a documentary about her life, in Washington, DC

1985: Receives honorary doctorate from City College of New York

December 13, 1986: Dies in New York City

Introduction

THERE WAS A TIME when I did not know Ella Baker. But that was a long time ago. Somehow she has permeated me and I feel a need to say. Her stories of her childhood and of her growing up have been with me for years and years. Oft repeated. They seem to now be coming out of my skin. I almost know Grandpa Ross, that aristocratic, very black man who paid five dollars an acre to the former plantation owner for a parcel of land on which he had been a slave. And he parceled out these acres to his relatives. I cannot say that Grandpa lives within me, but almost, almost. I can see him sitting behind his horse, Paul, with Ella sitting beside him as they ride the country roads to church. And I can see little Miss Ella sitting up there in the pulpit with her feet sticking out to face the congregation. And Mama, horrified!

Mama Baker. Straight and tall and no-nonsense. She is strict and upright. Not without love, but without a show of emotion. There were certain standards. Of elocution, of behavior, of sharing, of caring. But letting a child sit in the visiting minister's seat was unconscionable. Yet Grandpa's choice was what held. It could not be challenged, even by Mama. Mama accepted that defeat.

And then there was Aunt Carrie. And Uncle Carter and innumerable relatives who shared the extended family plantation. I know Aunt Lizzie who sang wild songs in the woods and I know Grandma who refused to marry the man of the mistress's choice. She is one of my heroes. For she was then banished from the big house to the fields for insubordination.

1

The extended family settled on the land of the former plantation and some of them live there still. When I visited the church which Grandpa built, I felt the pulse of the sense of community, the sharing atmosphere in which Ella Baker was reared. I walked the path that little Ella took from Grandpa's house to the church. I attended services at the church Grandpa built. But it was when I saw the copper beech that I could envision the young Ella swinging there. A tranquil childhood with undercurrents of, perhaps some guilt about Papa and his forebears. The emphasis was on Mama and her father. They seemed to be more powerful.

Out of this comes Ella Josephine Baker. A dignified and awesome figure who, when I met her, had just set in motion a revolutionary movement which would change the face of the nation. For her it was important that the students who had shocked the world by sitting in at lunch counters in the segregated Southland and been arrested in droves should band together to share information on activities, goals, and tactics.

For Ella Baker, this was the time. The time for which she had been waiting, waiting for years.

Baker had come out of a family tradition of rebellion and now it was to come to fruition.

Traversing the path of Ella Baker's lifework has taken me on a long, invigorating, exciting, stimulating, inspiring way. It has not been a lonesome trek, since in some sense she has always been there sitting at my side. Sorting it all out, trying to make a pattern and crystallizing a life, has been difficult but rewarding.

Baker was a significant personage, the figure always present. Her lifework was one of rebellion, though sometimes she recognized the need for compromise. She gathered strength, courage, and determination from her slave forebears and applied the lessons she gained from her experience to the vagaries of the movement that she was involved in.

Essentially, she was a radical. She came out of a family that rebelled against the status quo, and she carried on the family tradition. But she was not against; she was for. She was for the participation of people in whatever affected their lives. She was for the best in all of us.

Ella Baker's family came out of slavery, and that fact lived with her. She grew up with grandparents and other family members who had been slaves. That is a difficult thing for people in the late twentieth century to grasp. What must it have been like to know that your immediate forebears were forced to work in servitude? How did one adjust to the idea that one's loved ones had submitted to such degradation?

Ella Baker concentrated on the acts of rebellion that she found in her family's background. It was with great pride that she looked back on the days of her family heritage.

But she came to revel in the glorious time of the 1960s. That was when she saw the possibility of creating a new society: the beloved community, created by a band of brothers and sisters in a circle of trust. It was an inspiring time for Baker.

In the mid-twentieth century, she was not the only pioneering woman fighting for civil rights. But only a few stand out as she does, among them Septima Clark and Anne Braden. None of these three sought out headlines. Each had a lasting impact. And significantly, they were coworkers and friends. The interaction of people was of paramount importance to Ella Baker.

I have tried to chronicle the story of one person's impact on her times, but she would not have accepted that as the whole story. She never forgot the role played by Harry Moore and his wife, Harriette, who were killed in their beds by a Ku Klux Klan bomb in 1951; or Emmett Till, the teenager brutally murdered in Money, Mississippi, in 1953; or Medgar Evers, gunned down in his driveway on June 11, 1963; or Ralph Featherstone, the young SNCC worker killed by a car bomb in Cambridge, Maryland, in 1970. She never forgot the many who gave their lives or the work of countless others who miraculously survived the frightening time of the 1940s through the 1960s.

The story of Ella Baker begins in the last century. She came from a long line of strong women: her mother, Georgianna; her grandmother, Betsy; her aunts, Lizzie and Carrie. There were strong men, too: her grandfather, Mitchell Ross, who forged a community life for them, and Uncle Alpheus, who stood tall amid the people. She carried these legacies with her into the race discord of the twentieth century.

I met Ella Baker in Atlanta at the founding conference of the Student Nonviolent Coordinating Committee in October 1960. Our association as coworkers and friends lasted until her death in December 1986. I made a film about her in 1981, *Fundi: The Story of Ella Baker,* but that did not seem to be enough, and so this book. She needs to be explained, to be honored, to be learned from and followed. Ella Baker was not a media figure, but her influence can be measured by the fact that there are now institutes, lecture series, and training centers across the country that bear her name. I cannot list them all since they keep springing up, but these are a few that I know: the Ella Baker Intern Program of the Center for Constitutional Rights in New York (the first); the Harvard Divinity School's Ella J. Baker and Amzie Moore Memorial Lecture Series; the Azuzu Christian Community's Ella J. Baker House in Dorchester, Massachusetts; the University of Michigan's Ella Baker–Nelson Mandela Center for Anti-Racist Education; the Children's Defense Fund's Ella Baker Child Policy and Training Institute at the former Alex Haley farm in Clinton, Tennessee; and the New York City Board of Education designated an elementary school in the Julia Richman Education Complex as the Ella Baker School.

Though she did not want to be a teacher, in fact, she became one—not in the institutional sense but as an organizer and nurturer of future activists. She even taught Dr. Martin Luther King Jr. a thing or two—despite his resistance—by insistently nudging him to reach out to ordinary people. King saw the need to mobilize the masses, but he did not understand the need to organize them. Baker did her best to try to turn him into an organizer.

Her dignity won her a measure of respect from the ministers of the Southern Christian Leadership Conference (SCLC), who balked at taking advice, let alone direction, from a woman. The respect that she garnered from young people was exemplified by the way they addressed her: as Miss Baker. Only one of the students called her anything remotely like her first name. He was Charles McDew, who claimed that he knew a secret about her name and called her Miss Jo Ella. In fact, she had not been named Jo Ella but Ella Josephine. Another movement activist, Dorothy Burlage, recalled one time when she unthinkingly addressed her as "Ella," and then she was so embarrassed that she apologized for using her first name. Miss Baker immediately soothed her, saying, "That's all right. You know instinctively when the time has come when you can call me Ella."

This was Miss Baker, a dignified personage, a gifted woman who emerged from the rural environment in which she was reared and from which she gained her strength, and who in a significant way challenged the racial and economic barriers that faced her African American comrades.

Her life story needs to be told. The role of women in the movement has not been fully delineated. But perhaps more importantly, Baker's ideas about how to organize need to be in the forum: we need to discuss them. Baker was blanked out by the media, and so we have little record of her words and deeds. She avoided the press because she believed that the creation of organizations that would fight for change required dedicated work, not headlines. In fact, she felt that the media spotlight could halt, alter, detract from the organizing effort.

She believed strongly in the importance of organizing people to formulate their own questions, to define their own problems, and to find their own solutions, and throughout her life she worked to set masses of people in motion. She was primarily responsible for the establishment of the Southern Christian Leadership Conference, the organization that grew out of the Montgomery bus boycott of 1955–1956, but her most significant contribution to the civil rights struggle was SNCC—the Student Nonviolent Coordinating Committee, the cutting edge of the 1960s movement for civil rights. She is also an important figure because she constantly fought to make the voice of the ordinary person heard. She held firmly to the concept of group-centered leadership rather than a leadership-centered group, and grappled with the civil rights leaders of her day to make this paramount. Though she struggled unsuccessfully for this precept in the NAACP and the SCLC, she eventually succeeded in SNCC, which organized local groups accordingly.

Baker is well known within the civil rights movement, and should be more recognized outside it. During the past few years, undergraduate and graduate students have been discovering her and making a study of her lifework. For this I cheer.

CHAPTER ONE

Roots of Rebellion

[In] my grandpa's community there was this sense of indepen-
dence. . . . When they were beginning to permit the Negroes to
vote after Emancipation, he and his sons got into quite a battle
with somebody who called him "nigger." You see, they would fight
back. Now, whether this was good or bad . . . it provided you with
a sense of your own worth and you weren't brow-beaten.

THE COPPER BEECH FILTERED the sunlight speckling the small girl on the swing. Flashes of light and shade danced off her white cotton dress and twinkled in her braids. She was singing to herself, to the birds, to the tree itself. Perhaps to God.

Guide my feet while I run this race.
Guide my feet while I run this race.
Guide my feet while I run this race.
So I won't have to run this race in vain.

She was alone. Having a fine time. Not looking after her sister Maggie or her brother Curtis. Just by herself under her tree. It wasn't often that she got the chance to swing there by herself. And she thought of the times when she got to be alone with Grandpa Ross and Grandpa's horse, Paul. Paul wouldn't let any other horse pass him, and Ella and Grandpa chuckled as Paul let out so as not to be overtaken by anyone else.

Grandpa Ross had a special relationship with his granddaughter, whom he called Grand Lady. She thought he found her special because she liked to engage in conversation. Grandpa enjoyed the

Grandfather Mitchell Ross. (From: *Fundi: The Story of Ella Baker.*)

talks, and thought his granddaughter should be shown off, so he put her in the pulpit. Mama Baker did not, definitely did not, approve of her daughter sitting in the pulpit with skinny legs sticking out in front of the congregation. But Grandpa did. Grandpa was the founder of the church, the Roanoke Chapel Baptist Church, and what he said was law. So Miss Ella sat in the pulpit in the chair that Mama said should be designated for the visiting preacher.

For Ella the trips to the church were glorious, as were the visits to parishioners or even to the post office. She and Grandpa had the whole world to themselves. On these trips he would tell her about slavery days, about what it had been like to be a slave.

"You know," he said, "that the master wanted your grand-mother to marry Uncle Carter?" "You mean, instead of you?" interrupted Ella. "Um hum," said Grandpa. "But, why?" "Because he

Ella Baker's grandmother, Betsy Ross. (From: *Fundi: The Story of Ella Baker.*)

was the right color. But you know what? Your grandmother just plain refused, and you know what? The massa, whose wife wanted your grandma whipped, just said no. So they put her out of the house; she was a housemaid. They put her into the field. But the master would not let her be whipped. No, sir. You know why? 'Cause she was his daughter. And that's why the missus wanted to punish her. Because she was the master's daughter. But anyways, that's how I got you."

Grandma Ross went out to the fields. As the story goes, she plowed all day, and when there were social occasions, she danced all night to demonstrate her unbroken spirit.

For Ella Baker this spoke of rebellion, particularly because it delineated the color lines: The mistress wanted the lighter skin tones to be perpetuated, but Ella Baker's forebears said no.

Ella Baker's grandmother, Betsy Ross, with a grandchild. (Courtesy of Jacqueline Brockington.)

This is one of the stories with which Ella Baker grew up. She never ceased telling it, and she told it with great relish, because Uncle Carter, her grandmother's intended, was a light-skinned man and her grandpa was very dark. Ella Baker termed this the Dark Side of the Marriage.

After her grandfather's death, Ella asked a neighbor if he would be her godfather. When he asked why, she replied, "Because you are so nice and black like my grandfather." He agreed, but Mama said no, that as a Baptist she did not have a godfather, and most certainly she could not have a Presbyterian one.

There were other heroes in her family's past whose stories became a part of Ella's fiber. She remembered Uncle Alpheus as being nearly seven feet tall. Uncle Alpheus was second in command on the plantation under the white overseer. He and the overseer had been in the business of siphoning off some grain, selling it, and sharing the profit. In a dispute over how much money was due to Alpheus, the overseer shot him. According to Ella, as Uncle Alpheus lay wounded, he told the master: "If that had been you who shot me, Master, I would have died right away. I wouldn't die for that damned poor white man." Uncle Alpheus was not about to die from a mere overseer's bullet. While she told the story with great relish, Ella acknowledged that Alpheus's words might be considered Tomming. Yet what it does indicate is the independence that the family felt. Uncle Alpheus did not think the proposed settlement was fair. He argued, and then turned his back on the overseer; the overseer shot him as he started to walk away. (Incidentally, the typist who transcribed the tapes in which this tale was related transliterated Uncle Alpheus into Uncle Al Fierce, which I rather liked.)

Aunt "Stracted" Mary was another rebel. She used to go to the fields to chop cotton, and when she felt she had done enough she would leave the fields and fake a rampage. No one restrained her because she was distracted, or crazy.

Family stories proliferated, partially because the extended family was large. Shortly after Emancipation, Grandpa Mitchell Ross purchased part of the old plantation in Elams, Warren County,

North Carolina. In 1872, he and four other relatives purchased 250 acres,[1] which were parceled out to family members, thus creating the extended family enclave in which Ella grew up. Ross also deeded land to the church,[2] the Roanoke Chapel, of which he was pastor. On several occasions he put up acreage as collateral for loans, using the money to feed people in the community whose crops had been damaged by a flood or other natural disaster.[3] Ella's maternal aunts, uncles, and cousins lived on the shores of the Roanoke River, which bordered the fertile land. From this extended family she learned the values that would sustain her throughout her life: a sense of community and a deep-felt recognition of the importance of sharing. Baker often emphasized the importance of sharing food with anyone in need, white or black, pointing out that the sharing of food related to the sharing of ideas and hopes. "If you share your food with people, you share your lives with people," she would say. That is what she cared about. It was her credo.

ELLA BAKER WAS BORN on December 13, 1903, in Norfolk, Virginia. Only nine years earlier, Norfolk became the first U.S. city to switch from horse-drawn trolleys to electric cars. At the turn of the century the city had a population of under 50,000; 43.5 percent were black. Bordered by the Chesapeake Bay and the mighty Elizabeth River and invaded by many smaller rivers and creeks, the city was once a quagmire of muddy flats and stagnant pools. But by 1900 many streets had been built on fill and were passable except after heavy rains, when flooding was the norm.

Norfolk was one of the country's busy deep-sea ports. On December 17, 1903, a bill was introduced in the U.S. Senate to deepen Norfolk's channel by 35 feet so that it could float the largest of warships. Previously the port had been host to any number of four-masted barks and paddle wheelers. That same day, the Wright brothers lofted their plane above the North Carolina coast, less than a hundred miles away. These events marked the birth of the air age and the birth of a major port. Then as now, one could watch men and women tonging oysters with an instrument that looked like two rakes tied together.

Ella's parents, Georgianna Ross Baker and Blake Baker, had married in 1895 and immediately moved to Norfolk where Blake was already settled. Blake's job as a waiter on a ferry took him from Norfolk to Washington and back in 24-hour stints, so he was home every other day. Ella remembered him as being warm and caring. He would lift the children in his arms and take them on his lap, which her mother would never do. In later years she did not call up many memories of her father, but she married a quiet, warm, self-effacing man much like Blake Baker.

Ella did not see much of her paternal grandparents, Teemer and Margaret, who lived about twenty miles away from Elams, but she often visited Aunt Eliza, Blake's sister, on her large farm nearby. Ella said that the bone structure of Aunt Eliza and her father reflected their Cherokee background. Ella spoke of her father in almost apologetic tones, trying to summon an image of a fighter, such as her maternal forebears seemed to be. She often mentioned the time when Blake became incensed when an acquaintance said that he was "free issue"—born of free parents. To him it was insulting to be thought of as not having slave forebears.

Her admiration for him showed in the way she described the difference between the way her mother and her father related to the children. Papa always made sure that the children went to the circus: this seemed to be totally outside Mama's list of priorities. "He was the one you would depend on to take you to the zoo. Even though he came in and had maybe just a few hours in the city . . . you would expect him to come and sleep, but if the circus was in town he saw to it that we went to the circus."[4] Papa took them on other outings as well: to Uncle Peter's farm in Campostella, a ferry ride across the river, where they reveled in the number of farm animals Uncle Peter had: cows and a bull, pigs and horses.

Georgianna, who was called Anna, had forsaken school teaching to raise a family. The Bakers first lived on Norfolk's Chapel Street but later moved to 38 Lee Street (the corner of Lexington and O'Keefe)

Grandparents, Margaret and Teemer Baker. (From: *Fundi: The Story of Ella Baker.*)

in the neighborhood known as Huntersville. The two-story house must have been quite large, as it accommodated Blake and Georgianna, the three children—Curtis, Ella, and baby Maggie—and two boarders, Fred and Chester A. Williams. Ella remembered a house with substantial furniture, silver, and good china.

Anna took in boarders, but also kept up with her major calling, ministering to the poor. The family was relatively prosperous, having milk and fruit and eggs in abundance—all of which they shared with whoever was in need. Even in prosperous families the infant mortality rate was high, however. Four children had died before Curtis was born, and one more between Curtis and Ella.

Each summer the Bakers went back to North Carolina to spend the hot months with uncles, aunts, and cousins at the old homestead: the acres and acres of rich farmland along the Roanoke River where Grandpa reigned supreme. This was home to Anna and Blake;

Ella Baker's mother, Georgianna Baker. (From: *Fundi: The Story of Ella Baker*.)

both had been brought up and educated in nearby Warrington, and it was, therefore, home to Ella and her siblings. Blake commuted between Warren County and his job in Norfolk, and was often away from home for long stretches.

At Elams the farming families shared a threshing machine and worked together harvesting the crops. Ella was proud of the fact that she came from "a family who placed a very high value on people . . . if somebody came by who needed something, you got something; you got food."[5] Race was not a question. The family fed white people and black alike. If you were in need, the Ross family was there for you.

Curtis and Ella probably attended the Huntersville school at Wilson and Gordon avenues, the closest colored school to their residence. Ella, either by parental decree or most probably because of her feisty nature, was designated as the protector of her older brother. Curtis often came home from school disheveled after being knocked down in the mud by bullying classmates, so Ella walked her brother there and back to ward off attackers.

Ella often recalled an incident from the Norfolk years. Papa was taking Ella and Curtis to see Santa Claus. As they walked along Church Street, Ella stopped to look in a store window and a child of 6 or so, the same age as she, called her a nigger. She hit the youngster. Her father and brother looked back and saw her fighting, but Papa did nothing to dampen her spirit. Fortunately, she was generally protected from provocation because she was "shielded from having too much contact" with white people.[6]

The Bakers lived in "a complete black community . . . even the store, the store on the corner, Mr. Forman's store, was black. The ice cream store . . . was owned by Mrs. Evans. The fish man was black. . . . He still had his fish place in the same general vicinity [in the 1940s]. So this is the kind of insulation that was provided by black people themselves by trying to set up their communities or stay in an area where they gave evidence of being in charge, you see. To some extent at least, you didn't have to run afoul of a great deal of insults."[7]

Nevertheless, whenever a white salesman came to the door and addressed Mrs. Baker as "Auntie," she would draw herself up and archly say, "I didn't know my brother had a son like you."[8]

The incident with the white youngster on the streets of Norfolk was not the first time that she had exhibited her feistiness, and it most certainly was not the last: Shortly after the family's return to North Carolina the sheriff's son called her a nigger. She chased him through the yard and "rocked" him. "I got some rocks and started throwing [them] at him. If you have an aggressive nature you respond to the circumstances that provide opportunity for this aggressive nature to express itself," she said.[9]

The family moved to Littleton, North Carolina, in 1910 and settled in a house on East End Avenue. Anna was the grand dame of the neighborhood and dispensed her largesse. While this seemed to be noblesse oblige at times, when it filtered down to the children, it was simply helping out. So it seemed natural to Ella to minister to the less fortunate. She recalled being wakened in the night by knocks at the door and people asking for "Miss Anna," who always responded to calls to attend the sick. Ella, as part of her weekend "pleasures," went to round up the rambunctious children of a neighboring widower to bathe them and retrieve their clothes for laundering. "We'd chase them down, and bring them back, and put 'em in the tub, and wash 'em off, and change clothes, and carry the dirty ones home, and wash them. Those kinds of things were routine."[10]

Anna Baker did good works. She fed the hungry and bathed the unwashed. She ministered to the needy women giving birth. She was an awesome figure who, nonetheless, inspired admiration and gratitude. "She had her ways," said neighbor and close friend Helen Gilchrist. "She was sort of snobbish."[11]

Even in her late seventies, Ella Baker spoke of Mama as a force. Anna Baker had strict standards—of speech, decorum, religiosity, and neighborliness.

Anna was there for the education of her children, but according to Ella, she did not have her husband's practical sense. "If you follow Mama's pattern we'd all be home watching the sick and nobody would be ready to bury the dead because nobody had made any money to pay for the burial."[12]

Mama reigned in the neighborhood and in the home. It was she who made sure that Ella got the education that Anna felt was required. Education, the use of proper English, and oratorical skills were all important to Anna Baker. She taught her children to read before they went to school.

Anna Baker took pride in the fact that the *Norfolk Journal and Guide* (for which Ella later became a correspondent) was born right across the street at the home of its founder, P. J. Young. She would also point to family members who had held office during Reconstruction: a first cousin who had been postmistress in Macon, North Carolina, and another cousin, M. R. Thornton, who had been registrar of deeds in Warrington. She also claimed some relationship to Reconstruction Congressman Henry Plummer Cheatham, though this connection seems fairly tenuous: Cheatham owned land in Warren County where she had gone to school.

Eventually the family moved from Norfolk back to North Carolina because Anna felt that North Carolina was more "cultured." But while culture was an important part of the reason for the move, Anna Baker's respiratory health was also a factor. (Respiratory troubles also plagued Ella throughout her life. She would often sit in civil rights meetings with a cotton mask over her nose to keep out the smoke.) The lowlands of Norfolk did not agree with Mama and added to the pull of what she thought of as the more cultured atmosphere of North Carolina, which lured the family back to the old homestead. As Ella put it: "There was quite a family bit of bronchial business so in all probability there was a health factor which could be exaggerated by the emotional degradation of Norfolk in terms of its culture as far as she was concerned."

So the family returned to North Carolina and the days spent in Elams were punctuated by rural concerns. There were plowing and planting, reaping and harvesting, and above all, ministering to the needy. Much of this help was through the church, though much of it was at Mama's behest. Ella explained: "In an environment where aggressive leadership existed largely in the church, I responded to the church." The women, needing an outlet where they could function apart from the males in their families, were active in missionary societies, and the children were often taken along to meetings of the missionary groups. Ella spoke frequently at such gatherings. At the age of 7 she had become a leader of the Sunshine Club, a church-sponsored missionary adjunct. By the time she was 10 years old she had read the Bible two or three times.

She joined the church at 9 and decided that the one thing that she must do was control her temper. (When one joined the church it was customary to make a pledge to change one's character.) She would go out into the fields to do some heavy work—cutting wood, for instance—and accompany her work with loud, melodious song. Early on, she developed a sense of fairness that was expressed in this form of escape: Let me out of this; let me go away by myself and rage, privately, against what was seen as injustice. As she recalled it, the singing gave the impression to the neighbors that she was an extremely happy child. "Yeah," she said, "I guess I was. They would hear me when I was the most angry."

In church she honed her oratorical skills. "The early speech-making was oratorical—something you learned," she said. "But after I had gone to school, I added other dimensions—things I thought."

This became one of Ella Baker's themes: Don't just spout in cadences; say something that has meaning. This had struck her when she was 7 or 8 years old when she heard a noted speaker, Charles Satchel Morris Jr., lecture in Norfolk. Then she heard him speak again some months later and he gave "the same darned speech."[13] This impelled her to make certain that her talks had content, were tailored to her audience, and were not simply rhetoric.

While her early speeches have not been preserved, enough of her later addresses indicate that she was true to her resolve to maintain a high content level. In her early years the church was her platform. There were missionary unions in most counties, and Anna Baker, who was active on the circuit, often took Ella along. In 1924, they both spoke at the Women's Union State Convention of North Carolina in Ayden. Ella gave the address at the first night's session and Anna spoke the following morning at a panel on "The Needs of the Hour and How to Meet Them."[14]

Throughout her life she maintained a sort of distance from the accepted role of religion in the black community. She participated but did not succumb to the general fervor. "I am always happy to think," she said, "that to some extent I was saved from the worst aspects of religiosity because my family was not emotional in its religion." This attitude carried on throughout her life. She disdained the preacherly speech, which often lacked content but had cadences, and the shouting and testifying were anathema to her. There is no doubt that Ella's approach to speechifying stemmed to a great extent from her grandfather's example. "Grandpa, who was a pastor of four churches, had an unusual manner about him in that he did not countenance shouting. He'd stop people and tell them to be quiet and listen. Or when a young minister came to preach at his church and felt he had to act as some ministers acted, which was to put the 'rousement' over you, Grandpa would catch him by the coattails and pull them and say, 'Now you sit down and rest yourself while I sing this hymn and then get up and talk like you got some sense.' "[15]

Yet she had a theatrical sense and participated in oratorical contests. At one of these contests she was chagrined to find that one contestant after another had chosen to recite the same piece that she had prepared. Luckily, no one had delivered "The Curfew Shall Not Ring Tonight," so she breathed a sigh of relief and went on to dramatically declaim the saga of the maiden who saved her lover by clinging to the clapper to prevent the curfew from ringing. On another occasion her theatrical inclination landed her in trouble. She slipped away from home to a vacant lot next door, where a visiting acting troupe had erected a tent and was rehearsing for a performance. She joined the actors and when Mama found her a while later, she was singing along: "My mother-in-law is named Helen Gone, Helen Gone, and now she's dead and to hell and gone."[16] For this she got a spanking.

BECAUSE THERE WAS NO public schooling for Negroes beyond grammar school in her town, but also because Mama considered the local Negro academies to be inferior, after she finished grammar school, Ella left the idyllic atmosphere of Elams and Littleton for a more challenging one at Shaw University in Raleigh, North Carolina. She entered Shaw, not as a scholarship student but as one who had to work her way through the boarding school. She worked in the chemistry lab and as a waitress, but held her own and became valedictorian of both her high school and college graduating classes.

At the beginning of the twentieth century Shaw was a Baptist school, so the emphasis in the curriculum was on the classics. Shaw was founded in 1875 as the Baptist Institution for Negroes, as the plaque on its main gate states. The rules were strict. Dancing, profanity, intoxicating liquor, tobacco, card playing, earrings, and French heels were all forbidden. Special rules for females included a period of work daily with no compensation and no visits to the city. The dress code for women was a white middy blouse and full black satin bloomers. Ella immediately launched a protest against the dictum that young ladies could not wear silk stockings. Though she herself could not afford silk stockings, she felt that those who could and, as she said, "had good legs" should not be denied the right to wear their silks. For this she was called into a dean's presence, but though she did not seem penitent, this came to nought.

With Ella, causes were primary but baseball ran a close second. "I would rather play baseball than eat," she said. She often explained that she felt herself to be one of the guys and, therefore, didn't think about feminine wiles for attracting males.[17] While matchmaking was a frequent campus activity, Ella resisted it. Often friends tried to pair her up with this or that football star or campus leader, but it never seemed to work out. She had a relationship with a member of the football team, but she made it clear that the game came first. She packed lunches for the fellow and one of his teammates when they went off to a game and, to their chagrin, put a rose in each lunch box. "When they came back, the issue came up," she said, "but it just didn't seem to have meaning. I liked both of them. I liked one one way, I liked the other another way. As far as I was concerned, this was a situation where a team was going out, and I was, at that stage, team conscious, winning conscious. They needed all the morale building they could get to win this game, so if I could fix lunch for both of them, what the devil?"[18] She demonstrated the same objectivity when she voted against her then-designated beau for a campus office, saying that she did not think that he was the one who was most qualified for the job. Period.

The Bible was proclaimed the principal Shaw textbook, and Ella took courses in it. Over the years her grades slid progressively from A− to C−, but one suspects that this drop had more to do with the teaching than with a slip in her acuity. After all, she had been imbued with Bible studies from a young age and was no slouch as a student.

She took courses in Latin, English, French, history, and logic, along with the natural sciences. She took all of the science courses she could. She was a B student in sociology, which she had intended to pursue in graduate school, and a fairly consistent A student in chemistry, mathematics, and Latin. Throughout her life she would quote Livy and Shakespeare freely. As a cap to a conversation she would often quote these lines from *The Tempest* in her melodious voice:

> Our revels now are ended. These our actors,
> As I foretold you, were all spirits and
> Are melted into air, into thin air;
> And, like the baseless fabric of this vision,
> The cloud-capp'd towers, the gorgeous palaces,
> The solemn temples, the great globe itself,
> Yea, all which it inherit, shall dissolve;
> And, like this insubstantial pageant faded,
> Leave not a rack behind. We are such stuff
> As dreams are made on, and our little life
> Is rounded with a sleep.

Though her relationship to the church and organized religion was a complicated one, she wrote of God and his will in much of her correspondence and often sprinkled her conversation with Biblical quotes—no doubt a testament to her relationship with her grandfather, her early upbringing, and her education at a Christian college.

Perhaps following the church's mandate for social action, she showed signs early of developing into the fighter for social justice she became. As a child she had felt that fairness was supremely important, while Mama, the strict disciplinarian, meted out punishment according to her own rules. One day, while Mama was out at the front gate bargaining with a turkey seller, the children were amusing themselves in the house, which was set back a ways from the road and not quite within Mama's range of vision. Curtis and Ella, who had seen torchlight parades in Norfolk, had taken to marching around the house when no adults were present with torches made of lightwood, a resinous pine that ignited easily. Maggie, Ella's 4-year-old sister, made a torch, and while she sat on the couch marveling at the flames, the curtains caught fire. Ella rescued Maggie, put out the torch, and, throwing the curtains to the floor, stamped out the fire. Mama came racing in and, no questions asked, gave Ella a spanking because she was the eldest and the person responsible when Mama was not present. Ella deeply resented the assumption of her guilt when she had in fact been the rescuer. "She should have been giving me at least a word of approval for having saved the child and the house. But I got a spanking."[19]

In college Ella continued her pursuit of fairness and often took up the causes of students who she felt were wrongly accused. She began her political efforts, too, at Shaw, where she fought for the right of male and female students to walk across the campus together. President Joseph L. Peacock considered her a troublemaker and tried to have her expelled during her senior year. Since she was an excellent student, however, the faculty argued against expulsion and won. She was well thought of and had been sent to New York and Indianapolis as a delegate to YWCA conferences. She was an outstanding debater, winning honors for the school in debating meets. But she came up against the president directly on several occasions, one of which showed her indomitable spirit. He had asked her to sing for some visiting dignitaries, and she had refused. She resented being "shown off" for visiting whites.

Her experiences in college led her to think politically. This thinking stemmed from "what I considered contradictions in what was said and what was done," she said.[20] By now Ella had definitely decided against becoming a teacher. Teaching was an easy way out. In the first place it was expected of a Negro female college graduate, and this went against the grain for her. In the second place, she felt from her experience with teachers that they always shied away from confrontation if their jobs were at stake.

And so, armed with her B.A., in June of 1927 she entered the exciting atmosphere of the Harlem Renaissance. Here came a 24-year-old free spirit who had blasted into the new New York to pursue whatever came her way. She had come to live with her cousin, Martha. Ella and Martha called each other "sister," as Martha had been adopted by Anna and Blake and raised in the Baker family. She moved in with Martha and her husband at 277 West 152 Street into a spacious railroad flat where she had her own room. There was a dining room, a sewing room, and three bedrooms, all furnished in the dark 1920s style of heavy mahogany and antimacassars. Ella now ventured out of the coziness of her "sister's" place into the whirl of social ferment: Harlem of the twenties.

CHAPTER TWO

Reveling in New Ideas

New York was the hotbed of—let's call it radical thinking. You had every spectrum of radical thinking. . . . We had a lovely time! The ignorant ones, like me, we had lots of opportunity to hear and to evaluate whether or not this was the kind of thing you wanted to get into. Boy, it was good, stimulating!

HARLEM! In 1927 that was a name that conjured up a thousand—no, ten thousand—thoughts, feelings, emotions, ideas. And it brought to mind countless images: lights, dancing, laughter, gaiety, swirling tempestuous movement. A metropolis of black people all engaged in a rollicking rebirth. It spelled excitement, growth, and learning.

To a young black woman venturing north for the first time it spelled freedom. Freedom to be alone, on her own. Freedom to taste the excitement, to be part of the vitality of new songs, music, ideas, new relationships, new thoughts—new freedoms.

There was a vitality in the air. Black poets had said:

Come
Let us roam the night together
Singing

The songs declared that, come what may, there was no place like Harlem. A tune by the famed blues composer W. C. Handy, "Harlem Blues," proclaimed:

You can have your Broadway, give me Lenox Av-en-ue
Angels from the skies stroll Seventh, and for that
    thanks are due . . .

And another from a revue, "Strike Me Pink" by Lew Brown and
Ray Henderson went:

> Take me Home to Harlem, Harlem's in my blood,
> Let me see my heaven Lenox Av-e-nue,
> I'm in love with Harlem, Harlem loves me too.
> I need music, I need lights,
> Tired of slaving for these whites.
> They feels bigger, I'm plain nigger
> But up in Harlem I'se got rights.

Coming into this atmosphere, a serious person with a vision of
her future, Ella Baker soaked it all up. She went uptown, downtown, all over town, anywhere just to be where there was activity,
especially a speech to be heard. "Sometimes I was the only woman
there; sometimes the only black person, but I didn't care. I was there
to learn," she said.[1] At a meeting in Washington Square Park, where
she "liked to smell the fresh-turned earth . . . indulging [her] nostal-
gia for the land," she fell into conversation with a Russian Jew and
had her first discussion on communism. "He wasn't too keen about
the Soviets," she said. "He was basically approving of the concept,
but highly critical of the implementation of the concept as far as the
Russian revolution was concerned."[2]

When she first arrived in New York she worked as a waitress at
a nearby resort in New Jersey for most of the summer. She then did
a short stint as a domestic in Westchester County, but found soon
enough that that was not the job for her. She landed a job as a waitress at the Judson House across from Washington Square Park and
now lived on 143d Street. She would take the elevated train downtown to West Fourth Street and do breakfast, then "run up to the
Forty-second Street library and then go back and do lunch." She
soon discovered the Schomburg Library, where she "began to learn
some things."[3] She had hoped to attend the University of Chicago
for graduate study leading to a career as a medical missionary, but
her lack of financial support precluded that. Instead she pursued her

education in the streets of New York, but also took courses in sociology at Columbia University and the New School.

She made time as well for speaking at church services, and on at least one occasion she sang a solo and in a trio as well as delivering an address. Scrabbling to make a living, she organized tours to the Chicago World's Fair, touting a Labor Day Special at $25.50, which included a "round-trip ticket to Chicago, 2 nights' hotel accommodations, meals for three days, admission to the Fair and two major exhibits, free tickets to Noble Sissle Pageant and several other features."[4]

She had come into a Harlem that James Weldon Johnson described as an area that had gained "a place in the list of famous sections of great cities . . . known as being exotic, colourful, and sensuous; a place of laughing, singing, and dancing; a place where life wakes up at night."[5] This was true, but it was also true, as Johnson and others pointed out, that Harlem was the home of more than 200,000 black people, hard-working people who spent their time like most other hard-working people—at making a living. The glamour passed the majority of Harlem citizenry by, though some of it permeated to the people who had Saturday night and Sunday off.

On Saturday afternoons and Sundays, Baker would stroll Harlem's streets meeting friends and acquaintances. Harlem was one of the areas where the pastime of strolling developed to a fine art. It opened up a view of one's neighbors, creating friends. "The hours of a summer evening run by rapidly. This is not simply going out for a walk," Johnson wrote, "it is more like going out for adventure."[6] And that is what it was for Ella Baker. Here she was in Harlem, the center of black culture, and here was where she met the people who were creating it. Never shy, she would accost people during her stroll, "Hello, brother," she would say. "And where do you hail from?" It didn't matter that she had never set eyes on the man; she wanted to know. So a conversation would ensue about where they hailed from and who they might know in common. This was the object of strolling, and it was true for Baker even in her later years. Sixties activist Bob Moses recounted a walk across 135th Street he had taken with Baker in the late 1960s in which she accosted passersby with many of the same queries. "Hello, brother. And where do you hail from?" Moses was dumbfounded. "It was amazing, the rapport she established—with total strangers!"[7]

It was just as Johnson wrote: "Strolling in Harlem does not mean merely walking along Lenox or upper Seventh Avenue or One Hundred and Thirty-fifth Street; it means that those streets are places for socializing. One puts on one's best clothes and fares forth to pass the time pleasantly with the friends and acquaintances and most important of all, the strangers he is sure of meeting."[8] One of Ella Baker's friends of the time, Lee Simpson, said exuberantly many years later: "We took over Seventh Avenue, dressed in our finest." (Simpson described an even more exuberant takeover of Seventh Avenue during the 1935 Harlem riot: "We closed it down," she said.)[9]

But a 1927 Harlem Saturday night was especially alive. There were clubs that catered mainly to whites and others that were exclusively black hangouts, integrated only when some party from downtown decided to really go slumming. But there was music everywhere. "The noises of Harlem. The sugared laughter. The honey-talk on its streets. And all night long, ragtime and blues playing somewhere,"[10] wrote black poet Claude McKay.

The music and the gaiety swirled around Ella Baker and she thrilled to it, but mainly she thrilled to the groundswell of ideas surrounding her. She joined the staff of the *American West Indian News* and there was free to pursue her interests in the social and economic conditions of the Negro, or as it was called at the time, "the state of the race." She and the editor, A. Merrill Willis, put the paper to bed each week, and sometimes when they were short of copy she would write a poem to fill the space. In 1930 she became office manager of the *Negro National News,* published by George Schuyler, a leading Negro intellectual who would become her mentor. She also wrote for other papers, including leading black newspapers like the *Pittsburgh Courier* and the *Norfolk Journal and Guide,* the paper dear to the heart of Mama Baker, and for a Harlem news service called *Judkins,* for which she wrote a piece on the activities of Father Divine, an early guru with a wide following. Her comments were sardonic. She wrote: "The 'Father's' final message which brought the celebration to a close at about 10:30 o'clock assured his followers that the divine (perhaps it was 'Divine') emotions were 'transmittible, reincarnatable and reciprocatable.' The applause and smiles of relief which greeted this announcement led a mere outsider to wonder why the 'Father' had kept his flock in doubt so long upon this very fundamental point."[11]

She got into some trouble with her newspaper contacts since she had a tendency to run a bit late and sometimes missed her newspaper deadlines. An exchange between her and the managing editor of the *Norfolk Journal and Guide* bristled with underlying annoyance on both their parts. Baker wrote: "You stated that copy on happenings of Saturday 'should have been mailed sometime Sunday, at least.' She pointed out that covering the event had taken all day Saturday and added, "I have other duties and am not always free on Sundays."[12] She insisted that she had sent her copy in by deadline time, but perhaps out of sheer stubbornness she sent her copy by post rather than by wire, the method he preferred and urged her to use. Yet, despite the deadline problem she remained a correspondent for the paper, and wrote sporadically for others as well. Her tendency to make her own time schedule was a fault that dogged her for the rest of her career—though "dogged" is probably not the right word, as she sailed through doing her best in all circumstances, despite the complaints of those who preferred to hear from her in a timely fashion.

The pall of the Depression descended on Harlem gradually. Gone were the days of jazz, blues, conviviality, singing and dancing, cavorting, and spending. The Depression brought an end to the great cultural upsurge of the Harlem Renaissance. Langston Hughes wrote: "That was really the end of the gay times of the New Negro era in Harlem, the period that had begun to reach its end when the crash came in 1929 and the white people had much less money to spend on themselves, and practically none to spend on Negroes, for the depression brought everybody down a peg or two. And the Negroes had but few pegs to fall."[13] Yes, Harlem suffered: More than 60 percent of Harlem's population was out of work.[14]

But a casual comment from a friend one day taught Ella Baker a lesson in politics and sociology that influenced her for the rest of her life. She had said: "Look, Ella, a society can break down; a social order can break down, and the individual is the victim of the breakdown, rather than the cause of it."[15]

The remark had a profound impact, stirring Baker to radical thought. She was grateful forever after to her friend, for that kernel of understanding made her realize that there were certain social forces over which the individual had very little control. "It wasn't an easy lesson for me to learn," she said, "but I was able to learn it." This was the beginning of Baker's radicalization. "It was out of that context that I began to explore more in the area of ideology and the theory regarding social change," she said.[16]

Among the attempts at solving the economic problems of the people of Harlem was the consumer cooperative movement, which flourished during the 1920s and 1930s. In 1930, George Schuyler launched the Young Negroes' Cooperative League with a flowery pronouncement:

> Twenty-five young men and women from widely separated parts of the United States have now signified their intention of joining with me in putting over this movement which promises to be the most truly revolutionary the Negro race has launched in its entire history. The FIVE YEAR PLAN is destined to emancipate the Negro economically by 1936, or at least materially better his status as a working man. This is the only movement I know of among Negroes that is actually offering some hope to our bewildered young brothers, sisters, cousins, nephews and nieces who eagerly come out of school with absolutely no hope of employment commensurate with their education. The educational program will revolutionize Negro thinking.[17]

Ella Baker was a founding member of the YNCL, its first secretary-treasurer, and chairman of the New York Council in 1930.

She became YNCL's national director the following year; George Schuyler was president.

Schuyler's cover letter, which accompanied a mimeographed description of the organization, proclaimed that the Mutual Defense Department "will protect the Negro from persecution and injustice, give him a strengthened backbone, save many a member from prison and death, actually save the membership tens of millions of dollars in five years' time, help us more than anything else to get members among the more virile and independent youngsters and make the Negro more respected by the police and the judiciary."[18]

Schuyler was a newspaperman and radical thinker. Echoing Langston Hughes's sentiments, he said that the reason the Depression "didn't have the impact on the Negroes that it had on the whites was that the Negroes had been in the Depression all the time. . . . It wasn't such a blow to Negroes because they didn't have anything to begin with; and moreover, those that had something frequently suffered the same things even during times of prosperity."[19]

Schuyler, who often excoriated the established Negro leadership, had great faith in the young. His oft-quoted article in *The Nation,* "Negro Art Hokum," was an iconoclastic blast at the establishment. Ella Baker was his protégé. He hired her for the *Negro National News* and for several jobs up through the 1940s, when he recommended her to the NAACP and urged her to apply for the job of youth secretary.

Baker became a close family friend, and on several occasions Schuyler urged her to visit his wife, Josephine, when he was away on a business trip. "Try to visit," he would urge. Baker always did. She was in attendance at the birth of their daughter, Philippa, and was named her godmother. She remained close to all three until the untimely deaths of Philippa, in 1967, and Josephine, two years later.

Josephine Schuyler was a food faddist who believed in serving only raw foods. She introduced Baker to health foods "as a way of preserving yourself." In a letter to Baker in 1941 she included a recipe: "unsweetened grape juice, beaten egg, whipped cream, honey. It comes out orchid. Too delicious!"[20]

Baker never abandoned her allegiance either to Josephine's health foods (though a recipe for coq au vin is to be found among her papers and she never gave up bourbon) or to Schuyler himself even when their political views became so divergent. By the early 1950s Schuyler had become an archconservative, while Ella maintained her radical stance—which was only developing when they had first met—to the end of her life. In interviews in the late 1960s Baker staunchly defended George. Joyce Ladner, one of Ella Baker's protégés in the 1960s, cited Miss Baker's allegiance to Schuyler as an example of her ability to transcend the political and relate to the human being underneath the political verbiage. Her loyalty to Josephine remained intact as well. Josephine's painting of an African woman with a gun at her feet remains in Ella Baker's apartment— now occupied by her grandniece, Carolyn—to this day as a reminder of the power of black women. She cherished the painting and often pointed it out to visitors as a symbol of the independence and fighting spirit of women.

At the first national conference of the YNCL in 1931, Ella Baker, now an attractive, vibrant young woman, presented, in addition to her financial report as secretary-treasurer, a talk on "Educational Work in the Council: Its Value and Necessity." She also tackled the question: "What Consumers' Co-operation Means to Negro Women," thus signaling what would become a major theme in her later work. Indeed, one of the resolutions of the conference was "that we seek to bring women into the League on equal basis with men" and, in addition, "that where necessary Housewives' Leagues be formed and that where they are already formed the closest cooperation possible be established and maintained between them and the Y.N.C.L." A major resolution adopted declared that the YNCL should remain "separate and distinct from the Co-operative League of the U.S.A."[21]

Baker was unanimously elected national director of the YNCL, and no wonder. She had fired up the membership with her prose in "Straight Talk," the group's newsletter, where she declared: "Every great movement started as we have started. Do not feel discouraged

Ella Baker at age twenty-eight. (Courtesy of Jacqueline Brockington.)

because in our few months of life we have not rivaled some long established Co-Operative venture. Each successful Co-Operative enterprise has taken much time and energy and sacrifice to establish. Nothing worth accomplishing is ever achieved without WORK." This little note was headed: COURAGE![22]

In 1931, she was the first black to be awarded a scholarship by the Cooperative League of America to the Brookwood Labor College, a trade union–supported institute in Brookwood, New York. She had been preceded by Floria Pinckney, who had graduated from the college and whom Baker cited as an influence on her development. Baker had met Pinckney during her work with the Works Progress Administration and they had become friends.

As the struggle to get the cooperative movement off the ground in Negro communities went on, the YNCL showed steady growth despite a shaky financial base. By the beginning of 1932, the YNCL had local councils in twelve communities and a membership of four hundred. Membership was restricted to Negroes between the ages of 18 and 35, though older people could be admitted by a two-thirds vote. According to Schuyler, the age requirement was set in order to keep organizational control in the hands of young people. Schuyler wrote: "We consider most of the oldsters hopelessly bourgeois and intent on emulating Rockefeller and Ford on shoestring capital."[23]

As the YNCL national director Baker developed a fund-raising scheme that she would use for other causes later on: the Penny-a-Day Plan. The goal of the plan was to reach between five and ten thousand people in twenty cities who would raise or contribute a dollar over a 3-month period. Though her math was slightly off, the plan did raise some funds for "the promotion of Consumers' Cooperation among Negroes" and "to stimulate interest in existing co-operatives, and to lay the basis for a more permanent Consumer program in schools, colleges, churches, and civic organizations."[24]

Soon after, the YNCL put out a call for sponsorship of a national tour to be made by Ella Baker to "awaken the Negro consumer to the ENORMOUS POWER that is his as a consumer; and it will act as an antidote to some of that hopelessness with which the inarticulate masses of Black Americans face the question, 'After the Depression, What?' But it will be more than a mere barnstorming tour. Miss Baker will spend at least two days in your community, studying with you your problems, organizing groups where there are none, pointing out from the experiences of others what plans to make and what steps to avoid."[25] This trip was a precursor of the many that Baker made when she joined the NAACP. More important, through her work with the YNCL she made the initial contacts that would aid her in her later work with the NAACP and other civil rights groups. For example, J. L. LeFlore, whom Baker knew when he was on the board of the YNCL, and later, when he was president of the Mobile, Alabama, branch of the NAACP, became a close ally.

Though membership doubled in little over a year after its founding, Schuyler and Baker thought it was time to expand the League's influence, so they began to encourage the formation of "buying clubs," sometimes called "consumers' clubs," to extend the outreach. Such clubs could have fewer than the twenty-five members needed to form a YNCL chapter. At least one buying club grew to become a full-fledged cooperative, Harlem's Own Cooperative, which functioned into the 1940s. It had started under the auspices of the Dunbar Housewives' League in 1935 and functioned primarily as a distributor of milk. Other buying clubs around the country struggled along for years, some developing into cooperatives that functioned until the late 1970s. Baker remained active in Harlem's Own Cooperative until she joined the NAACP staff in 1941 and her new job took her out of the city for much of each year.

Suffering under the problems that can arise when operating with a largely volunteer or underpaid work force, Harlem's Own Cooperative had its troubles. It was accused of unbusinesslike procedures and mishandling of funds in 1941 by the Eastern Cooperative Wholesale, Inc. Baker replied to a letter from Eastern's manager, L. E. Woodcock: "I must say that even my worst fears would not justify the picture painted in your letter. I hope that the situation has been remedied to some extent. . . . I am still very much concerned that the Cooperative name does not receive a death blow from the lack of businesslike practices by Harlem Cooperatives."[26]

Indeed, some matters were handled in a less than professional way. There had been other complaints of the difficulties involved in managing a cooperative. In a hand-wringing letter a member outlined problems of delivery and collection, pointing out that "delivery of milk by 'boys' and subsequent collection of bills by Manager is costly and inefficient, inasmuch as it does not afford a personal touch between the delivery man and the customer and being immediately on the spot to answer complaints and facility [*sic*] in canvassing for new business." The writer sought changes in administration, because "I feel that we have been too co-operative practically to the point of being unbusinesslike and that until we throw sentiment out of our affairs we cannot hope to approach the goal we are hoping for."[27]

There was considerable outreach by both the Young Negroes' Cooperative League and Harlem's Own Cooperative. Both were in touch with the Co-operative League of the United States of America, and the Consumers and Craftsmen Guild of Harlem. They also maintained contact with smaller groups, such as the Ethiopian Welfare Foundation of Brooklyn, Philadelphia's United Consumers' Cooperative Association ("The Grocery Store Owned by Its Customers"), and Harlem's Pure Food Co-operative Grocery Stores. They kept in touch with the Harlem Consumers' Cooperative Council and had a working relationship with several national organizations.

Harlem's Own Cooperative distributed weekly tips on what were good buys; in October 1932, good buys included "pure vanilla extract, 4 oz. 37 cents" and "light meat tuna fish, 7 oz. 17 cents."[28] Schuyler himself issued YNCL press releases in which he examined various products and recommended best buys of such items as razors, razor blades, and fountain pens. There is no indication in the press releases that the testing purported to be in any way scientific; nonetheless, both the listing of best buys and the effort to evaluate products were attempts to aid the consumer.

Among the smaller enterprises, effective as community organizing aids and of no small benefit to the consumer, were the milk cooperatives. (Bob Moses, who later worked closely with Baker and became a key leader of the 1960s civil rights movement, was a milk cooperative delivery boy in the early 1940s.)

Along with the day-to-day activities there were conferences and other forms of networking. In September 1933, "Harlem's First Economic Conference" was sponsored by The Problem's Cooperative Association. Called "The Consumer's Opportunity," it had as its theme: "Where There Is No Vision, the People Perish!" The invocation was read by the Reverend William Lloyd Imes, prominent pastor of St. James Presbyterian Church and a leader of the co-op movement. The welcoming address was delivered by Ella Baker and the keynote speech by Schuyler. The stated general aims were "To

provide means whereby we can assure ourselves of the basic necessities of life (food, clothing and shelter) on the Rochdale plan of
Consumer's Cooperation" and "To go from cooperative buying and
selling into the field of cooperative production."[29]

Besides her work with the cooperative movement, Baker was involved in numerous other community activities. She was chairman
of the Youth Committee of One Hundred, which among other activities carried on an antilynching campaign. She never let up on her
drive to inspire everyone to their best efforts. Thus, in a call to a
conference in 1936, she wrote: "Prepare to do some of your best
thinking at the conference on the 19th. REMEMBER, this is more
than a lecture; it is an occasion for exchanging opinions. So let's be
sure that our opinions have the highest possible exchange value."[30]

Baker also worked extremely hard with the Young People's
Community Forum, which she set up under the sponsorship of the
Harlem Adult Education Committee. She took an active part in
other community issues, such as the effort to get the New York City
Public Library to employ Negroes in its 135th Street branch. The librarian, Ernestine Rose, who was soon to become her boss, made
an appointment to discuss the matter with her, saying, "I personally
should be very glad to have a special request made for Negro workers in this library."[31]

She joined the library staff in 1934. Among her activities was
one that seemed to suit her perfectly. She worked with Mothers in
the Park, a group concerned with parent education. Imagine, a 30-
year-old, young-looking, unmarried woman meeting with mothers
to discuss any problems they might have with their children. They
met in St. Nicholas Park and were sponsored by the Harlem Adult
Education Committee, a library adjunct. She was also an adviser to
the New York Youth Council of the NAACP and helped organize
forums such as "How to Make Our Fight against Lynching Most
Effective," held in May 1936.

That year she was a speaker at the NAACP's twenty-seventh annual conference on the subject of consumer cooperation. Her level
of energy and commitment propelled her into a number of activities

simultaneously—a way of functioning that remained with her throughout her working life.

As part of her job at the 135th Street library Baker was part of the Works Progress Administration's Library Project. This connection led to her move to the WPA Consumer Education Project in 1936, first as a teacher and later, in 1937, as assistant project supervisor.

From these early days her abiding interest was to encourage the development of grassroots leaders. This interest manifested itself nearly a quarter of a century later when Baker worked with student activists in the civil rights movement. She felt that the students needed their independence to express their ideas, to grow and develop into community leaders. The roots for this belief can be seen in her background as well as in the way she carried out her early organizing efforts. In one of her proposals from this period, she stressed that her aim was to empower ordinary people. In a prospectus for her "Guide to Consumer Cooperation," which suggested courses and was requested by consumer educators across the country, she wrote: "The main objective is to aid the consumer to a more intelligent understanding of the social and political economy of which he is a part. The approach is to be more informational and suggestive than dogmatic and conclusive, yet the aim is not education simply for its own sake, but education that leads to self-directed action."[32]

IN 1935, ELLA BAKER AND MARVEL COOKE wrote an article for *The Crisis* called "The Bronx Slave Market." The article described the street corner mart where Negro women waited to be approached by white housewives seeking domestic help:

> The Simpson avenue block exudes the stench of the slave market at its worst. Not only is human labor bartered and sold for slave wage, but human love also is a marketable commodity. . . .
>
> Paradoxically, the crash of 1929 brought to the domestic labor market a new employer class. The lower middle-class housewife, who, having dreamed of the luxury of a maid, found opportunity

staring her in the face in the form of Negro women pressed to the wall by poverty, starvation and discrimination.[33]

Being a good journalist, she invited one of the prospects on the slave market to lunch, the better to get to know her—an early illustration of her drive, so prominent in her later life, to become more closely connected with the people about whom she was concerned. Lee Simpson, who worked with Baker in the thirties, said that as a political activist, Baker was not content merely to write about an injustice but took her criticisms of the Bronx market to New York City Councilman Adam Clayton Powell Jr. for redress.

While Baker was constantly on the go throughout this period, either attending meetings or arranging them, listening to speakers or making speeches, and working at a number of jobs to make a living, she was also in touch with a young man at Shaw, T. J. Robinson, commonly known as Bob, who wooed her by mail and Western Union. He had been two years behind her in college, but they had been close when she was at school. By September 1927, after she had moved to New York, he was addressing her as "sweetheart," and by November of that year he wired: "Am still loving you."

Robinson graduated from Shaw in 1929 and informed her in a telegram dated July 14 that he would be in New York that week. (Curiously this wire is addressed to "Miss Ella J. Baker, colored.") Ella had moved to a "bachelor pad" on 139th Street and Bob stayed with her when he visited New York. Initially, she resisted his proposals of marriage, but finally succumbed in 1940, after a courtship that lasted more than a decade. They moved to a light and airy one-bedroom apartment at 452 St. Nicholas Avenue across from St. Nicholas Park. Almost immediately they began work in the building's tenants' association and remained active in it throughout the years they lived in the building. Baker signed all of her letters written on behalf of the tenants' association "Mrs. T. J. Roberts," but she continued to use the name Baker in her other activities. (Bob changed his name to Roberts and left the railroad, where he had been a member of the Brotherhood of Sleeping Car Porters, to become a refrigeration mechanic.) Explaining in a somewhat

Baker and husband, T. J. Roberts, and an unidentified person. (Courtesy of Jacqueline Brockington.)

convoluted fashion why she maintained her name as Baker, she said: "I had something of what you might call a name. And I think as I look back in reflection, there may have been a factor of, uh, it may have been an ego factor. I don't know. I never considered myself a feminist in the sense of championing the rights of women, but I may have felt the need to exercise this right by retaining my name. In terms of what conversation took place with Bob . . . I think there were two veins: one was the right of the individual to be an individual. . . . We said something like this: since I was public . . . that it would be less of a question of his being Mr. Ella Baker, than it would if I used the Roberts name. If I changed my name to Mrs. Roberts then he would have been more closely identified and could have been faced with being the husband of the wife." This may be an acceptable explanation, but given Baker's hems and haws in delivering it, I wonder. In any case it was an unusual arrangement in the 1940s. Baker, clearly, was clinging to her independence. Maintaining her name was a statement. Elaborating, she said: "This is the way, I think, we looked at it, or at least, discussed it. I'm not sure he accepted this emotionally, although verbally he did. And I don't recall any occasion where we had any problems about it."[34]

Baker's political activities continued unabated, as did Bob's. Though Bob had not been active in the Brotherhood, he plunged into Harlem political life. Baker had always been disappointed that Bob had not pushed for his ideas in the Brotherhood, but he always maintained that it was run by a clique, so protesting was useless. Baker, of course, did not agree. She was always in favor of fighting for her point of view.

They both were exhilarated by the political turmoil of the time. Baker maintained that the political atmosphere of the late 1920s and the 1930s was freer, more open, than later years. This was borne out by the curious amalgam of forces that established the National Negro Congress (NNC) in 1935. The NNC brought together churchmen like the Reverends Adam Clayton Powell, Jr. and Sr.; socialists like A. Philip Randolph; and communists like Ben Davis. The sponsoring committee was a cross section of the Harlem intellectual and professional community. The NAACP and the Urban League were both represented. Baker served as the publicity director of the sponsoring committee. She was just over 30 years old, already crossing paths with the elite of Harlem activists and becoming acquainted with radicals across the board from Ben Davis to the anticommunist labor leader Frank Crosswaith.

Randolph was elected president at the first congress, which was called to unify existing organizations around issues affecting blacks ranging from discrimination in employment and trade unionism to the fight for a federal antilynching law.

The congress drew eight hundred delegates, and thousands more attended the plenary sessions. Every political stance was represented, from Republicans and New Dealers to Garveyites, socialists, and communists. The NNC flourished until 1940, when Randolph resigned with biting criticisms of the Communist Party USA, which he saw as dominating the organization. Although it continued to function until the end of the war, Randolph's prominence and the reluctance of the NAACP to actively participate led to a diminution of NNC influence.

The NNC represented the height of activism in Harlem during the 1930s. More than one commentator summed up the Harlem Depression experience as a burgeoning of radical thought and action. Historian Cheryl Lynn Greenberg, for instance, described Harlem as having an "activist black and leftist political community that protested inequality at every point." She wrote: "Already organized through their churches and service agencies and long involved in local politics, blacks had the experience necessary to mobilize successfully on their own behalf. The Depression fostered this culture of political activism. Harlem residents took the skills they had developed and fought for better job opportunities in both private and public employment, and for fairer treatment by relief agencies. Harlemites flocked to picket lines and demonstrations in support of dozens of causes, led by integrationists, nationalists, Communists, and trade unions. . . . These protests brought black issues into the public eye, as did the 1935 riot."[35]

This was, indeed, a time of intense political activity in the Harlem community. The historian Mark Naison posited that the Depression was as important as the Harlem Renaissance: "Harlem experienced an unprecedented explosion of protest activity"[36] from mass marches protesting the Scottsboro arrests, the " 'Don't Buy Where You Can't Work' campaigns, rent strikes, relief bureau sit-ins, unionization drives, rallies against discrimination in education and cutbacks in the WPA." He stressed that all these "became *common* features of Harlem's political landscape."[37] No wonder that a young woman from a rural Southern background invigorated by the sights and sounds and activity of Harlem would respond to such ferment. Baker described the period as being an open, energizing atmosphere in which many approaches to the problems facing the populace were offered at every street corner. The activity buoyed her. The times were exciting precisely because the atmosphere was so open to the acceptance of ideas from every quarter.

Baker continued her organizing efforts giving aid to the American Labor Party (ALP), which was organized in 1936 with an eye to capturing the labor vote, particularly in New York City, to support President Franklin D. Roosevelt in his fight for reelection. She helped organize meetings and, together with Bob, was a stalwart ALP supporter—though in later years she always proclaimed that she was not a joiner and did not adhere to any political party. In 1938, she helped organize a large ALP gathering at P.S. 136, writing to various political and public figures, including the local assemblyman, the Reverend Adam Clayton Powell Jr., and Lester Granger of the Urban League, urging them to address the assemblage.

But her connections with radical causes were of less importance than her own approach to political action, in which she consistently pushed for a grassroots base. Urged on by Schuyler, and armed with an impressive number of letters of introduction, Baker applied for the job of youth director of the NAACP in 1938. She did not get the job, but was asked in June 1940 by the outgoing Acting Youth Director, Rev. James Robinson, to apply for the position of acting youth director. She had an impressive roster of recommendations: from Ernestine Rose, librarian of the 135th Street branch of the New York Public Library; the Reverend William Lloyd Imes, pastor of the prestigious St. James Presbyterian Church; A. Philip Randolph and Ashley Totten of the Brotherhood; the Urban League's Lester P. Granger of the New York City Welfare Council; and Isabel Taylor, managing project supervisor of the WPA.

Unintentionally forewarning the NAACP of Baker's interest in mass involvement, Rose wrote, "It was Miss Baker's plan always to place emphasis on increased participation by members themselves . . . many [of whom] still show an active interest in the library's community program."[38]

In September she was informed that Madison Jones had been selected for the job, but Robinson wrote her: "The Committee was very much impressed with you and has requested that I ask you to come in to see me again, relative to some other work which the Association has in mind and believes you would be the person best suited to do it."[39] So two years after her first approach to the NAACP, she joined the staff as assistant field secretary in February of 1941 on a six-month trial basis.

This was for Baker a trial run. She was about to enter into the mainstream, to become, for the first time, a major player in the civil rights struggle of a national organization that was in the forefront of the fight. She joined in the battle with her usual vigor.

Putting People in Motion:
The NAACP Years

The NAACP [had] the best framework for developing a mass organization in that it had all these branches and youth councils and college chapters scattered throughout the country. . . . My first move when I was drafted into the directorship of branches was to get an okay for the development of leadership training. . . . This was predicated on the idea that people needed to know what to do . . . and how to go about doing it . . . we argued for the concept of putting people into areas and letting them work there. You know, really work there, instead of having people . . . just going down to have membership campaigns and move on.

HER LARGE PURSE FIRMLY TUCKED under her arm, her beaded hat set at a jaunty angle, Ella Baker strode forth with determination in her eye, her gait, her whole demeanor. Wherever she headed it was always with this hell-bent look. Given her horrific schedule, it's no wonder that she took off at great speed.

Often she left behind a bewildered secretary who wasn't sure of Miss Baker's itinerary, whether she had all of her train tickets, whether she would get to the right place at the right time for her next appointment. The hierarchy was equally confused—the executive director of the NAACP, for instance, who thought she should be in Virginia when in actual fact she was headed for North Carolina. No matter. She had her own agenda.

And wherever she went, she created a whirlwind, leaving a scatter of papers, notes, leaflets, church programs, and phone numbers in her wake. The more disciplined people in the office always found her takeoff breathtaking, unorthodox, and disorganized. Yet she championed orderly procedures and her reports were meticulous—though they were often late. Her informal communications with the national office often contained insightful political analyses of the NAACP programs.

When she set off she was always impeccably dressed, usually in a trim suit, a neat, white blouse, sporting gloves and, of course, a hat. Her correspondence is filled with requests to railroads to search for her missing hats, and she had a retrieval rate that was about 90 percent successful. She was a petite woman with dark skin and flashing brown eyes that glinted ferociously when she was annoyed. Her deep voice could be quite intimidating, and she used it to good effect when she was crossed by a rude trainman or bus driver who sought to "put her in her place." But she charmed the local people whom she set out to organize, never frightening them with her presence, her voice, or her steely-eyed look. Her rich, resonant laugh always evoked a warm response.

Baker could communicate with the people who didn't wholeheartedly identify with the civil rights struggle but who were going along in a desultory fashion. She easily established rapport by expressing her genuine interest in their lives and concerns, always inquiring into the welfare of their families, especially the children. In the small towns particularly, she was revered as the one national officer whom the people could relate to. Out of nowhere there would be a moment of shared experience, as when a rank-and-file NAACP supporter announced with great pride that she owned the same dress that Baker was wearing. She was one of them.

This touch, the ability to relate to local people, was vital to her work. Baker knew, as she often said, that the struggle was continuous, and so she cherished such contacts. She built on her relationships with local people, who would become, she hoped, local or even national leaders. These were the people who would be there for the battles to come.

She never let up on her struggle to increase the role of the rank and file. The NAACP was a tightly structured organization that functioned from the top down. Walter White, the executive secretary, was an astute administrator who was expert at maintaining his control over the organization. White was primarily interested in establishing a massive national organization as a power base from which he could deal with the white power structure. He was not interested in the participation of local people in policy making. While delegates from branches (the term for local chapters) did attend the annual conference where plans for the coming year were adopted, these local people had little say in the final resolutions, which were decided upon in advance and adopted by the board of directors.

From her earliest days with the NAACP Baker tried to make the organization more democratic. Time after time she proposed that local branches have a say in the program and policies of the organization. She lobbied for a regularization of personnel policies, linking this with her pursuit of more democratic procedures. A few months after she joined the staff, she wrote a memo calling for job descriptions and salary specifications to end the inequities that she perceived in the organization.

Baker later sought this kind of order in other organizations with which she worked—the Southern Christian Leadership Conference and the Student Nonviolent Coordinating Committee. She felt that no matter how an organization was set up there must be some structure, some rules within which it functioned. She was blocked in all three organizations, for different reasons in each one, though SNCC struggled to establish a structure consonant with its purposes and thus came closest to Baker's concept of how an organization should function.

As she would later fight for SNCC to maintain its independence, she continually fought for some measure of independence for local NAACP chapters and sought to expand the input of branches in the formulation of a national program. She hammered away at the concept that the grassroots membership should have a greater voice and should, moreover, emphasize local problems in their own programs.

Her work in the NAACP met with much praise. After her first membership campaign kudos came into the national office from the branches. In March the president of the Washington, D.C., branch, C. Herbert Marshall Jr., wrote to Walter White: "I am happy to have this opportunity to give my personal appraisal of the work of Miss Ella Baker during her first Membership Campaign. We feel fortunate in having had her with us this spring. . . . Your office is to be congratulated for such a fine selection and I predict for her a very brilliant future as a member of our NAACP family."[1] A handwritten note by White on the letter reads "Delighted etc. Show to TM, MSJ, RW." On June 26, 1941, the NAACP board voted to extend Baker's position until the end of the budget period, December 31, 1941. Among those who praised her work were Dr. E. W. Taggart, who told the board how pleased the Birmingham branch was with the membership campaign she conducted, and the field secretary, Daisy Lampkin, who said that she found Miss Baker to be a valuable addition to the staff.

In her first six months Baker produced impressive figures both in membership growth and in funds raised. But she had her own agenda. A larger but passive membership was not her goal. From the beginning she stressed the need for greater participation by the membership, and she consistently pushed for an expansion of the base, stressing again and again the desirability of strengthening the NAACP as a mass organization. She wrote in a June 1941 report: "In general the work this fall serves but to emphasize a previously expressed opinion that the masses of Negroes are ready for the program of the Association. . . . As gratifying as might have been the success of the Baltimore, Balnew-Sparrows Point and Norfolk campaigns, when compared with the number of potential members for those centers, we are definitely challenged by the need for a more dramatic and mass-encompassing technique to capitalize upon our opportunities of the moment."[2] Presaging organizing techniques of the 1960s, Baker added: "We must have the 'nerve' to take the Association to people wherever they are. As a case in point, the mass-supported beer gardens, night clubs, etc., were invaded on a small scale. We went in, addressed the crowds and secured memberships and campaign workers. With results that are well summed up in a comment overheard in one club, 'You certainly have some nerve coming in here, talking, but I'm going to join that doggone organization.' "[3]

The list of stops on her tour in July 1942 is impressive. In her field work report she noted that "between February 11th and July 8th, thirty-eight branches and 178 different groups were addressed in the States of Florida, Alabama, Georgia, Virginia and North Carolina." While the tour was geared to increasing branch membership, she pointed out that "it would be preposterous to claim that campaigns were 'conducted' for all of the thirty-eight branches." Realistically and characteristically, she was pointedly saying that giving uplifting speeches at numbers of gatherings was not equivalent to the nitty-gritty of running a membership campaign, and she was informing the national office that a drop-in visit did not constitute a struggle to increase local activity. At odds with the self-congratulatory tone of some reports she said that "a visit of a few hours or even a day or two was not enough to credit or discredit a national officer with the results of a membership campaign." She always felt that digging in and really working with the local community was the only way to bring results.

She spoke of the need for branches to emphasize local issues, pointing out that this was the key to growth and effectiveness. "The prevailing attitude is no longer one of hoping and waiting for the effects of national victories to trickle down to the South; but it is increasingly one of working and fighting for victories against local injustices and discriminations," she said.

A concrete example was the experience of the Birmingham branch. Baker had suggested to the branch the previous year that it might function more effectively if it were to break down its citywide branch into smaller units. Birmingham was a city of over 200,000 separated into neighborhoods by race and class. The city's labor force numbered over 100,000. Baker felt that branch work could be more effective if neighborhood units were established. She found that "the speed, enthusiasm and the results of the 1942 campaign" proved the value of the new structure. "Concretely," she said, "of the 150 or more persons attending a unit mass meeting, at least one hundred of them probably would have made no effort to attend a citywide branch meeting, but did respond to direct community leadership."[4]

Nevertheless, she would not have pursued this struggle had she not recognized that the NAACP had an unrealized potential for becoming the mass organization that she envisioned. It had the resources to focus the attention of thousands of black people on a single issue if it so chose. Further, the local branches had an allegiance to a larger entity that gave them an enlarged base for action. As often happens in national organizations, local mass action was discouraged by the national leadership; nonetheless, branches took on local fights. The Chicago branch launched an all-out struggle against restrictive covenants, and Newton, Kansas, tackled discrimination at lunch counters. In Council Bluffs, Iowa, it was theater segregation; in Roosevelt, Alabama, it was voter registration; and in Topeka, Kansas, the NAACP staged the nation's first lunch counter sit-ins.

The sociologist Charles Payne has pointed out that the 1960s civil rights movement evolved from earlier efforts, which were mass-based despite the elitist attitude of some of the national leaders. The fact remains that the NAACP, notwithstanding its emphasis on legal action and in spite of its lack of real attention to local issues, was the largest, most effective organization fighting for Negro rights until the emergence of the 1960s civil rights movement. It is a gross mistake to minimize the mass character of the NAACP. While the national NAACP was reluctant to participate in the most radical aspects of the 1960s movement, many from among its membership of half a million supported the upsurge. NAACP Youth Councils took part in the massive demonstrations, and many adult members of local Southern chapters supported the young people by giving food and shelter and, often, taking part in the demonstrations themselves.

Baker encouraged the work of the NAACP Youth Councils after she joined the national staff. She kept in touch with developments in the youth councils through her great friend Ruby Hurley, the youth secretary, but she emphasized the development of adult chapters. Her main concern was the overall functioning of the organization. Though she had been on staff for only a few months, Baker spoke her mind in uncompromising terms after attending her first annual conference, held in Houston in July 1941. She politely praised the meeting for the "orderly and smooth manner in which the business and meetings of the conference were carried out, . . . the regularity with which the delegates and community folk attended all sessions," and the geographical and social cross section represented by the delegates. But after these laudatory remarks, she immediately plunged into the matters she considered most important, pointing to "the challenge to gear our organizational machinery to meet the demand for an expanded program."[5]

She then emphasized the importance of substantive participation by the rank and file, urging that members be given greater opportunities to express their views. Pointedly, she suggested that the "session used by staff members might evoke greater response from delegates if, instead of staff members making speeches, several delegates be designated to talk out of their branch experience on some phase of branch work." She urged that some method be devised to give the delegates "a larger voice in mapping out program and tactics to be followed after the conference."[6]

There was, however, tight control by the national office; it was a rare thing for a resolution to come from the floor, and even rarer that such a resolution should pass. But Baker never gave up on her goal of expanding the role of the membership in policy making and programs.

Baker traveled for six months each year, usually beginning in February in Florida and working her way from Tampa to Jacksonville to Tallahassee. From there she would travel to Mobile and on up through Alabama to Georgia, South Carolina, North Carolina, and Virginia. As often as she could fit it into her schedule she would stop in Littleton to visit her mother and her niece Jackie, who was in Anna Baker's care. Often her husband would join them in North Carolina for a day or two.

Her schedule was rigorous; she sometimes made ten speeches in a day. Her schedule for April 1941, for example, was typically hectic:

April 11: Richmond, Va., meeting with staff of Richmond Beneficial Insurance Company

April 12: Baptist Ministers' conference

April 15: 9 A.M., Southern Aid Society staff meeting; 9:30 A.M., staff meeting of N.C. Mutual Life Insurance; 7 P.M., campaign report meeting

April 16: Independent Order of St. Luke meeting

April 17: 10 A.M., Apex School of Beauty; 11 A.M., School of Modern Beauty Culture

April 17: Peaks, Va., 8:30 P.M., staff meeting, Peaks Industrial School

April 18: Peaks Industrial School student assembly

April 18: Richmond, Va., meeting with staff of Mutual Insurance Company

April 21: Meeting of Interdenominational Ministerial Alliance; 2 P.M., luncheon meeting of branch

April 21: Victoria, Va., 8 P.M., meeting at Lunenburg County Training School re organizing branch

April 22: Richmond, Va., closing meeting of branch campaign

April 24: Mass meeting of student chapter, Virginia Union University

April 24: Danville, Va., 7:30 P.M., conference with branch officers to plan campaign

April 27: Opening mass meeting of Danville branch campaign

April 28: Meeting held in county

April 28: Martinsville, Va., meeting with group interested in organizing branch

April 29: Youth council meeting at high school

April 29: Farmville, Va., meeting with branch officers, mass meeting of branch, Moton High School meeting

April 30: Nottoway County, Va., branch meeting held at Blackstone, Va.

Her schedule every month of her six-month swing through the South was just as full. She found time, however, to fill in the national office on local situations. Roy Wilkins, the assistant secretary, wrote her: "Your letters are a delight to this office." Sometimes she spoke of the arduousness of the travel. In a letter to her friend Lucille Black—a clerical worker who was soon to become membership secretary—she wrote: "Today, I am worn to a frazzel [*sic*]. Train connections are not so good; and I am stopping at a home with three women of leisure whose major pasttime is idle chatter. That, with being shown off this morning to residents who were *too busy* to attend the meeting last night, but whose curiosity was piqued by the reports from the meeting, leaves me quite frayed. At the moment, I could wish my worst enemy no greater torture than to have to be nice under such circumstances."[7]

She described the conditions in small southern towns: in Pompano, Florida, the NAACP president lived in a house where "you could count the stars as you lay in bed." The migratory farm workers were living in very bad situations: the kitchen door could be facing the outhouse.

Baker continued her travels through the South in 1942, agitating for greater concentration on a program devoted to local issues and for salary schedules and job descriptions. In January she sent a memo to the executive staff asking support for her proposal that the board discuss the establishment of salary and job schedules.[8] While the board did discuss a report by the finance committee on the matter at its February 9 meeting and again in a September meeting, Baker in a memorandum dated September 28, 1944, wrote: "It does not appear that any report has been made on this as yet."[9]

She proposed that in her visits to "pool-rooms, boot black parlors, bars and grilles [sic]" she seek a subscription to the NAACP magazine *The Crisis* from the business. But she did not proceed with this as, she said, "it occurred to me that we might not O.K. having memberships sent to Big Joe's Bar and Grille." She added: "This is but another offshoot from my desire to place the N.A.A.C.P. and its program on the lips of all the people . . . the uncouth MASSES included."[10] This was a lighthearted comment (one to which in those days the writer would have added "smile," as she often did), but she was deadly serious about involving the "uncouth." She found that she often had to work hard to persuade the sometimes staid Southern membership that defending the town drunk "caught in the paws of the law," an action which some felt would not enhance the organization's reputation, was in essence a defense of the black population in general. Baker reminded the more comfortable members of the community that they were not immune to abuses, that they must stand up for the rights of the most vulnerable members of the community to protect the rights of all.

To this end, she tried to activate the branches to concern themselves with local issues. At the annual conference held in Los Angeles in July 1942, Baker made a strong appeal to the branches, asking: "What are the things taking place in our community which we should like to see changed? What one thing can we be relatively certain we will be able to accomplish in a certain period of time?" She urged: "Take that one thing—getting a new school building; registering people to vote; getting bus transportation—take that one thing and work on it and get it done." She concluded: "Branches should take the initiative in developing leadership in all social and economic problems and problems of discrimination, job employment and the like, which confront Negroes today. Any branch which says it has nothing around which it can build a program is simply too lazy to concern itself with things on its own doorstep."[11]

By this time the United States was concentrating on the war effort and powerful forces were attempting to dampen the fight for Negro and labor rights; such struggles were felt to be a distraction from all-out pursuit of the war. Baker was working at her job of increasing NAACP membership and funds, but both she and the organization itself faced the problem of how to address the war effort. Some members of the NAACP board felt strongly that a total commitment to the fight against the Axis powers—Germany, Italy, and Japan—was of paramount importance, even if it meant suspending the fight for Negro equality. Others felt that given the rigid segregation in the armed forces, abandoning the fight for Negro rights was a betrayal of all that the NAACP stood for. Civil rights activists were in the anomalous position of wanting to be patriotic Americans giving full support to the war effort yet at the same time continuing the fight for the rights of Negroes at home and in the armed services. But there were dissenters, just as there were those in the labor movement who resisted the call to join in the "win the war" frenzy, a call which asked labor to abandon its fight for the right to strike for the war's duration. The "no-strike pledge," grudgingly accepted by the labor movement, was not formally proposed to the Negro rights movement, but was tacitly understood to apply. The "double V" slogan evolved out of this dilemma: victory for democracy at home and victory abroad. So the question became, How to keep the focus on civil rights without distracting from the war effort?

The first major controversy arose over A. Philip Randolph's proposal for a march on Washington in support of equality for Negroes in defense industries, which had been in full production for some months before the United States declared war. The demonstration was scheduled for July 1, 1941, and had the backing of all the leading figures in the black community, many white leaders, and leading social action organizations. But the United Auto Workers opposed the action because of its "all-black character," threatening to wreck the march or, alternatively, to support it financially "if Phil [A. Philip Randolph] will get in line."[12] Not to be left out of such a mammoth undertaking, the NAACP did participate in the planning.

The march was "postponed" when, on June 25, President Roosevelt issued an executive order prohibiting discrimination in defense industries and establishing a Committee on Fair Employment Practice (FEPC) to "receive and investigate complaints of discrimination in violation of the provisions of this order" and to "take appropriate steps to redress grievances which it finds to be valid."

Whatever the symbolic significance of the presidential order, its practical effectiveness is questionable. Just as the need for an expanded work force led to the employment of women, so it led to employment for Negroes. And when war industries were converted to peacetime production at the end of the war, both groups suffered unemployment. The FEPC did, however, have some impact in private industry. The struggle for the adoption of fair employment practices legislation continued in Congress over the years with Southern senators filibustering and Northern Democrats making only halfhearted attempts to end filibusters in the interest of keeping the support of Southern Democrats. FEPCs were eventually established in several states.[13]

Within the NAACP, the issue of declaring a moratorium on the fight against segregation for the duration of the war came to a head over the question of the tenure of William Pickens, the NAACP's director of branches, who favored a concentration on the war effort to the virtual exclusion of the fight for equality. Baker, though generally a supporter of Pickens, straddled the fence. She fought for the rights of black servicemen and battled for their rights when they were charged—often falsely—with rape, murder, and other crimes. One memo she sent to branches and youth and college councils urged letters to the President to intervene against death sentences for three black soldiers convicted of rape.[14] Baker continued to fight against segregation while at the same time supporting the war effort. She took on some patriotic duties, accepting an appointment to the Consumer Advisory Committee of the Office of Price Administration, which while helping the war effort, also monitored consumer rights and in particular sought employment of blacks by the OPA itself. The numbers of blacks employed did show an increase over the years, and by 1945 1,250 blacks were employed in regional and district offices of the OPA out of a total of 58,507—2.1 percent. In the national office blacks made up 13 percent.[15]

The debate over civil rights versus the war effort eventually created a crisis within the NAACP. Pickens had taken a leave from his position as director of branches to go to the Treasury Department. A request to extend his leave arose in conjunction with his stand on training Negro soldiers at segregated facilities in Fort Huachuca, Arizona, and of Negro airmen of the 99th Pursuit Squadron at segregated facilities at Tuskegee, Alabama.

In an article in the New York *Amsterdam Star-News,* January 31, 1942, Pickens said: "Fort Huachuca is not a plot for getting rid of Negroes who want to join the Army. It is an efficient institution for integrating colored Americans into our armed forces." The article lauded the two bases as efficient and well appointed and said of the 99th Pursuit Squadron: "These black boys are going to get into the air and prove their equality."

It is not hard to see that the article did, indeed, seem to accept segregation. "Segregation based on skin-color or eye-color is damned nonsense, of course," Pickens wrote, "but this man's Army is not planning to break or to make segregation: it is planning to win a war, in spite of segregation or of those who oppose segregation."

On February 9, the NAACP board voted to notify Pickens that he could not be reappointed to the executive staff because his position on segregation was contrary to that of the association. Pickens, in his letter appealing the decision, wrote: "I have never 'advocated' racial segregation anywhere, in the Army or out of it. But I look with realism upon the dilemmas which face us in these times—these times which bristle with dilemmas: for Negroes, for labor, for pacifists, and for others."[16]

Board member John Haynes Holmes wrote Pickens expressing his shock at the board's action and proposing "to see Walter White and also Mr. Spingarn, for I am unhappy beyond words." Commenting on what he termed "the general situation," Holmes wrote: "I must say that I have never been able to understand the picking and pecking which have always seemed to be your unhappy lot. I know of no one who has worked harder than you have for the N.A.A.C.P., or been more effective and self-sacrificing. Yet, in one way or another, there has always been this peculiar attitude of criticism or even out-and-out hostility. I feel guilty that I have never gone into it, so to speak, but have always rather taken it for granted that your position was secure and that you were amply able to take care of yourself."[17] Holmes's letter is an indication that others besides Baker were aware of the "hostility." In the editing of the article Pickens's position was perhaps distorted. Pickens wrote Wilkins on March 24 saying that the problem arose from the editing. Board member Thomas Griffith urged Pickens to show the board his original article, saying that it would clear up any misunderstanding.[18]

On April 13, 1942, after Pickens presented his statement, the board voted "that Mr. Pickens be notified that his article on the matter of segregation in the United States Army is contrary to the repeated stands taken by the NAACP and officially taken by the Association's Board of Directors." Drs. John Haynes Holmes and J. M. Tinsley were recorded as abstaining and Mary White Ovington voted against. Mrs. Ovington felt that Pickens should resign. In a letter to Pickens dated May 24, 1942, she wrote: "I do so wish that you would resign. You could so [do] it in so dignified and patriotic a way. You would be the person in the right. You are not hindering the Asscn in any way and you are doing a patriotic duty. Everything would be left in the finest way for you as well as for us. You are so big a man and have such excellent judgment that I wish we saw eye to eye on this."[19]

Pickens, in his statement, said: "In spite of the pros and cons on any domestic problem, it is the business of the army, especially in time of war, to win that war; that it is neither the duty nor the capacity of the army to settle our peacetime social problems, even in peacetime. . . . Priorities must be given to the plans for the defense of the United States as a whole. No passion or emotion can shake the fact that no domestic issue, however dear to its own propagandists, can be more than secondary to the great national and international interests."[20]

While the board's action seemed to put an end to the matter, the dust had barely settled when Pickens became the center of a new storm barely a month later. Virginius Dabney, editor of the Richmond, Va., *Times-Dispatch,* published two editorials on "The Negroes and the War," which, while generally praising Richmond Negroes for their activities around the sale of war bonds and stamps, criticized African American newspapers and organizations for pressing for Negro rights. The *Times-Dispatch* blamed *The Crisis* and the NAACP for what it termed "race riots" near army camps and for "interracial tension." The paper was widely criticized, but happily published a letter from Pickens in which he said that the editorials were "full of goodwill for the Negro race." He called the "Negro masses" loyal but said there were "some few traitors, and some very foolish persons in their midst." This comment raised a storm of protest. His argument was, however, that while the country had been unjust to blacks, "only a fool . . . would exchange American democracy for European fascism. . . . We of all races are on one ship, the United States. If any enemy wants to sink that ship, even if we have been fighting all over it—only idiots would debate whose business it is to keep the ship afloat and sailing."[21]

The Committee on Administration presented to the board at its June 8 meeting a memorandum summarizing the controversy, and the board voted to terminate Pickens as of June 15.

Although Ella Baker admired Pickens she certainly did not support the manner in which he expressed his opinion. She tended to be much more judicious in her public utterances, but she certainly respected him for his interest in and ability to work closely with the masses of people. She pointed out that Pickens was a draw at local branch meetings, and that he went where no one else from the national office had ever gone—to small branches in rural communities. She felt that Pickens was the most popular national officer in the local chapters, as he was the only national officer who even visited remote rural outposts until Baker began her own visits. She noted that local chapters had photos of Pickens in their headquarters, not Walter White. White was always critical of Pickens for not bringing in more funds, but Pickens's efforts had been to encourage the participation of local people in the work of the NAACP, thus endearing him to Baker. "Some of the places I visited in Florida were places that people had never been. That was not only true of Florida, but also some of the other smaller towns. Nobody from the national office had been there. There were many places I went that didn't even know Walter was the executive. They had pictures of Pickens. They knew Bill Pickens, but they didn't know Walter."[22]

Though Pickens's title had been director of branches, White appointed Frederic Morrow coordinator of branches. Baker thought that White "had made Morrow the branch coordinator as a kind of nullifying of Pickens' effectiveness or role."

Looking back, she said that she thought the firing of Pickens was part of White's efforts to rid the Association of people in the public eye whose stature might detract from his own. "It was a very strange thing," she said. "What was the difference between coordinator and director. I don't think it was very clear. What was happening was that this was part of . . . Walter White's effort to get rid of everybody who had been there before and had had some public presence." Baker felt that White had also put James Weldon Johnson and W. E. B. Du Bois in the same category.[23] In Pickens's case there was a good deal of tension leading up to his severance, as John Haynes Holmes noted when he wrote of the "peculiar attitude of criticism or even out-and-out hostility."

Yet, careful not to burn bridges, White, in a letter accompanying his official notification of the board's decision to terminate Pickens, adroitly wrote: "This letter is a personal one to express my very keen regret that increasing differences of opinion between yourself and the Association necessitated this step. You and I have disagreed from time to time but then, now and in the future I have been and always will be certain that these differences were of the head and not of the heart. It is my hope that though we are no longer associated in the work of the N.A.A.C.P. we shall continue to remain friends whether we are in agreement on specific issues or not."[24] To Baker this was a sop, a public relations ploy not meant seriously.

CHAPTER FOUR

The Travel Was Bum

If he [Walter White] had spent as much time . . . developing a program and an organization as he did trying to cultivate people in high places, he would not have found it necessary to go out and try to reach these people. They would have been beating a path to his office, reaching him.

IN THE POPULAR RECOLLECTION OF HISTORY, the problem of travel by blacks could perhaps be singled out as the cause of the outpouring of the 1960s, for one of its sparks was the refusal of Rosa Parks to move to the back of the bus, in defiance of Southern segregation laws. Baker's memory of her travels through the South in the 1940s may have come back to her when early on she saw the significance of Rosa Parks's action. Parks's stance was, of course, not about travel alone, nor was Baker's response. There had been a long history of struggle by blacks over the issue of segregated transportation, a history going at least as far back as Sojourner Truth's refusals to abide bad treatment on Northern streetcars in the mid-nineteenth century. But her protest and those that followed were not solely about the problems of mistreatment in public transportation. They were concerned more with the general position of black people in society. The fight for dignity in travel was an important step toward a recognition of African Americans as equal citizens.

During the war years Baker kept up her heavy travel schedule, sometimes suffering the indignities in silence, and sometimes fighting back. Travel for African Americans in the Jim Crow South was difficult, and often hazardous. In war conditions travel became even more fraught with tensions. Space shortages, limited Pullman accommodations, late trains and buses, and the priorities of the military all combined to make the journey arduous for a young Negro woman traveling alone, especially so for a person as feisty as Ella Baker. As Baker put it, "The travel was bum." She said, "The first time I went to Pompano nobody had ever gone there from the national office. The train came in before day, maybe 4 or 5 o'clock in the morning, so I sat by the side of the railroad till [the local officers] came, for two or three hours, because I just didn't like the idea of sitting inside the station. I didn't know what kind of town it was, anyway."[1]

In April 1942, she wrote to Roy Wilkins, "I am now in Montgomery after staying up all night to get here. I remained in Mobile last night to meet with the International Longshoremen's Association. We expect to get at least fifty new memberships from the group, and I think my delay in coming to Montgomery was justified. It only meant that I had to leave at 2:20 a.m. in order to be here today; and because the coach fare was only $3.10 as compared with $8.72 for pullman accommodations, I resignedly suffered the companionship of a group of noisy soldiers and a high-pressure news butcher for the five-hour trip. However, I was able to get about two hours' sleep today in forty-five minute relays."[2]

Some travel problems she took in stride. One day in Sanford, Florida, after a couple of buses had passed her by, she finally started to board one when she saw a white soldier stretched out on the backseat—the seat for Negroes—so she didn't board. At other times when the buses were full, she would sit by the roadside and wait for the next bus. But she did not always suffer silently. On one occasion she made a Pullman reservation to travel from Birmingham to Richmond; when she arrived at the station she was told that no berths were available. She went to the Traveler's Aid desk, where the man in charge said to her, "Listen, miss, the president of Tuskegee never takes a Pullman."

Drawing herself up to her full five feet, two inches, Baker responded: "It does not matter to me what the president of Tuskegee does. It has nothing to do with the fact that I have made reservations for a berth. I expect to get one." In recounting the incident, she said: "I made such a stink they gave me a berth in a bedroom, a double bedroom, in fact."[3]

She sent the national office detailed reports of problems. A typical example is a note she wrote in 1942: "Train 108—Seaboard. Leaving Columbia, S.C., between 4:30–5:00 A.M. About 5 asked conductor about turning [off] lights (came in and turned on lights—every other one was off before). Had to do his work. Refused to give his name. Seaboard—(Sunday, Dec 13, 5:00 A.M.)"

In a long memorandum dated July 22, 1943, and entitled "Memorandum on: Difficulties Encountered in Securing Dining Car Service on the Seaboard Airline Railroad,"[4] she recounted two incidents: On May 4, she sat at a table in the white section, as the colored section was full and included two tables where four white soldiers were seated. The dining car steward told her she would have to wait for a free table. She demurred and suggested that he ask the soldiers to move to the nearly empty white section, but he refused. In the end she asked the soldiers to move, which they did, but the steward refused to give his name, so she could not include it in any complaint she might make.

There was a more serious altercation on May 29, when she was traveling between Sebring and West Lake Wales, Florida. When she took a seat in the dining car, the dining car steward told her, "You have to wait. You can't sit here. It's against the law for white and colored to eat in the same room."

Resolutely facing up to the challenge, this slim, demure-looking young woman attired in a neat suit and a jaunty hat asked, "Where is the curtain that is usually here to divide the dining car into white and colored sections?"

"It hasn't been put up yet," the steward said.

He then called on two military police to oust her. One of the MPs pulled her up from her seat, bruising her leg. "Get out of here," he said. Baker, outraged, replied: "You are overstepping your bounds." Since he seemed to be unimpressed by this remark, Baker appealed to the other diners, loudly declaring: "This man is over-stepping his authority." This "seemed to shock him into the realization that he was manhandling me without any right to do so," said Baker.

She did not eat breakfast or lunch. At dinner time she attempted to get service again, stopping a steward who had heard about the incident as he walked through her car. The steward told her that he would serve her at her seat. "I told him that would be all right, providing he didn't make me wait until all hours to get service."

Several people in the dining car offered to testify on her behalf if she wanted to institute a suit. Baker was deeply upset by the incident and wanted badly to sue, but to her dismay, the NAACP's attention was in other directions, and no suit was started. Instead, Thurgood Marshall, then the NAACP attorney, wrote letters of protest to the railroads on Baker's behalf and received some apologies, mostly excusing railroad employees.

Similar incidents followed and the experiences remained with her, strengthening her resistance. By the time I traveled with her in the 1960s I was never surprised at what she might take offense to and would humbly tag along as she upbraided a train conductor who she thought had been less than polite.

During the war the NAACP greatly increased its membership. This growth was partly due to the staff efforts, but also resulted from the program: the emphasis on employment for Negroes in defense industries, the fight against discrimination in the armed forces, and the rigorous legal pursuit of civil rights—voting rights, equal pay for black teachers, an end to segregated public accommodations. One important case was *Smith v. Allwright*, in which the U.S. Supreme Court voted 8 to 1 to outlaw the Texas all-white primary. With the end of Reconstruction as the nineteenth century came to a close, Negroes were systematically denied the vote in the South by law and by intimidation. *Smith v. Allwright* was a major step toward reopening the polls to Negro voters.

As increasing numbers of blacks went into the armed forces, agitation for equal treatment mounted. While the NAACP protested segregation, much of its fire was aimed at gross injustices in the services and violence against Negro servicemen, both on base and off. The preamble to resolutions adopted at its 1942 convention stated: "We fervently believe that our citizens will fight more successfully for freedom in proportion as we carry out our ideals of democracy in the armed forces and the war industries. . . . We will not abandon our fight for racial justice during the war."[5]

Baker publicly stressed the need to fight for democracy at home. In a 1943 radio broadcast she strongly urged that the war at home be one against racism. "The fight for democracy for Negro Americans is not limited to Negroes," she urged in her compelling and resonant voice. "It is a fight for all Americans. For it has been truly said that the National Association for the Advancement of Colored People has battled to save black America's body, but it also battles to save white America's soul."[6] In a 1945 broadcast she said, "America cannot hope to lead the peoples of the world to freedom, justice and equality without achieving for all of its own citizens a full measure of these virtues. Hence, the fate of the minority groups in America is bound with the fate of the peoples of the world; and the prevalence of human freedom and peace throughout the world will be conditioned by the extent to which democracy and freedom are enjoyed by all Americans, regardless of race, creed or color."[7]

Other NAACP activists struck the same chord. Organizers like Osceola McKaine of South Carolina "encouraged black southerners to act on America's war aims; now was the time, as the country emerged on the international scene as a self-proclaimed bulwark of democracy, to lay claim to the guarantees of citizenship." As Baker's coworker, Madison Jones, told historian Patricia Sullivan: "If America meant her war aims . . . if full democracy was to be brought to all peoples, then surely America in good conscience was compelled to begin at home with her thirteen million underprivileged black citizens."[8]

The Association linked its support of the war effort to anticolonialism, proposing that loans to Great Britain stipulate that monies not be used "for the perpetuation of imperialism and human bondage,"[9] opposing the return of lands to colonial powers[10] and protesting the lack of inclusion in peace preparations of concern for "750,000,000 persons of color living under colonial governments."[11] (On March 5, 1946, Winston Churchill delivered his famous speech marking the beginning of the cold war, declaring that an "iron curtain" had descended across Europe and warning of a possible third world war.[12] The NAACP board denounced the speech as "one of the most dangerous and cynical made in contemporary history by a presumably responsible spokesman," saying that it "would virtually insure continuation of imperialism."[13])

On April 15, 1943, Walter White, who had assumed the role of director of branches when Pickens left, wrote Baker in Birmingham informing her that she was the new director.[14] She replied immediately, saying, "were I not more or less shock proof I would now be suffering from a severe case of hypertension caused by your letter." Though flattered by the offer, she suggested that she return to New York for a day to discuss the appointment and the job's parameters before accepting.[15] She expressed appreciation to him and to the board for the "vote of confidence," but wrote: "It is because of my desire to do any job as well as I possibly can that leads me to withhold commitment until I can have a full discussion on what directorship of branches involves."[16]

White answered by return mail, proposing a meeting at the end of Baker's tour and promising a memorandum on the work of the director of branches. "In the meantime," White wrote, "have no doubt about your ability to do the job. If you have any such doubts, you are alone in that regard."[17] A press release dated April 16 had already announced her appointment as director of branches.

For long afterward Baker pointed to the manner in which she was appointed as an example of White's high-handedness and lack of respect for her. She cited this in her memorandum of resignation in 1946, and in later years she speculated that her appointment was part of a political move by White, made not so much because of her merit but as a way to outmaneuver board member Alfred Baker Lewis, who had sought to remove White from the position. "White pulled a fast one," she commented, saving face by suddenly choosing her. There appears to be some support for this argument since at the April 12 meeting of the board, before he even wrote to Baker informing her of the appointment, White "reported that Miss Ella J. Baker, who has served the Association for two years as Assistant Field Secretary, has been appointed Director of Branches."[18] The letter to Baker was dated April 22. At any rate, under some pressure from board members William Hastie, Earl Dickerson, and Hubert Delany, who urged her to accept, Baker became director in May.

For two years she had been traveling in a South much changed from the one in which she had been reared. She had grown up in the relatively protected rural area of Elams and Littleton; now she worked not only in rural counties but also in the cities—and the cities were in the midst of great change. For one thing, the war had altered relationships between blacks and whites, though not without intense struggle. Negroes were employed in areas heretofore closed to blacks. A burgeoning trade union movement was, to some limited extent, challenging the long-standing rules of segregation. A new sense of resistance stemmed from the question, Why should the Negro not fight for democracy at home when he was called upon to fight for democracy abroad? There was also a new spirit in the country engendered by people's expectations of the New Deal, which held out the promise of major change in societal relationships and which had helped to open the way for the growth of progressive organizations, especially in the South.

In typical fashion Baker immediately plunged into her new job as branch director. In July, she set forth three of the goals she was to emphasize throughout her tenure: increasing membership participation, extending the membership base, and maximizing the NAACP's leadership role in local communities. In her most innovative proposal—to establish regional leadership training conferences—she argued that "many local issues are not met because our branch leaders do not know how to tackle them. Much of our failure to secure timely and sustained response to national appeals for branch action springs from the fact that our local officers do not know what to do."[19]

Baker envisioned an outpouring from local people who would change societal relationships. From early on, she consistently pointed out that the issues that plagued the country were linked, and that people could make this connection. She believed that the NAACP had an obligation to deal with issues other than those strictly based on race, and that branches should assume leadership on such issues as consumer goods pricing and antilabor legislation. She said: ". . . the fight for up-grading of Negro workers might well gain support if a given local branch would also take the leadership in support of the labor movement's fight against anti-labor legislation."[20] The Committee on Branches adopted the following as a working platform on the question of attacking antilabor sentiment: ". . . an effort should be made in southern communities to educate the Negro that his worst enemy is not the poor white but those who use segregation and discrimination to keep the black and white people divided for purposes of exploiting them, and that therefore the Negro and white must ultimately put their pressure together to defeat the oppressing class.

". . . it was agreed that we should continue our policy of supporting any labor union which admits Negroes on equality with whites, whether CIO or AFL, and that our branch officers and members should be fully informed regarding this policy."[21]

Baker's diplomatic skills were often called upon regarding the trade union movement since the recently formed (1935) Congress of Industrial Organizations (CIO) had begun organizing integrated locals in areas where the more conservative American Federation of Labor (AFL) already had established all-black locals. Since its founding in 1886, the AFL had made its base among the crafts and had fairly systematically refused to enroll blacks. The CIO, organized by John L. Lewis, president of the United Mine Workers, targeted semi-skilled and unskilled labor in major industries.

While Baker favored alliances with the CIO, which had a more militant approach to race relations, she tempered her support, recognizing that in some situations an AFL local, even one that was all-black, was a step forward. Baker was well aware that red baiting—branding opponents as communists—was being used against workers inclined to join the CIO, but she was trying to keep a foot in both camps, supporting the organizing efforts of both national union organizations in the firm belief that labor unions were vital to the survival of the black—and white—workers.

In Savannah, Georgia, for example, where the only Negro trade unionists were members of the AFL, NAACP branch officers made no secret of their support of the CIO. Of the Savannah situation, Baker said: "I am trying to aid the branch in avoiding an appearance of complete partisanism [*sic*] in this growing labor dispute, and yet at the same time make membership gains in both fields."

And while Baker was in the South struggling with the problems of labor organizing, there was considerable turmoil in the North. In 1943 there were dozens of race riots across the country, culminating in a major cataclysm in Detroit: Twenty-five Negroes and nine white persons were killed in Detroit; hundreds were injured and over 500 stores were looted. The riot began in a park when a fight between a white and a black led to a general melee. Almost immediately, a rumor spread that a Negro woman and her baby had been drowned, and fighting and looting spread to other parts of the city. The NAACP was called in on June 20, the day it started, and was active in trying to defuse potential riots in other cities as well as to stabilize the situation in Detroit. Detroit was especially ripe for racial violence because it was a center of the war industry. Thousands of blacks had migrated there seeking jobs in a city where anti-Negro sentiment was already intense. The previous year, there had been a smaller riot over the city's refusal to admit blacks to a public housing project, ironically named for the black antislavery leader, Sojourner Truth. (Actually it was so named because the project was built to house Negroes.)

Of Detroit's wartime population of more than 1.5 million about 210,000 were Negroes, 500,000 were Southern whites, and 350,000 were whites of Polish descent. Anti-Negro sentiment was high in

Polish districts, and there was considerable friction in war plants; a series of anti-Negro strikes had broken out prior to the riot in June. In the aftermath, government officials held innumerable meetings to reduce tensions. One solution offered by Attorney General Francis Biddle in a letter to President Roosevelt was that "careful consideration be given to limiting, and in some instances putting an end to Negro migrations into communities which cannot absorb them, either on account of their physical limitations or cultural background."[22] He continued: "This needs immediate and careful consideration . . . It would seem pretty clear that no more Negroes should move to Detroit."

Dowling, the county prosecutor, was of the opinion that the NAACP and the local black newspaper were responsible for the riot.[23] More positively, R. J. Thomas, president of the UAW-CIO, issued an eight-point program to relieve racial tensions, calling for a grand jury investigation into the cause of the riot, rehousing of Negro slum dwellers, and the creation of a biracial committee "to make further recommendations looking toward elimination of racial differences and frictions."[24]

In New York a riot in August did not reach such disastrous proportions mainly because of quick action by Mayor Fiorello H. La Guardia, who made five live radio broadcasts and immediately enlisted support from Negro leaders. But the riot left five Negroes dead. The *New York Times,* comparing Detroit and New York, said: "Both riots had similar powder-keg backgrounds in the rapid growth and overcrowding of Negro districts in recent years, charges of discrimination in the Army, Navy and war industry, demands for economic and social equality, and the rise of Negro and radical agitators, preying on these conditions."[25]

Baker was not in New York during the upheaval, but the outbreaks were on her mind. She thought that one of the ways to make the lessons of the riots useful would be to incorporate information on them into the organization's program. Baker proposed that the national office supply to the branches visual aids "of definite social significance." She gave as an example a short film on the Four Freedoms "utilizing the Detroit riot pictures to show the sharp contrast between the ideal and the present practices of some law enforcing agencies."[26]

One of Baker's first acts as director of branches was to set up leadership training conferences around the theme "Give Light and the People Will Find the Way." The conferences would "fill a definite need for information and instruction to branches not met by the annual NAACP conference." Between 1944 and 1946, ten such conferences were held. Typical programs covered such areas as "Techniques and Strategies of Minority Group Action," "Developing a Program of Action through Branch Committees," and "Postwar Problems and NAACP Branches." Baker sought to redress the problem of branch leaders not knowing where to turn or where to focus. She had to fight over the years for the leadership training program, stating often that the purpose was "to emphasize basic technique and procedure for developing and carrying out local programs of action."[27]

In addition to leadership training Baker also instituted in-service training sessions for staff members and paid branch workers. Because the needs of large branches differed greatly from those of smaller branches it became difficult to meet the needs of the two groups. According to a report by Baker, however, all the leadership training conferences recommended regionalization of branch work, together with paid regional directors, and "all regional meetings have attempted to become legislative bodies. This reveals," she concluded, "the increased demand for influencing national program and policy."[28] She operated like a gnat, always biting at vulnerable parts, never missing an opportunity to state the desperate need to involve the people in decision making.

She continually stressed that the in-service training seminars were designed to inculcate organizational procedures and program building to meet the economic, social, and civic problems that blacks faced, but she maintained that the emphasis should be on administrative techniques and procedures which she felt were definitely lacking among the staff.

For one such training seminar in January 1944, Baker proposed discussion on the NAACP's relationship with the labor movement, and on legislative and political action. Specifically, she suggested sessions on how the services of the NAACP's Washington bureau could best be used by the field staff, on how to generate mass pressure through the branches on upcoming legislation. She raised questions about labor relations such as: "At what point . . . does the NAACP branch take sides in local labor struggles?" and "What can and should be done in cases where branch leadership is found to be reactionary in its attitudes towards organized labor?"[29]

At her suggestion, the NAACP launched a national membership campaign with Baker as its national director. As a result of this effort NAACP membership increased enormously. By 1943, membership had reached the quarter million mark, and in 1944, with a membership of 429,000, the annual report noted: "This marked increase in membership was, in a large measure, the direct result of the First NAACP Annual Nationwide Membership Campaign. . . . Charters were granted to 136 newly organized units of the Association during 1944, setting a record in the history of the NAACP."[30]

Baker also continued to dream up fund-raising plans. Two months after she joined the staff in 1941, she sent White "a germ of an idea," a plan to raise $100,000 by soliciting dimes under the slogan "Draft a Dime for Race Defense" or alternatively, "Draft a Dime for Real Defense."[31] Later that year she proposed a fund-raising campaign around the issue of equal pay for black teachers; the aim was to rally teachers around the issue, and the slogan was "A Penny a Point for Equal Pay." She said that the campaign should be carried out among educators because it was a special-interest fight, and those most concerned should be rallied to fight for their own rights. "Despite the public interest involved, large sectors of the Negro public can hardly be expected to contribute generously to a group whose standards of living are so far above that of their own, and whose community spirit is too often clannish in expression." The campaign, like others she proposed throughout her career, was meant to reach large numbers who would contribute small amounts—she always went for the mass base.[32]

White's relationship with Baker was extremely cordial at this time. They exchanged Dear Ella, Dear Walter letters. In a 1942 note he wrote, "When I see you in Norfolk on Friday remind me to tell you of some of the things I heard in Baltimore last Friday night,"[33] clearly siding with her in a dispute with Mrs. Lillie Jackson, the crusty honcho of the Baltimore branch.

Problems with Mrs. Jackson had arisen early in Baker's work with the NAACP. In October 1941 Jackson criticized Baker's work in the Baltimore membership campaign in an extremely intemperate letter, accusing her of a "discourteous and contemptible" attitude and of encouraging dissension and confusion in the branch. Roy Wilkins, acting in White's absence, and later White himself, expressed astonishment to Mrs. Jackson. (The Department of Branches report for this campaign, during which Baker raised over $5,000 and signed up over 4,000 new members, called Baker's work "sensational.")[34] In a memo to White, Wilkins said that, in Baker's opinion, "the methods of the Jackson clique in running the Baltimore Branch have about attained the peak of productivity and that from now on the Jackson methods will show diminishing returns." White, acting on Wilkins's suggestion, wrote Mrs. Jackson asking if her letter was approved by the branch executive committee. He also said that he was turning the matter over to the administrative committee. Mrs. Jackson objected to this, but in the end tried to set the date of its meeting at her convenience.

The tone of Mrs. Jackson's letters indicates her imperious nature. Indeed, her high-handedness was legend within the ranks of the NAACP. She, her daughter Juanita, and other family members ran the branch in the manner of a small fiefdom. Jackson fairly snarled at White in a subsequent letter and complained that Baker had returned to Baltimore, staying in the office from 1 P.M. until 11 that night, to complete her report to the branch instead of submitting it the previous week at the end of the campaign. White urbanely replied: "As for Miss Baker stopping off in Baltimore en route to Norfolk where she is to conduct a drive, in order that she might put her records in such complete shape as to assist the Branch, it would appear to me that Miss Baker should be commended rather than rebuked."[35]

Wilkins felt that since the Jackson family found fault with any national officer, the branch should be left to conduct its own campaign and thus "probably hoist themselves by [sic] their own petard."[36] Nonetheless, Baker continued to serve the Baltimore branch and Jackson continued her criticisms. In 1942 she wrote to the national office: "This is another one of Miss Baker's errors which we think could have been avoided had her attitude in the campaign been different." The conflict raged on—even into 1945 when Baker in a memo to White spoke of "an effort to pacify the Baltimore branch" by sending a staff member, LeRoy Carter, to help with their campaign. Carter reported, as if in most reluctant captivity, "if any emergency shall arrive where my services could be used, please call to arrange my release." He added: "I will have loads to talk about when I come in."[37] By the spring of 1946 things had cooled and Jackson wrote Baker to "warmly invite" her to attend the Baltimore annual conference.[38]

But tensions between White and Baker had been slowly developing, and in 1944, while a successful national membership drive was rolling along, differences between them erupted over the proposed reorganization of Sydenham Hospital. Sydenham, located on Fifth Avenue in Harlem, voted to become an interracial institution. The hospital added Negroes to its board and projected the training of black doctors and nurses.

The question about the status of the hospital became a major controversy, with some NAACP supporters favoring the Sydenham proposal and others strongly opposed. City Councilman Stanley Isaacs, for example, wrote to White saying that he was "delighted to read of the conversion of Sydenham Hospital to joint White and Negro control."[39] He added: "My reasons are purely pragmatic. I do not believe that Jewish physicians would have been able to obtain the fine training that they receive in this City if it were not for the existence of hospitals financed and controlled by the Jewish community." Others, like A. Philip Randolph and Anna Arnold Hedgeman, felt otherwise. They wired: "The Sydenham plan will eventuate in the old pattern of segregation. . . . It is being disguised as an 'interracial project.' The result is the same. We resent, and will fight, this extension of Jim Crow into New York City."[40]

Tensions between Baker and White boiled over when Baker abstained at a board meeting on a vote on the hospital's plan. Baker, apparently, had abstained from voting simply because she objected to the procedure. By this time she had become disenchanted with the NAACP hierarchy and could no longer condone its rigidity.

Wilkins told White that Baker had abstained and White asked Baker for an explanation in writing, adding the self-serving remark: "In requesting this, let me make clear that this in no wise implies any necessity of your agreeing with the Secretary. It is, instead, a question of whether you agree with the Association's often affirmed opposition to every form of racial segregation."[41]

White sent a copy of this memo to Roy Wilkins, the assistant secretary, who apparently was a bit chagrined at having been named as a snitch, for the next day, May 18, White wrote the following to Wilkins: "Of course I did not mean to imply that you were informing—only that as Acting Secretary it was your responsibility to advise me of what had happened in my absence." He then went on to outline his view of the voting. He pointed out, with somewhat strange reasoning, that if Baker (and Ruby Hurley, who also abstained) had voted against sending the letter instead of abstaining, "the vote would have been a three to two to reverse the Association's 35-year-old policy on segregation."[42]

This was a typical NAACP contretemps, reflecting White's determination to keep everyone in line. At issue was a directive from the board to the Committee on Administration asking that it draft a letter concerning the integration of the board of Sydenham Hospital. Baker, with her strong sense of independence, and a stickler for the proper method of dealing with issues, said that she had abstained because she felt certain that when the board debated the contents of the letter it had been completely unaware that the letter had already been sent. Often adhering rigidly to her view of what was principled, she felt that this was an attempt to slip by her a plan that she did not endorse and that, furthermore, the board was unaware of: "I recall very vividly the heated discussion that took place at the January 3rd Board meeting on the context and phraseology of the Secretary's letter to the Mayor. This, with the directive that an appropriate letter be sent to the members of the Board of Sydenham Hospital, led me to question the degree to which the Board as assembled January 3rd understood that the letter had already been sent. It was this that prompted my request to be recorded as 'not voting'."[43]

Another rather testy exchange took place the following month when White, in a letter to Judge Hubert T. Delany, chairman of the Committee on Branches, objected to the fact that its report requesting board action was submitted to the board without his prior knowledge. Baker fired back a memo saying, "any seeming diversions from the norm would have been avoided had the procedures listed in your letter of June 16 been given to me in June, 1943."[44] At the time she had received an uncompleted memo in which White said that there was a need for "greater coordination of branch work" and for better allocation of fieldwork. Point three of the memo was blank.

Baker claimed that there had been other opportunities for spelling out correct procedures: for example, when she began functioning as director of branches, or when the Committee on Branches was enlarged, or when the committee announced that its regular meeting date would be the Friday immediately preceding the monthly meeting of the board.[45] At issue, ostensibly, was a request from over 100 people in Honolulu for a branch charter. (The Association's bylaws provided for charters only for branches in the continental United States.) What actually was at stake was White's fear that the branch department was making an end move around the secretary.

Despite such squabbles, Baker carried on her campaign for regularizing salaries and job descriptions, gaining ever more support until, by November 1944, she had twelve signatures, including those of Roy Wilkins and Thurgood Marshall, on a memo to White.[46] But it was not until after Baker's letter of resignation was read to the board meeting of July 15, 1946, that the board decided to establish either a personnel committee or a committee on staff relations. The board urged action and referred the matter to a committee for study.

In September 1944, the formidable Dr. W. E. B. Du Bois rejoined the NAACP staff as director of special research after an absence of a decade. Ella Baker's recollection of Du Bois years later was of an aristocratic man from whom one could not necessarily expect a response to "Good morning." Asked if she had known Du Bois, she replied: "I got to meet him, but not to know him. Knowing Du Bois was not the easiest." Hastily she added, "Although I understand he was a very charming person and not as hard to meet as one might have thought."[47]

Du Bois was the country's leading black intellectual. He had been a founder of the NAACP in 1905 when its precursor was known as the Niagara Movement. He had been the editor of its magazine, *The Crisis,* for 24 years. Du Bois had left the Association in 1934 following a serious disagreement with Walter White. Not only did he return at a time when White held even more power than he had in the early years, but according to his biographer, Arnold Rampersad, he returned with a misunderstanding of what his role was to be. Rampersad wrote: "He himself thought that he had returned to develop the NAACP's African policy, especially through revival of the Pan-African Congress. Walter White, Du Bois later believed, saw him as a potential ghostwriter and a personal representative acting entirely at the executive's discretion."[48]

From the outset there was friction. While there were substantive issues involved in their disputes, White and Du Bois expended considerable energy in a squabble over office space and furniture. The memos between White and Du Bois bristle with underlying rage. Here were two nationally known figures of no small egos, squared off as if predators in a territorial fight. In a fury over the cost of

Du Bois's office furniture, White wrote: "The desk in my office, which was bought while I was out of the country [whatever that signifies], cost only $125.00—less than half the one which you have just purchased."[49] Du Bois, obviously fuming over the space allocations, took himself off and rented offices elsewhere to accommodate his library and papers. "One of the requests that I made of the committee was that I should have for my work two offices: one for myself and my books and one for my assistant and other clerical help. . . . I was assigned a single office eight feet wide, separated by thin board partitions from two of the busiest and noisiest offices in the building." Apparently in a conciliatory move, White offered Du Bois the use of his office while he was away touring the U.S. forces in the Pacific. Du Bois settled into White's office for three months but was then displaced when White returned. Du Bois wrote to White: "In May the Secretary returned permanently to occupy his office. I was worse off than before. My books and part of my files were in the Secretary's office, to which I had no right of access. I made written and urgent appeal to the Secretary and received no reply."[50]

It was then that Du Bois rented nearby office space to house his books and files and provide what he deemed an adequate working space. Baker watched the denouement from afar. Learning that Du Bois had offered to pay a part of the rent, she commented: "They'll never buy it." And, indeed, the board voted against his use of the additional space and Du Bois some months later relinquished it. Nevertheless, the issue still smoldered, and colored other issues of substance on which the two men disagreed.

In the end Du Bois was relieved of his duties after a series of confrontations: over Du Bois's support of Henry A. Wallace's Progressive Party candidacy for the presidency in 1948, and ultimately over his push for an anticolonial statement at the United Nations.[51]

Throughout her tenure Baker had had similar experiences. Though her wants were not in the realm of larger office space or leather couches, she had often pleaded for more clerical and secretarial help. After she resigned in 1946, her successor, Gloster Current, who had been one of the few paid branch executive secretaries and who presided over the prestigious Detroit branch, sailed into the office with demands for increased control and increased staff. His furniture request, which was quickly granted, was put succinctly: "I note that the branch office furniture is light oak. I would prefer a larger desk in mahogany." He also said that he needed a file cabinet and commented that if all could be requisitioned before he arrived "there will be a minimum amount of importuning necessary."[52]

Baker, though she was seen by some as imperious, never matched this. She herself said that perhaps she had not been insistent enough in her requests for more clerical help, and though she was persistent in her pursuit of more democratic procedures, she was not successful in loosening the reins held so tightly by White. If she had been more demanding, would she have been more successful and, perhaps, have had an even longer tenure? When she resigned she told her successor, Current, that when she took over as branch director, she had received letters saying that "at last there was someone in the national office to look after the welfare of the branches." To Current she wrote: "If nothing more has been accomplished, we feel that during the past three years, the branch department has succeeded in making local branches feel that they are an integral and vital part of the N.A.A.C.P. machinery and that the national office was concerned with and would give attentive ear to their problems and needs."[53]

In the end Baker resigned because of White's strictures and the frustrations of coping with the general NAACP tendency to treat the membership in terms of numbers and dollars rather than as a mass organization. These organizational considerations were paramount, though Baker always added that she could not travel the way she had in the past because she was taking on the duties of motherhood—the rearing of her niece.

In her letter of resignation Baker said: "My reasons for resigning are basically three: I feel that the Association is falling far short of its present possibilities; that the full capacities of the staff have not been used in the past; and that there is little chance of mine being utilized in the immediate future. Neither one, nor all of these reasons would induce me to resign if I felt that objective and honest discussion were possible and that remedial measures would follow. Unfortunately I find no basis for expecting this. My reactions are not sudden but accumulative, and are based upon my own experiences during the past five years, and the experiences of other staff members both present and former." Referring with some bitterness to the way in which she was appointed director of branches, she said: "Almost simultaneous with the letter to me giving notice of the appointment, a story was released to the press."[54]

Baker pointed out that "no directive on the status of the branch department or on the proposed program was given me." She also said that "the department has been without constant, adequate, and/or efficient help almost fifty percent of the past three years." She commented further: "Perhaps I should have called louder for help; but my will to do a job and the amount of work to be done led me to expend my energies in trying rather than complaining."

Baker said that she had pointed out to the Association time after time that there was an "almost complete lack of appreciation for the collective thinking of the staff." She added: "Another demoralizing aspect of our staff relations is an indirectness that is too much akin to espionage. Members of the staff are asked leading questions about the work of other staff members."

She concluded: "The total effect of the attitudes and the practices to which I have referred is that a disproportionate amount of staff energy is consumed in fighting a sense of futility and frustration. I came to the Association because I felt that I could make a contribution to the struggle for human justice and equality. I am leaving because I feel that there must be some way to do this without further jeopardizing one's integrity and sense of fair play."[55]

Although the 1960s movement would without doubt be the high point of Baker's civil rights work, her stint with the NAACP during the crucial war years played an extremely significant role in her development as an organizer. It was through this work that she came face-to-face with the difficulties of bureaucracy, but at the same time, it was where she first met the challenge, on a grand scale, of developing grassroots leadership. This period provided her not only with contacts who would greatly aid her in her future work, but also with the experience of nurturing and developing the leadership qualities that she saw in ordinary people.

Baker said that she would remain committed to the NAACP's ideals: "I shall keep faith with the basic principles of the NAACP and with the faith vested in it by the people."[56] She remained a staunch NAACP supporter, becoming active in its New York City branch as a member of its board, as president, and as education director.

She also maintained her contacts with the national office. She was friends with a number of staff members, but socialized with only a few. Among them was Lucille Black, membership secretary, with whom she had grown up in Norfolk. On Sunday mornings it was traditional for people in Harlem to visit either on their way to church or on their way home, and Baker would often stop at Black's apartment. A former coworker fondly remembered one such occasion: Baker arrived with her niece Jackie, all decked out in her Sunday-go-to-meetin' finery. "It was wonderful to see Ella as the doting mother, fussing over her young charge, dressed, as I recall, in a pale blue coat and a flowery bonnet."[57]

CHAPTER FIVE

The Northern Challenge

The thing that I have bemoaned [in the NAACP] is that here you have the physical set-up . . . in 1941 there were 1500 units of the Association . . . that provided a mass base. But the machinery, organizational machinery, for taking advantage of that did not obtain . . . going into a community to raise membership, staying at the best a month . . . was not taking advantage of the fact that in that community there were sixteen hundred or, in some places, several thousand people who had memberships in the Association, and then leaving the community to the leadership of volunteers; that didn't take advantage of the physical base you had.

THE ORNATE MEETING ROOM of the Emery Auditorium in Cincinnati came to life as hundreds of NAACP delegates from all over the country milled around waiting for the session to begin. Ella Baker, handsome and trim in her blue and black plaid suit and blue pillbox hat, mingled affably with delegates, fending off urgent requests that she take to the podium to explain her resignation as director of branches. There was a concerted effort to get her to address the plenary. People with whom she had worked for the past five years wanted to hear it from her.

She was, after all, the only national officer with whom they had worked closely—indeed, the only one many of them had actually met and talked with. Pickens had been the only other staff person to whom they had related, and even that relationship had been more formal. Pickens had traveled in the South more than other national staff, and he was liked for his down-home speeches: he talked like folks. But it was Baker with whom hundreds of local people had developed a closeness, and they wanted to hear from her. Baker staunchly refused to, as she put it, "detract from discussion of program" by diverting attention to herself, and she did not speak publicly about her resignation. She did let people know that she would maintain contact with them and that she would continue to work for the goals of the NAACP. Typically, in her final official farewell letter to branches she had gently chastised them for hastily accepting suggested constitutional changes, urging them, since a final decision had been postponed until the following year's conference, to "make a more thorough study of the proposed revision" for submission to the national office. Then, under an all-caps heading reading "Thank You and Good-by," she wrote: "We did not accomplish all that we had hoped for, but we tried to be of definite service to all branches. . . . Now is the time to consolidate our gains and move forward to a brighter and more effective future."[1]

Old friends and coworkers like W. W. Law of Savannah and John LeFlore of Mobile had written to express "deep regret" at the loss of her counseling and comradeship. LeFlore said: "All of us here and people throughout the country to whom we have talked, and who know you, have nothing but statements of praise for the very fine work you have done for the Association. . . . We have grown to love you."[2] Similar expressions came to her from many places. The president of the Louisiana State Conference wrote that if the resignation was for any other reason than health, "I don't know how I can ever forgive you."[3] And G. F. Porter of the Dallas branch said: "It made me sick to learn that you are going to leave us, for I feel so close to you and think you are an ideal woman for the position you are holding." He added: "I hope the National Office will be able to persuade you to stay."[4] There was no chance of that. But Baker was gratified that each of the letters expressing sorrow at her departure nonetheless went on to discuss some aspect of branch work—an affirmation of her often voiced belief that the struggle continues. It was also an expression of the membership's faith in her continuing interest and support.

Baker had touched the lives of ordinary people, and they felt abandoned, left without that personal link to the distant national organization. Her departure left a gap that was never filled. Her successor, the energetic Gloster Current, didn't have the touch that would allow him to relate to local people and local concerns. Indeed, in 1964 he said, "I have been listening to crying of people from Mississippi for 17 years. I don't want to listen to Steptoe [an elderly local activist]. We need a high-level meeting so we can cut away [the] underbrush."[5]

Baker, on the other hand, had always listened to the local people and addressed their concerns. But no matter how much she was in demand by local delegates—and although this aspect of her organizational ability was recognized by the national leadership—she was criticized by some for procrastination and stubbornness. Some also said that she was too radical. Current, for one, said that he thought that one of her main difficulties with White was that her politics were too far to the left. This was not exactly correct. Her problems with Walter White mainly stemmed from her assessment that he spent too much time catering to the wealthy and influential. She felt that if he had spent more time on the program and dealing with the local people the "makers and shakers" would beat a path to his door.[6]

It is true that her reports were sometimes late, but given her drive to organize people, it is no wonder that she let the paperwork slide. It seemed to her more important to work with people than to do reports. Yet, she did get the reports in and they were filled with relevant information—much of it concerning the subtleties of relationships, the interaction of various forces, and the climate of whatever town or city she was reporting from.

The NAACP never recaptured that moment in time—the war years, when the local chapters were vibrantly connected to national policy—nor did it even come close until the 1960s, when NAACP youth chapters caught the spirit of the civil rights revolution and took part, as much as the tight NAACP structure allowed, in the movement that was sweeping the South and the nation. The NAACP did regain a measure of its place in the forefront of the battle for civil rights; but many of its bravest and brightest followed the dictates of the burgeoning new organizations—the Student Nonviolent Coordinating Committee and the Congress of Racial Equality—and defiantly challenged the national office's attitude of cautious cooperation with other civil rights organizations. The youth chapters had a difficult time when they came up against the powerful national apparatus. There was many an attempted revolt by youth chapters at national conclaves, but they were stifled. The young people wanted to take part in the excitement of the 1960s sit-in movement, but the NAACP leadership was reluctant to let them go off on their own. Some did, anyway. Had Baker been intimately involved with NAACP policy decisions at the time, the situation might have evolved differently, since she was always on the side of the new and developing promise of leadership. She would have found a way to support the young people in their eagerness to take part in the fight.

Baker came through the 1946 annual conference with good grace and left amid an aura of goodwill, though her reasons for resigning rankled within her. She always had a dichotomous view of the period: On the one hand, she was bitter because she felt she had been used by White to further entrench himself and consolidate his power. On the other hand, she felt confident that she had succeeded to some extent in approaching her goals. She had not succeeded in making the NAACP more democratic, but she had, by perseverance, expanded the leadership base. There were a number of local leaders, carefully nurtured by Baker, who would play an important role in the new movement of the 1960s.

Harried by the turmoil of her last trip through the South and wrung out by the annual conference, Baker returned to New York to assume motherhood. She had collected her 9-year-old niece, Jackie, from Anna Baker's home in North Carolina and installed her at 452 St. Nicholas Avenue, where her husband Bob immediately took on the role of surrogate father. Jackie remembers him as a friend, a pal who took her to the park to go bike riding and dig up worms to feed his pet snake. Bob was a gentle, soft-spoken person who left the disciplining to Aunt Ella, often interceding to plead Jackie's cause.

Jackie described the relationship between Uncle Bob and Aunt Ella as a loving one. "They sent love letters back and forth, when they were apart," she said, and when they were together Jackie sensed a commonality of outlook.

Sometimes there were tensions. Lee Simpson, a longtime friend who often played cards with Bob, recalled one Saturday when they had been playing canasta all afternoon. Suddenly there came a knock on the door, and there was Ella, angrily demanding to know where Bob was. Bob, in his usual noncombative manner, left with Ella, who had refused an invitation to join the party.

That was a minor ripple in an otherwise happy household. Bringing Jackie from North Carolina to New York was a wise move. Jackie's mother, Maggie, had been unprepared for motherhood, so the family had rallied. Jackie said that Aunt Ella had visited Norfolk, where she was born, when she was two days old. Just a few days later she was taken by her grandmother, Anna Baker, to North Carolina, on a pillow, Aunt Ella told her. Mama Baker raised her from birth until age 9. By that time Anna was 80 years old and judged by Aunt Ella to be too old to deal with a youngster. Jackie felt that Aunt Ella wanted to give her more educational opportunity than was available in North Carolina, so she moved her to New York and enrolled her in the School on the Hill, a private school run by the Lutheran Church. During the summer Jackie visited her grandmother in North Carolina and went to summer camp.

During the fall of 1946 Baker conducted a fund-raising campaign for the New York Urban League, the first joint campaign of the national and city Urban League. The following January she sent her resume to Edward Lewis, the New York executive director, following up on a conversation about the possibility of Baker's "helping to broaden the membership and financial basis of the Urban League." In her letter to Lewis, Baker wrote of attending a meeting of the Emergency Committee on Rent and Housing of which Lewis was a steering committee member. An action program was adopted and she expressed an interest in discussing Harlem's participation in it. She pointed out: "At the meeting, the articulate leadership from the area was from the left, and the Emergency Committee strikes me as offering a broader basis for community representation."[7] She always pushed for greater participation by the community, though her comment could be viewed as an attempt to create an opening for an out-of-work organizer. She was probably not so much objecting to the left presence, but pointing out that interest in the committee could be aroused in other parts of the community.

Six months later Baker again approached the Urban League, this time with a public relations scheme for a nationwide radio program "memorializing war servicemen whose hardest battle was to return to and face anti-democratic practices at home." Enclosed was a proposal for raising $25,000 for the vocational guidance program of the League.[8]

After the Urban League, she worked briefly for the Salvation Army, until the fall of 1947. In 1947, Martha, who had become part of the Baker family as a teenager, died of cancer. This in part motivated Baker to begin work as a fund-raiser for the New York City Cancer Committee. In the course of this work she wrote at least one radio script in which she was interviewed on the nature of cancer and the need for volunteers. She took part in seminars and forums and organized workshops to inform the public on cancer care and early diagnosis.

By this time Jackie was in high school. She often accompanied Aunt Ella to meetings and sometimes on trips. "In order to be with her you had to go to meetings," she said.[9] Baker was, as usual, lending her support to a number of causes. Foremost among them was her work for the NAACP as youth council adviser and as a dedicated member of the New York branch. She was much in demand as a speaker, and through the late 1940s and the 1950s, she traveled to NAACP branches around the country to fulfill speaking engagements.

The Atlanta *Daily World* heralded her as "electrifying" in her New Year's Day address of 1947. This was the Emancipation Day address to launch the Bethel, Georgia, membership drive, and Baker pulled no punches. She warned that the United States could not maintain world leadership and a pretense of democracy while keeping freedom from people at home. Starting way back in her history lesson, she pointed out that "the freedom of Negroes came as an incidental matter during the Civil War . . . their emancipation was an inevitable act of President Abraham Lincoln tied up with a larger crisis." She said that the same situation existed in 1947; the rights of Negroes were tied to larger issues—"the moral consciousness" of all the people.

In her hard-hitting talk she stressed that blacks must assert themselves vigorously for their own rights and went on to point out what must have seemed a radical idea: "The fight for unionization concerns the businessman, the doctor, the lawyer and other professional folk, because their fate is tied up directly with the fate of the working man. They cannot exist except with the money made by the working man." She urged black people to "support the NAACP as a frontal organization, press for fair labor laws, better health conditions, a fair employment practice committee, anti–poll tax legislation and against every measure, proposal and practice designed to oppress the underprivileged." Sounding her constant theme, she said: "The Negro must quit looking for a saviour and work to save himself and wake up others. There is no salvation except through yourselves."[10]

That year Baker began what was to become a close working relationship with activist Bayard Rustin. Together with members of the Fellowship of Reconciliation, a Quaker-oriented peace group, they organized the Journey of Reconciliation, an interracial bus trip to test segregation laws in the South. Planning meetings took place in Natalie Mormon's apartment at 555 Edgecombe Avenue. Mormon had worked with Rustin and Baker organizing the Prayer Pilgrimage to Washington that year, and she had been active in the fight against segregation in the nation's capital. Baker pointed out that Natalie had not only a brilliant mind but a record of courage, and that she herself had traveled for "the previous five or six years alone throughout

the segregated South." Baker, Mormon, and Pauli Murray naturally assumed that they would be participants. However, they
were overruled by the group, who felt that the trip would be too
dangerous for women. Rustin and Baker's longtime friend Conrad
Lynn, the attorney and ardent socialist, took the position that this
journey was different. "Your trips were solo," they argued, "and
this is a direct challenge. We will announce our intentions and therefore bring on the opposition. They'll be waiting for us," they
argued.

The Journey of Reconciliation, which proceeded without the
women and ended in Virginia when the riders were arrested, was a
precursor of the bloody Freedom Rides of 1961, which had a decidedly female presence. That year it was the persistence of the women
that ensured that the rides did not end prematurely. Baker encouraged the young women who sought to continue the rides after the
first arrests. She herself had wanted to be a part of the 1947 Journey of Reconciliation because she had ridden in the back of the bus
and been humiliated during her travels for the NAACP. She wanted
"to go back as part of the test," so the Freedom Rides became "an
extension of [her] own desires."[11]

In the postwar years Baker continued her ties to the Southern
struggle, remaining in touch with many of the people she had
worked with in the NAACP. Among these were Harry T. Moore and
his wife, Harriette, the main activists in their local NAACP branch
in Mims, Florida. Baker had often stayed with the Moores and remained close to them. She was devastated when the Moores were
murdered on Christmas Eve, 1951, killed by a bomb that was exploded beneath their bedroom. Year after year she would speak at
memorial meetings for the Moores. The Moores were among the
many people in whom she had put her faith. They were local heroes
who had dug in and remained in southern Florida even after Harry
Moore had been deprived of his job as school principal. They had
continued to fight.

Baker continued to relate to branches almost as if she were still
connected with the national office. In a letter to a chorus manager,

for instance, she outlined a schedule for the chorus in New York, Boston, "some other New England cities," and New Jersey. "I feel confident that we could arrange a Town Hall or downtown recital, or at least one to attract two thousand or more people here in New York," she wrote.[12] Such interest in the NAACP extended well beyond her allegiance to the New York branch. She continued to attend annual conventions, often as a workshop leader or resource person, and was a speaker at membership drives at branches around the country.

When Baker became adviser to the New York youth council in 1947 its membership had declined from seventy to twelve, according to the membership committee chairman.[13] A membership drive that fall was a shambles due to lack of personnel, lack of advance planning, lack of focus, and lack of funds. Baker began taking an active role, infusing the youth council with renewed vigor. On Mother's Day she was honored as "Mother of the New York Youth Council." Her portrait was featured on the cover of the council's news bulletin.

She also maintained her ties to a number of consumer organizations. She was on the board of directors and the program committee of the National Association of Consumers (NAC) from the late 1940s. NAC, which was chaired by Helen Hall, the director of the Henry Street Settlement and a longtime associate of Baker's, was set up to promote consumer education and to push for consumer representation in government agencies and in business, agriculture, and labor. NAC conducted such programs as "Your Money's Worth," a series of six sessions held at the Women's City Club in February 1950. Baker chaired the sessions on "Dollars and Sense: Modern Budgeting" with a talk by Sylvia Porter, finance editor of the *New York Post,* and "Areas of Joint Interest: Consumers and Retailers" addressed by Dr. Ruth Ayres, managing director of the National Consumer-Retailer Council. Always dear to her heart, the cooperative movement kept her interest until well into the 1960s.

Baker and her husband also worked with the tenants' association of her building, firing off letters to management on needed repairs, making a survey of tenants' needs, and complaining to the Housing Authority.

The cord connecting all of her activities was her deep involvement with people and her desire to infuse them with a sense of their own abilities. On October 24, 1953, Baker helped sponsor the Metropolitan Youth Conference on Equality. Over 160 young people from forty-four organizations took part in workshops on employment, housing, health, education, and veterans issues. Jackie chaired the workshop on schools and recreation.

Throughout her career Baker had devised fund-raising plans for whatever organization she was working with. Some of them were elaborate, but all of them were built around soliciting small amounts of money from large numbers of people. This was in keeping with her constant efforts to involve ordinary people in social causes. In 1952, she drew up a detailed plan for raising $25,000 for the New York branch of the NAACP in which she proposed recruiting l,000 volunteer fund-raisers committed to raising $50 each. Her proposed budget included an item of $100 per week for a director. Her memo to Russell P. Crawford, then president of the New York branch, said, "I have a personal interest in such a campaign and will discuss this at greater length at the meeting of the Branch Executive Committee, at which the proposal is presented."[14] Clearly what she had in mind was becoming the director of the campaign, which she eventually did. The campaign was apparently postponed until 1954.

In all of her fund-raising presentations there was always the possibility of a job for her. Though her need to earn a living often caused her to be on the lookout for a job, even though it might be a temporary one, she was always active as a volunteer for causes in which she believed, serving on the boards of many organizations. When she was with the Cancer Committee she also served on the Committee on Information Services of the Welfare Council of New York City. When she was director of branches of the NAACP, she had served as an adviser to the Office of Price Administration. In 1947 she had been invited to serve on the Consumer Advisory Com-

Board meeting of the W. C. Handy Foundation for the Blind on August 23, 1951, at Handy's Yonkers residence. Standing, Ella Baker, fourth from left; Noble Sissle, far right. W. C. Handy, seated, center in white; Prince in front row. Photo by Morgan and Marvin Smith. By permission of Monica Smith. (Courtesy of Handy Brothers Music Co., Inc.)

mittee of the President's Council of Economic Advisors. In correspondence with Caroline Ware of the committee, Baker wrote that she was "willing and pleased" to attend the first meeting scheduled for March 13 as "I am interested in consumer problems and welcome every opportunity to serve that interest in a more effective manner."[15] She also pointed out that she was identified as being with the NAACP and that the letter of invitation "was not too clear as to whether membership on the committee will be on an individual basis or an organizational one." Ware replied, asking Baker to please just accept.[16] She did and regularly attended meetings that year.

But during this period—1946 to 1958—her energies were mainly focused on school desegregation. Her interest in schools had started during her tenure in the national office of the NAACP, when she perceived that Northern NAACP branches were rather more comfortable in dealing with Southern problems than with those in their own areas. As early as 1941 she was critical of the Albany, New York, NAACP branch for being much less concerned with the discrimination in their own locale than with helping the "poor" Negroes of the South. She was appalled to find that there were three levels of training in the high school: a college preparatory course, education for a trade, and a third which simply indicated that the student had made it through. "The majority of Negroes were being put in that last category. And nobody was challenging it."[17] Her concern was twofold: for the quality of education that Negroes were getting and for the lack of attention the branch was giving to problems in its own backyard.

It seemed natural, therefore, that after her long stint traveling for the NAACP she should concern herself with de facto segregation back in New York. She threw herself into the school fight and in her typical way concentrated on involving people in the struggle at the grassroots level. As education chair of the NAACP New York branch she instituted a survey called "Check Your School," which contained such questions as, What year was your school built? When was it last painted? How many toilets are there for boys? For girls? The questionnaire asked signers to describe the conditions of play areas, lunchrooms, auditoriums, teachers' rest rooms, and classrooms. It asked what were the most needed repairs (heating, plumbing, electrical), what was the student-teacher ratio, how many children were behind in reading and arithmetic, how big classes were, and how many substitute teachers were employed. The survey resulted in a broad parents' movement to improve New York City schools. It also identified the existence of de facto segregation, which came under increasing attack by such organizations as Parents in Action and, later, In Friendship. Baker was a founder of both organizations.

The Reverend Milton A. Galamison, who had organized the Parents' Workshop for Equality, came to know Baker mainly through a mutual friend Annie Stein, a teacher and stalwart in the fight for school integration and a leading member of the Brooklyn NAACP. Galamison was pastor of the Siloam Presbyterian Church in the Bedford-Stuyvesant section of Brooklyn and president of the Brooklyn branch of the NAACP. He and Baker worked together on the Intergroup Committee on New York Public Schools. Baker was a member of the New York City Board of Education's Commission on Integration, and as a member of the subcommittee on zoning, she fought for a clear definition of the relationship between housing and schools: since neighborhoods were segregated, so were the schools. The report of the zoning committee was drafted by June Shagaloff of the NAACP; it was amended by Baker and Ethel Schwabacher of the Urban League, who were critical of the role of the assistant superintendent of schools and who sought a clearer definition of how segregated housing blocked school integration. At issue was the familiar one, the opposition to change by those in power versus those who felt the need for remedies. Baker's and Schwabacher's suggestions reflected the stance of the most militant advocates of desegregation, who were adamantly opposed to Dr. William Jensen, head of the Board of Education. In the end, Dr. Jensen prevailed and the connection between housing and school segregation was not addressed.

In her continued association with the national NAACP office, Baker was a consultant at an Eastern Regional Training Conference in March 1953, which held workshops on police brutality and other civil rights violations and on enlisting community support for NAACP activities. At the New York State conference that year she presided at the testimonial dinner for Dr. James E. Allen, a past president of the conference. Walter White was the guest speaker.

Her first and only foray into electoral politics came in 1953, when she ran for New York City Council on the Liberal Party ticket. An explanation of why she took this step is hard to come by. (Prominent businessman and politician Percy Sutton said in an interview that perhaps she took "Liberal" to mean liberal.)[18] She herself said that she had always found it difficult to align herself with any political party. For Baker, "it was a question of whether you can maintain your integrity and be a good politician, [but] I was finally drafted." She resigned as president of the New York branch of the NAACP in order to run. She was encouraged to run by Russell Crawford, who was vice president. Always looking for hidden motivations, she was a bit cynical in remarking: "I guess Mr. Crawford who was my vice-president was helping me to get out of the way so he could become president."[19] But Baker gave a stirring speech in favor of Crawford's candidacy, and he won overwhelmingly.

The Citizens Union endorsed the incumbent, Earl Brown, but pronounced Ella Baker qualified, commenting: "Sincere and well-informed, interested in health, racial and consumer matters. She has a good comprehension of the problems confronting the city and her area." In an election statement Baker called for a stepped-up low-rent housing program, long-range planning for slum clearance, full budgetary support of day care, and utilization of schools for both adult and young people's community activities. And here once again she urged a job reclassification plan and equalization of salaries. Baker received 8,155 votes and Brown, who had the endorsement of both Republicans and Democrats, received 47,808.[20]

After her defeat Baker rejoined the executive board of the New York NAACP and functioned as chair of a Special Committee. The Special Committee was part of an ongoing NAACP anticommunist campaign. Since the 1930s, when it sparred with the Communist Party over several trials, including those of the Scottsboro boys, Willie McGee, and Angelo Herndon, the NAACP had been vehemently anticommunist. In 1944, board member Buell Gallagher had written from Berkeley, California, to inform White that "at least two of the branches in the Bay area have been strongly influenced by the infiltration of White Communist [sic], many of them CIO workers and officials." Subsequently both the West Coast Regional Conference and the national NAACP in 1947 adopted exclusionary resolutions regarding Communists.[21] In 1950, controversy had erupted over the refusal of the Credentials Committee of the Civil Rights Mobilization in Washington, D.C., to accept New York branch delegates. Then in 1951 there was a furor over the participation of Communists in the New York branch's celebration of Josephine Baker Day. By 1956, a full-scale witch-hunt was underway, and a directive came down from the national office demanding a clean sweep of Communist Party influence, including "fellow travelers."

The report that Baker submitted, in September 1956, seemed to waffle. It sought to safeguard the civil liberties of people "accused" of being Communists, arguing against public disclosure. But it did not challenge the fundamental premises of the witch-hunts, "Past experience has shown that an individual often resigns when given the choice to do so, or to face incriminating evidence." In the end some branch officers resigned. At least one was bitter about this well into the late 1980s; she expressed gratitude that Baker said many years after the expulsions/resignations that she had perhaps been wrong in having accepted a directive of the national office and acting on it. In interviews in later years Baker recalled going down to the national office to argue against the expulsions, but "I followed a national office directive to the letter, and I should not have," Baker said in a later interview.[22]

Longtime civil rights and civil liberties activist Anne Braden recalled a wide-ranging discussion she had with Baker in 1956. At that time Baker said she did not think that Communists should be members of the NAACP, but that the NAACP should participate in the defense of anyone under attack by a segregationist entity no matter what their politics.[23] Braden had met with Baker to elicit support for Andrew Wade, an African American for whom the Bradens had purchased a house in an all-white neighborhood. Baker organized a support meeting at the Community Church in New York and solicited support from leaders of organizations from a broad political spectrum.

Baker turned her attention to the South once again. In the wake of the 1954 *Brown v. Board of Education* decision, which called for the desegregation of schools "with all deliberate speed," African American parents were meeting with intimidation and economic reprisals when they attempted to enroll their children in all-white schools. While she had earlier been critical of Northerners who failed to attend to local problems, choosing rather to aid their Southern brethren, Baker felt in 1955 and particularly in 1956 during the bus boycott in Montgomery that aid to Southern freedom fighters was crucial.

So in 1955, Baker, Bayard Rustin, Stanley Levison, and others formed In Friendship, a liberal-labor coalition to aid those pushing for school integration in the South. In Friendship established an office at 122 East Fifty-seventh Street in Levison's offices. Cochairs included A. Philip Randolph, Rabbi Edward E. Klein, Monsignor Cornelius J. Drew, Dr. Harry Emerson Fosdick, and Dr. James H. Robinson. As one of its first projects, in 1956 In Friendship sent funds to the movement in Clarendon County, South Carolina, where the black community was among the earliest to face segregationist opposition to the *Brown* decision. In Friendship and the Brotherhood of Sleeping Car Porters supplied the bulk of the organizing personnel for a massive civil rights rally that was held in May 1956 and jointly sponsored by several organizations. Baker, Levison, and Rustin spent six weeks organizing full-time. The rally raised $4,000 for the NAACP and $2,000 for the Montgomery Improvement Association.[24]

Another huge rally was held in December at the Manhattan Center, a large meeting hall at Thirty-fourth Street and Seventh Avenue. Baker was executive director of the event at which Duke Ellington and Harry Belafonte performed. This was Belafonte's first serious involvement in the civil rights movement and out of this association he and Baker became lifelong friends.

The aid that In Friendship provided to the Southern school desegregation movement gave Baker an additional entree to Southern activists, and it was through In Friendship that she came to know Amzie Moore, the longtime fighter for Negro rights in Mississippi, whom she had met briefly during her NAACP days. Moore was among those whom In Friendship helped to sustain financially. Moore, who became a key person to the students of the 1960s movement, was introduced to the young people by Baker. He became a good friend, and Baker maintained a relationship with him and his wife for many years. She often stayed in their home and shared their troubles.

In addition to helping individuals in the struggle directly, In Friendship also provided more than $10,000 to a black-run bank, the Victory Savings Bank in Columbia, South Carolina, to provide loans to needy families. This was the bank run by Modjeska Simkins, a lifelong fighter for black rights. Simkins was the first black female bank president in the country, and she always aligned herself with radical espousers of the rights of blacks and poor people.

Baker, seeing the importance of the solidarity the Montgomery, Alabama, black community was exhibiting in the bus boycott, had become intimately involved. She spent many weeks in Montgomery and in her words "meeting night after night" with Bayard Rustin and Stanley Levison to discuss, Where do we go from here?

The Montgomery bus boycott had electrified the nation, doing more to stir the national conscience than the sight of young black children facing screaming mobs to attend school, for it involved almost the entire Negro community of a major Southern city. What had sparked the boycott was the determination of Mrs. Rosa Parks, who sat down in a seat at the front of a city bus and refused to move to the back where Negroes rode, by law. Parks, a seamstress, was an active NAACP member and she had just returned from a Highlander Center civil rights workshop led by Ella Baker, but her decision to defy the segregation laws was her own. She was arrested and bailed out by E. D. Nixon, the local NAACP president, and the lawyer, Clifford Durr, and his wife, Virginia. Her action began a yearlong boycott of the city's buses, a boycott which took on heroic proportions. Over 40,000 black people walked to work and to school; the city buses were almost empty.

Baker helped where she could and worked with E. D. Nixon and Virginia Durr, a member of the white aristocracy who had long since thrown in her lot on the side of integration, to further the boycott. Baker had met Durr during the fight against the poll tax in Virginia in the early 1940s, and they had become staunch allies.

Baker had met Rosa Parks in 1946 when Parks attended one of her leadership training sessions in Jacksonville, Florida, and she often stayed with her when she was in Montgomery. Soon after the boycott began Baker and Parks made a fund-raising and promotional tour through the Northeast in support of it.

Baker felt that the boycott was a signal event that must be followed up. Always yearning for a mass movement, she saw in the boycott the possibility of its emergence at last. Levison and Rustin agreed. Moreover, they felt strongly that here was an opportunity to provide a base for Martin Luther King Jr. Indeed, four days after the boycott began the Montgomery Improvement Association was formed and King was elected president.

In Baker's mind the whole thrust of the burgeoning Southern movement of defiance took its emphasis on nonviolent resistance from the essentially Northern tactic of nonviolent protest, the historical technique of the Fellowship of Reconciliation. She said that conversations with FOR representatives had "strengthened whatever germ of an idea about a nonviolent movement Martin had." Bayard's influence became paramount, according to Baker, in the "articulation of the nonviolent concept coming out of Montgomery."[25]

Whether or not King was wedded to the idea of nonviolence before the emergence of this Northern push for a Southern organization is not clear, but the organization was set up because those three New York intellectuals—Rustin, Levison, and Baker—pushed for its establishment.

Baker's main aim was to create a *movement* out of the Montgomery events. This does not mean that she was ignorant of previous or concurrent actions—Baton Rouge, Louisiana, and Tallahassee, Florida, boycotts. It means that in this, the Montgomery action, she saw the outpouring of community support as decisive.[26] The eventual outcome of the consultations that she, Rustin, and Levison held in the Levison kitchen in New York was the creation of the

Southern Christian Leadership Conference, SCLC.[27] (John Britton in an interview asked Baker, "So what you're saying then is that the genesis of the idea for SCLC started in the minds of people in the North, not in Montgomery?" To which Baker replied: "That's correct.")[28] The first step was the organizing of the Southwide Institute on Transportation, later known as the Southern Negro Leaders Conference on Transportation and Non-violent Integration held in Atlanta on January 10 and 11, 1957.

That meeting launched the SCLC. Rustin had prepared a series of working papers for the conference, which were edited by Baker and Levison. According to King biographer David Garrow, "King, Abernathy, Rustin, and Baker were still polishing Rustin's handiwork in Atlanta the evening before the meetings were to commence."[29]

"At this meeting there were over 100 men present," Baker recalled. "I don't think that there were any women there except me. There may have been one or two others. And these men were willing to do something I had never seen Negro ministers do before: they were willing to analyze each of the papers we presented." She felt that King could have utilized this willingness to study and learn, but he didn't. She said that she, Rustin, and Levison "had lots of arguments" because she felt that they ought to confront King to try to get him to "face up to the potential that was in the movement." She did point out that when he was on the cover of *Time* magazine, he did acknowledge that it was the 50,000 marching feet which made the boycott a success, not him. She said that this was the first time that there was evidence of his recognition of the fact that "the movement was making him, rather than him making the movement."

Baker felt that both black and white Southern ministers didn't need to know how to organize because of the structure of their church hierarchies "so all you need to do is carry on as before . . . but I think they would have been willing to learn had their 'leader' had the understanding."[30]

After the Atlanta conference and a follow-up in New Orleans, many discussions ensued. King wanted Rustin to head up a voter registration drive, the Crusade for Citizenship, but realized that Rustin would likely come under heavy attack because of his homosexuality, his former membership in the Young Communist League, and his stance as a conscientious objector during World War II. The upshot was that Rustin and Levison promised to deliver Ella Baker as the organizer of a Crusade for Citizenship and furthermore as the organizer of an office for SCLC. She reluctantly agreed, though, once again, she felt used—foisted into a position about which she had not been adequately consulted.

Yet, she went along. She felt that the promise of a movement was worth the sacrifice of her pride. She had been guaranteed to be there without her agreement—but she went.

The Southwide Leadership Conference was transformed into the SCLC, and Baker was destined to get it into operating order, put it in motion, and, as she hoped, transform it into the mass organization for civil rights.

CHAPTER SIX

Confronting "De Lawd"

Our concept of the need for extending this mass action [the Mont-gomery bus boycott] in the South was also predicated upon the re-alization that the NAACP had the mechanics in terms of the spread of its membership for the development of mass action. But its philosophy had not been expressed in the direction of real con-frontation or using mass action as a means of confrontation. . . . I began to feel that my greatest sense of success would be to suc-ceed in doing with people some of the things that I thought would raise the level of masses of people.

PRESSED INTO A JOB for which she had not applied, Baker was yet mindful of the promise open to her: here might be her chance to fashion a mass organization for civil rights. She grasped the oppor-tunity to maintain some of the momentum generated by the Mont-gomery movement and, in January 1958, moved to Atlanta, now the center of activity in the new Southern-based movement.

She was disconcerted, though not altogether surprised, to learn that the newly formed Southern Christian Leadership Conference didn't even have an office. For a week or so she operated out of her room at the Savoy Hotel on Auburn Avenue, using a coin telephone for her business calls and the nearby King family church, Ebenezer Baptist, to copy documents. She was permitted to use the mimeo-graph machine after five o'clock, when the church office officially closed. With the help of the Reverend Samuel Williams, she was fi-nally established in a small office at 208 Auburn Avenue.

Such circumstances were not new to her. She had seen the dingy offices that most of the leaders of the civil rights movement worked out of: creaky staircases ascending to minuscule second- or third-floor quarters with no amenities. But, as she saw it, she had a job to do, so for the time being her surroundings didn't much matter. She had just six weeks to organize the Crusade for Citizenship voter registration drives in as many cities as possible by February 12. This was not a publicity stunt, but an organizing opportunity.

Plunging into the work, Baker pushed SCLC board members to campaign in their communities. She traveled to several of the targeted cities to rally the forces for the voter drive, fired off letter after letter to urge local workers on, provided such literature as was needed, and kept the press informed of progress.

The concrete objective of the Crusade for Citizenship was to get more Negro voters on the rolls, but it was also a crusade to encourage black people to stand up to the white power structure. A February 4, 1958, memorandum from King—which was probably drafted by Baker, as she drafted most statements that emanated from SCLC—stated that one of the aims of the Crusade was to double the number of Negroes who vote in the South and "to set up at the local level the type of action and organization that can struggle, come what may, to obtain the right to vote where it does not exist."[1] While there had been activity around voter registration in earlier years, the right to vote had begun to take on a new emphasis by the mid-1950s. As the memo went on to claim, with a bit of hyperbole that must have come from King, since it was not Baker's usual style, "When Negroes have won and fully exercise their right to vote many changes can then occur. . . . Segregated buses will disappear, wages will be increased, police brutality will be a thing of the past, men who believe in justice will be sent to congress, 'mob violence' will fade away, Justice will be established in the courts."

Despite Baker's efforts, the Crusade apparently failed to produce much of an increase in voter registration, though a report from In Friendship in the spring of 1958 seemed to rebut this view. It said that according to Ella Baker's diary, voting rallies were held in twenty cities in fourteen states on February 12. "In several cities—Jacksonville, Houston, Memphis—the meetings were the largest and most enthusiastic held in many years. In Houston, the Mayor participated by introducing the Rev. Adam Clayton Powell to an audience of over 3,000."[2]

Baker herself also reacted to counter criticism of the Crusade. In a March 26, 1958, letter to Ralph Abernathy she wrote: "Despite the Associated Press story that there has been a drop in the number of Negro registrations since the Crusade was launched, reports from the cities I have reached show that some good sound work has been and is being done, and that the results are far from negative."[3] To King she wrote: "I talked with New Orleans, Baton Rouge, Shreveport, Mobile, Tallahassee, Jacksonville, Nashville, Chattanooga, Knoxville and Durham. All of these places had something to report."[4]

By the end of February 1958, the task she ostensibly had gone to Atlanta to do was essentially completed, but there were people working with SCLC who wanted her to stay on and run the organization. Among these were her old allies Stanley Levison and Bayard Rustin and some of the board members: Ralph Abernathy, Fred Shuttlesworth, C. O. Simkins. In the end she stayed pending the successful conclusion of a search for an executive director. She suggested the Reverend John Tilley, who was eventually hired after the first choice, Dr. Lucius Pitts, head of Tougaloo College, the black college in Jackson, Mississippi, declined.

Long before she had taken on the job of director of the Crusade, Baker had had serious questions about the SCLC. She had gotten depressed ("or certainly irritated") by what she saw of the leadership in Montgomery. While it was important that a Southern-based organization should be developed as a counterpart to the NAACP, which was Northern-based, "in terms of its national office, . . . it was apparent that what was developing in Montgomery was this cult of personality.[5]

"On one occasion, an anniversary, they had this meeting in Montgomery, and there was nothing, nothing, but nothing in the call to the meeting that dealt with people or involving people," said

Baker. "The basis of the call was the honoring of our great leader, and even the achievements, if there were any, of the association, were not highlighted. Everything was a reflection of the greatness of the individual. . . . I spoke to [King] about that, which was not very bright. And I spoke to people who were sponsoring it. When I spoke to him, he said, 'Well, I can't help what people do.'"

Later, at an evaluation workshop, Baker asked a question about the lack of machinery for getting a continuing program that would provide opportunity for people who had given much in the initial boycott. She pointed to a number of women who had participated and said: "These were women who had demonstrated a kind of dedication, and who had enough intelligence, and had enough contacts with other people to have been useful, to have found a role to help move people along." However, she continued, "no role was provided for them, and that's the way it went."

Baker had been thinking of the nurse she had met who would work all night at a hospital, but who was there in the morning to do whatever needed to be done. On one occasion, after the boycott was over, King was arrested and Baker was in a demonstration outside the jail. The nurse was there too, despite having worked all night. "Now that kind of dedication could have been utilized," Baker said. She spoke of the woman who baked pies and sold them and brought the proceeds to the Montgomery Improvement Association each week. "That woman may never have developed to the point of being a leader of a workshop, but she could have been integrated into a program and her talents could have been developed," Baker said. When asked, "What do you suppose happened to all of those people?" she replied, "Nothing. That's the tragedy of it."[6]

Dissatisfaction with what she saw as King's inability or unwillingness to organize remained with her. For a time after the Crusade, more or less cordial relations existed between Baker and King.[7] Yet Baker seemed always to prod, and her prodding rankled. In a letter dated May 19, 1958, for example, Baker wrote concerning a mass meeting in Clarksdale where King was to be the main speaker. Pointedly she wrote to King, "I know that you would hesitate to be the only speaker and would like to suggest the possibility that one or two others be requested to deal with specific points, such as explaining the provisions of the 1957 Civil Rights Act and procedure for making use of the act or some similar informational emphasis."[8] What she was saying between the lines was, "In addition to your inspiring talk, we need some factual information to help the organizers."

Baker consistently pushed for mass organizing. In a July 1958 administrative committee meeting, where the discussion centered around what type of organization SCLC should be, Baker said: "The decision to have an executive type or a mass organization will determine the extent to which we aim to meet the demands of the period. We are really passing through a revolutionary period. We have no mass movement. Because of present restrictions on leftist groups, existing organizations have not found it necessary to compete with them. Now SCLC has a real opportunity to develop the mass action that we must have to implement school decisions, the 1957 Civil Rights Act, etc. But if we fail to act, sooner or later some other group will provide the leadership, because mass action is sorely needed."[9]

She was increasingly irritated with King, complaining that often she didn't even know where he was, so she could not consult him when she needed to. She was also annoyed by King's tendency to delay decision making. "Martin had to consult a whole lot of people before he could make up his mind. . . . Sometimes, to me, they were very small decisions that should not have necessitated the wide consultation that he felt he had to involve himself in." On the other hand, everyone awaited King's final word. The result: "No decision can be made until he makes it. But this does not mean that he has been the one to analyze it and to think it through."[10]

From the outset there was a clash. Baker attributed it to her being a woman—not a young, alluring female, attractive to libidinous men in their thirties and forties, but a mature, self-assured woman who did not tolerate sloppy work or sloppy thinking. She was impatient with King, almost as if he were a recalcitrant youngster. This was one source of their conflict: King's resistance to being "mothered." In reality, however, Baker was trying to be a mentor, not a mother. She was trying to shape him into an organizer, though she had little hope of success.

Neither King nor Abernathy had any organizing experience, whereas Baker had a lifetime of experience in organizing people. But she was not part of the old-boy network of Southern black ministers, and she was not "church," at least in a manner to which the young ministers were accustomed. She was a commanding personage who did not kowtow to the ministerial presence. "I was not the kind of person that made a special effort to be ingratiating," said Baker in a 1974 interview. "I didn't try to insult, but I did not hesitate to be positive about the things with which I agreed or disagreed."[11] Ralph Abernathy's widow, Juanita Abernathy, concurred: Baker was "a resourceful woman, perceptive, candid, honest, forthright." With a smile she added, "If you didn't want to know what she thought, don't ask her."[12]

Yet despite the difficulties, she continued working. In November, Baker organized a major SCLC conference in Norfolk. There she met with Harris Wofford, who was on the legal staff of the recently established U.S. Commission on Civil Rights. The CRC was scheduling hearings on voter rights violations. When Baker learned from Wofford that it had not received enough affidavits on violations, she returned to Atlanta and fired off a series of letters to local leaders around the South to encourage the gathering and filing of affidavits. She visited several Alabama counties to assess local preparations for the hearings scheduled for December 8 and prepared a detailed memorandum for King and Abernathy, ending with "After the hearing, what? Special attention should be given to this question, with special reference to Alabama. I have a few ideas when we meet and can discuss them."

There was a working relationship between SCLC and the commission at this point. Baker and Rufus Lewis of the Montgomery Movement met with Colonel A. H. Rosenfeld, head of the Surveys and Investigations Division of the CRC to discuss the complaints from the various counties. Baker felt that it was important to have representatives from other Southern states present at the Alabama hearings because, as she wrote in a memo to the executive board of SCLC, "It is highly important that this hearing reflect the widespread and intense interest that Negroes of the South have in registering and voting."[13]

Having made a decision to remain with SCLC, at least temporarily, Baker steadfastly continued her fund-raising and voter registration efforts. In a letter to A. Philip Randolph in November she asked for his advice on approaching the AFL-CIO. In a postscript she noted: "I submitted your name as one of my personal references in connection with an apartment application. I don't think this will be too involved and hope you don't mind."[14] Randolph replied by return mail saying that he would approach the AFL-CIO for funds and added: "You are free to use my name at any time if it may be helpful to you."[15] Randolph and Baker had a long-lasting friendship. He spoke of his great admiration for her and stressed her "quiet respect of other individuals' points of view."[16]

Later he said: "Ella has the unique quality of having the necessary sense of struggle for an oppressed people to achieve the alleviation of oppression, and at the same time she is capable of understanding . . . certain principles of organizing that [are] necessary to achieve an objective. Many militants don't understand that. They think that a part of militancy is to disregard organized procedure."[17] Here Randolph hit upon one of Baker's strongly held beliefs. Throughout her career she pushed for organized procedure, and the lack of it was especially frustrating to her in SCLC. She agitated perpetually for simple things like office tools, a mimeograph machine, stationery, an air conditioner. She complained, often bitterly, about King's inaccessibility; sometimes she could not reach him for consultation for days.

She was in demand by local groups precisely because of her professional organizational skills. In late 1958 she spent several weeks with the United Christian Movement of Shreveport, Louisiana, working on their voter registration campaign. The director, C. O. Simkins, who openly appreciated Baker's organizing ability, was on the SCLC board and managed to get her to return the following February and stay on into March through the CRC hearings in Louisiana.[18]

The campaign in Shreveport climaxed on R Day, March 19, 1959, when 250 persons went to the Caddo Parish Courthouse to attempt to register. A letter to registered voters signed by Reverend R. C. Thomas, general chairman of the voter registration drive, and by Baker as director, urged them to bring at least one person to the courthouse to register. They should do this, Baker prodded, to "show our unity with our brothers and sisters in other parts of the South" as well as to "show that we are determined to become first-class citizens."[19] They wanted a massive turnout.

As director of the Shreveport voter campaign Baker ran the office, organized mass voter registration efforts, coordinated the work of committees, and wrote leaflets. Just before she returned to Atlanta she outlined for the steering committee a plan for future work. Opening with praise for their work, she stressed the need for resources "to help provide prospective voters with information and confidence." She advocated that clinics and workshops be held during periods when the registration books were closed and recommended that churches and civic clubs be asked to assume responsibility for taking a specified number of people to the courthouse on days when the books were open.[20] She then pointed to two areas that needed further attention: organizing registration committees in churches and increasing the number of block canvassers. As to the first she said: "It may be highly advisable if the ministers already associated with the organization would jointly sign a short statement as to why ministers and churches should be interested in voter-registration, with Biblical references pertinent to their position." True to form, she noted, "There is a definite need for more training machinery."[21]

Baker coordinated any number of large meetings in the various Southern states to plan voter campaigns. The agenda for an Alabama meeting was typical: 15 minutes for opening devotions and 15 minutes total for remarks on "Why This Meeting Is Important." The Reverend K. L. Bufford, acting president of the Tuskegee Civic

Association, W. C. Patton, president of the Alabama State Coordinating Committee on Registration and Voting, and King were allotted no more than 5 minutes each! She was running a tight ship and not giving time for oratory.

Baker said that once before she had spoken to King about limiting speakers and he had said, "Well, you know that if Joe gets up there and turns them out, that Ralph's got to get up there and do that, too." So, Baker said, "I asked whether it's just a matter of being a sophomoric oratorical contest. Of course none of this endeared me to anybody. . . . I know that people do listen and can respond to information with the same degree of enthusiasm that they respond to just sound."

In April she was in Birmingham at a meeting of the Alabama Christian Movement for Human Rights. "Mrs. Ella Baker was in our midst and briefly told us of her struggle to help make our people conscious of the worth of the ballot in hand," the *Pittsburgh Courier* reported. "She was given a standing ovation."[22] President Shuttlesworth said that she would be back soon as a keynote speaker. She did return in June to give a major address at the third anniversary meeting of the ACMHR. Speaking on "What Price Freedom?" she warned the audience to "beware of the accommodating type of Negro leader who says what he thinks local southern officials want to hear." She said that the leader who limits the goals to one aspect of the movement such as voter registration, while ignoring other issues, "is as dangerous as those white persons who lump together the NAACP and the White Citizens Councils as the 'two extremes.' Both are misrepresenting the facts and therefore befuddling the issues." She pointed out that legal victories can be implemented "only if people make use of every right won, and continue a determined battle against segregation wherever and whenever it exists."[23]

One of her main tasks that spring was organizing a dinner honoring Tom Mboya, the Kenyan leader; it was to be a tribute to him, a bow to African solidarity, and a fund-raising event for SCLC. By now Baker was officially executive director of SCLC. Tilley had departed on April 15, having been fired on April 2 by a unanimous decision of the administrative committee. On April 4, after conferring with King and Abernathy, Baker agreed to stay on until a permanent director could be found.

In a May 15 report to the board[24] Baker outlined her activities since October 1958, reporting on her five-week stint in Shreveport and her work with the CRC and outlining plans for the imminent Southwide Institute on Nonviolent Resistance to Segregation. She briefly touched on the letters and telegrams of protest that SCLC had issued. Among these were protests on the bombing of a Jewish temple in Atlanta and numerous missives regarding the lynching of Mack Charles Parker (on April 25, 1959) in Poplarville, Mississippi. Parker had been taken from a jail cell where he was being held on rape charges and his body was later found in the Pearl River. SCLC and other organizations demanded a federal investigation. In one of the few instances of FBI diligence in a civil rights case, agents obtained confessions and tried to get the evidence introduced in court, but it was suppressed.[25] Such brutal lynchings affected Ella Baker deeply. (Years later when I was filming her for a documentary on her life and work she began to weep as she recounted the 1955 lynching of Chicago teenager Emmett Till in Money, Mississippi. This was the only time I saw her cry.)[26]

Dealing with long-range goals, she reiterated the need for leadership training and pushed for "real coordination" of civil rights groups. She also called for greater emphasis on promoting the participation of women and youth. A significant proposal was for the distribution of thousands of pieces of literature in the North, urging Negro voters "not to let their Southern brothers and sisters down by failing to vote."[27]

Baker maintained her contacts in the North, writing to her many associates. In May 1959 she sent a letter to the Reverend Thomas Kilgore of Harlem's Friendship Baptist Church, enclosing a check for $160 "to cover church contributions for the 17 Sundays" that she had missed while in the South with SCLC.[28] Kilgore replied, saying that he would not be in town when she arrived for services on May 31, 1959, but "we still claim and cherish your membership in Friendship and though we miss you a great deal in the immediate life of the church, we are happy to lend you and your service for the wider outreach and for the things which we stand and promote." Kilgore then suggested that Baker be given a few minutes at the morning service "to bring us up to date on what the Southern Christian Leadership Conference is doing."[29] Baker was also in close touch with Levison and Randolph, especially in regard to fund-raising. She was particularly anxious to take advantage of Northern outrage at reports of violent reprisals against Negroes who tried to register to vote.

Baker suggested to King a fund-raising campaign in selected northeastern cities. "It is quite clear to those of us who have had occasion to present the Southern cause to audiences in the East," she said, "that the people are eager to respond to a going program in the South, especially one that creatively and dynamically involves the masses to act to secure their civil rights."[30] To buttress her argument she pointed to three talks she had made in the previous few months. One to the executive committee of the New York chapter of Christian Action had resulted in more than $2,200. A ten-minute talk to the Empire Baptist Missionary convention had produced a $200 collection on the spot and a promise that a statewide appeal would be forthcoming. In a talk at Friendship Baptist Church, Baker had asked for 20 people to pledge to raise $25 each and 56 had volunteered. The number was later increased to 100 and "in ten days raised more than $1600."[31]

She continued to push her concept of the need for and possibilities of a wider base for SCLC and pursued this idea in the *Pittsburgh Courier* columns she wrote, substituting for Shuttlesworth while he was abroad. She claimed that the "most salutary difference" between the early 1940s and 1959 was that "the leadership base has broadened and continues to expand; and that more and more it is recognized that people, in large numbers, must act."[32]

In the meantime she continued her travels and speaking engagements—while also organizing the Southwide Institute on Nonviolent Resistance to Segregation—speaking at a mass meeting of the

Montgomery Improvement Association on voting and participating in a workshop on citizenship at the Penn Conference Center in Frogmore, South Carolina, where she gave the main Saturday evening address on "First Class Citizenship: It's [*sic*] Rights and Responsibilities." She was described in the program as executive director of the Crusade for Citizenship, illustrating the confusion that still remained over her title and position in SCLC.[33]

Over forty leaders from organizations such as the NAACP, the YWCA, and the PTA attended the Penn Center meeting, which was sponsored by the South Carolina Council of Human Relations. The meeting was important as a prelude to SCLC's annual conference, scheduled to be held in Columbia, South Carolina, in September. Baker pointed out that through "the contacts made at this meeting we are in touch with the representative community leadership of South Carolina." She reported that at a planning meeting in Columbia with the Reverend Matthew McCollom and I. S. Leevy, SCLC board members who would chair the statewide committee, it had been decided to hold the sessions at Benedict College. "There are several large churches in the city, but as you know, it is possible to have them vying for the meeting, and it is also possible that this can breed disaffection," Baker stated.[34]

The aims of the Southwide Institute, which was jointly sponsored by the SCLC, the Congress of Racial Equality, and the Fellowship of Reconciliation, were to explore the philosophy and practical application of nonviolent resistance and to develop leaders who would return to their local communities and train others to resist segregation without violence. Baker presided at the opening session and participated in a panel on "Allies and Opponents of the Negro's Drive for Equality." She reported that it was attended by sixty-five persons from sixteen states.[35]

Consistently and constantly pushing for a greater emphasis on organizing, Baker restated some of SCLC's basic aims: "to facilitate coordinated action by local groups and to assist in their sharing resources and experiences" and "to develop potential leaders." She insisted that to "achieve even minimum coordination between local groups calls for spelling out quite clearly action that should be taken, and agreeing on what action should be taken where, when, and how." She added: "Since the job cannot be done with a few hands, it seems timely to plan for expanding the office staff." Trying to goad the ministers into action, she concluded: "These observations and suggestions have been advanced because I am convinced that SCLC can and should play a unique role in the struggle for human rights; but I am equally convinced that this cannot be done by following, or even approximating 'usual procedures.' SCLC must present creative leadership that will bestir dynamic mass action."

These conclusions followed a rather indirect plea for more staff in a memo to the board in which she delineated the tasks performed since April, "when the executive staff was reduced to one person," and noted: "When added to our other activities, this has been not only physically exhausting, but intellectually frustrating and spiritually depleting."[36] The tone of the memo seems to indicate that Baker was willing to stay on to bring about what she envisioned as SCLC's goals. They were, indeed, the stated goals, but it is doubtful that the top leadership took them as seriously as she did, mainly because of their interest in other matters: establishing a nationwide presence for the organization, and King as a national figure. During Baker's tenure no more executive staff was added, though some additional clerical help was hired.

Baker was by no means the only person concerned about the future of the SCLC. Others, including King, were not happy about the organization's lack of success in its voter registration efforts, lack of focus, and shortage of funds. Yet Baker approached the problems from a different point of view. She was not so much concerned with the longevity of the organization as she was with the development of a movement. She did not envision the SCLC as a leading civil rights organization with national recognition, but rather as a vehicle for the creation of a mass movement with indigenous leadership. This difference was the main cause of the breach with King that eventually led to her resignation.

Baker put her case strongly at the Columbia meeting. In her address to the plenary on September 30, 1959, she stressed the need to pressure the U.S. Congress for action on civil rights and to concentrate on organizing for voter registration, urging mass demonstrations at registration places.

She pressed once again for one of her primary goals: adult literacy. In October she pursued this goal by writing to the Department of Health, Education and Welfare, seeking help in setting up an adult education program. Edward W. Brice, a specialist in fundamental and literacy education, recommended that she contact the National Commission for Adult Literacy and provided statistics on literacy. In South Carolina, for example, one out of two Negroes over 25 years of age was functionally illiterate.

Baker used this information as ammunition in a hard-hitting memorandum dated October 23, 1959, and entitled "SCLC as a Crusade," in which she tried to shake SCLC leaders out of their drive for national civil rights prominence.[37] She outlined her thoughts on a literacy program, proposing that SCLC "stimulate religious bodies, civic and fraternal organizations (composed of women, especially) to utilize the facilities for reducing functional illiteracy among Negroes." She suggested that SCLC interest such groups as the Women's Division of the National Baptist Convention, the National Council of Negro Women, and national college sororities. She noted: "The literacy project could well serve as the basis for calling a Southwide meeting of women, as we proposed before," adding, "Incidentally, the Laubach method [for teaching literacy] is being used in 80 countries and 253 languages with phenomenal results. The slogan 'Each One Teach One' certainly has crusading value."

But the main thrust of her message was the need to develop a mass movement. Having grown increasingly less patient with SCLC's lack of program, she again challenged the organization to put people in motion. She wrote: "The word CRUSADE connotes for me a vigorous movement with high purpose and involving masses of people." She suggested the recruitment of one thousand ministers "and/or other leaders" who would give 8 hours a month for person-to-person contact with people in their communities to push voter registration, arguing that "it could take on crusading proportions." Using a formula that she had used countless times in the past, she argued: "It is possible to contact four persons an hour; and in eight hours a month, one minister could reach 30 persons, at least. If one thousand gave 8 hours it would mean 30,000 persons in one month. For 10 months this could mean 300,000 persons. If initiated and accepted by the leadership of SCLC it is quite possible, I believe, to commit 1,000 leaders to give eight hours a month to work directly with the people."

Her emphasis was, as always, on the need to search out and develop indigenous leaders, especially in the hard-core states. She proposed the development of "action teams" to train people in the techniques of nonviolent resistance. To bolster her proposals with facts and allies and make her arguments more palatable and persuasive, she had spoken to Brice and other experts in literacy education, and to the Reverend James Lawson, the foremost advocate of nonviolent training. She had done her homework well.

Baker didn't let the question of SCLC's program and methods rest with the October 23 Crusade memo, but continued to warn the leadership of ongoing criticisms of SCLC. In a handwritten note dated December 1, 1959, she wrote about a conversation she had had with I. S. Leevy and Alice Spearman, enumerating questions raised by both whites and Negroes: "Is King so philosophical and naive that he is being used by radical and questionable forces (ex. F. L. Shuttlesworth, Ella Baker), or does he surround himself with less trained and erudite to bolster his own status and is he thus 'using his co-workers'?" Another comment was, "The organization is shot through with radicals."[38] Spearman had written to Baker saying that the competitive feeling regarding SCLC was strong in other major civil rights organizations. Referring to the NAACP, Spearman observed that the feeling of rivalry, "which goes almost to the point of resentment, is being fed from higher up—from beyond state boundaries."[39]

In her report to the executive board for the period September 30 to December 8, 1959, Baker reiterated her concerns about the SCLC's goals. She said that priority should be given to fund-raising, pointing out once again that the office should be expanded, since a one-person office with extremely limited office equipment was inadequate to the tasks already at hand. Still, she soldiered on and some of her proposals were adopted. A prime example was the literacy project. Baker worked out an arrangement with Septima Clark of the Highlander Folk School. Clark and Esau Jenkins ran a citizenship school to teach adults how to read and write and to prepare them for the testing they would face when they attempted to register to vote. (It was not until 1961 that the citizenship school at Dorchester Center near Savannah, Georgia, was taken over by SCLC, to be run by Clark and Dorothy Cotton under the supervision of Reverend Andrew Young, who had become SCLC executive director.)

Given the real differences she had with the SCLC ministers one wonders why she stayed in the job so long, especially because her marriage was breaking up. In 1959, Baker and her husband agreed to live separately. He had not recovered from the death of his mother and had become depressed and morose. They decided to make a change, but Baker and her niece maintained contact with Bob, visiting him from time to time.

Baker and Jackie moved to Lenox Terrace apartments at 10 West 135th Street, a prestigious address, easily accessible to transportation and a draw for many prominent politicians and activists. Their apartment appeared to be a repository for old newspaper clippings and leaflets. James Forman had a similar impression of her Atlanta apartment: "a living room cluttered with newspapers, which she was in the process of clipping."[40] One of Baker's favorite ploys was to stash her dirty dishes in the refrigerator. Thus, she reasoned, she both foiled the cockroaches and kept the unsightly things out of sight.

Though her home base was New York, Baker remained with SCLC for another year. A prime reason, of course, was her abiding interest in the movement and in the local people who were on the front lines. They were embattled. After the *Brown* decision in 1954, opposition to the Negro struggle increased steadily year by year. The NAACP was under fierce attack, outlawed in Alabama and virtually out of business in other states. Segregationists who were more middle-class than the typical Klansmen formed White Citizens Councils to fight integration, using economic reprisals and intimidation rather than lynchings. President Eisenhower had finally sent federal troops to Little Rock to enforce the law around school integration and prevent full-scale rioting. The 1957 Civil Rights Act had been passed; weak though it was, the new law did establish the Civil Rights Commission. Nevertheless, by 1959, the federal government had shown little inclination to look for a remedy to Southern segregation.

Just as when she was with the NAACP, Baker's prime aim was to be of service to the grassroots leadership, and thus to a mass movement. Whatever her reasons for staying, her dissatisfaction grew. Reflecting on Baker's relationship to SCLC, Bob Moses said: "What I take as important in terms of Miss Baker's relationship to SCLC was her different concept about leadership. First, the idea that leadership would emerge in the community and second, the idea of helping leadership grow. . . . That was something different from the SCLC version of leadership . . . [which was] to project the national leader. There's a tension between projecting a national leader and creating local leadership. It was in that tension that I think Miss Baker wasn't able really to function within the SCLC organization. If you're spending all of your energy trying to project the national leader, you have very little energy left over to actually develop a local leadership."

Moses went on to point out that projecting a national leader lends itself very well to mobilization, whereas developing local leadership is much more tied to organizing. This represents a "difference in philosophy and a difference in style as to how you approach the community."[41]

But her niece Jackie felt that she had other reasons for remaining with the organization. "She was eager to prove that she could do the job, to prove herself as a woman, as an equal."[42] Janet

Jamott, who had been an active participant in the 1964 Mississippi drive, confirmed the existence of male-female tensions. She thought that there were three reasons why the Reverend Wyatt Tee Walker was subsequently chosen to replace Baker: he was a minister, he was a media figure, and he was male.[43]

Baker was the first person to suggest Walker for the job. She had invited Wyatt and his wife and the Reverend George Lawrence to her home in New York for dinner to discuss the possibility long before the December 1959 Birmingham meeting at which the decision was taken. She recalled later: "I am very vulnerable as far as young people are concerned, and I can perhaps be very easily misled when people give the impression of being dedicated. And I had begun to think of Wyatt as having great dedication." She thought that Wyatt had been under the illusion that he would become the organization's spokesman, just as executive directors of other civil rights organizations were, but "he soon learned that this could not take place." This led to "dissatisfaction" and "some strains." After Walker left the SCLC, Baker "never raised the question as to the extent to which he felt he had been screwed," but she thought that Walker had erroneously assumed that the reason for projecting the president as the central figure before Walker's arrival was because "there was nobody else in the organization worthy of being projected."[44]

In an interview for the film *Fundi*, Walker said that Baker had a difficult time in the SCLC because she wasn't a minister and so didn't have the ministerial skills of maneuvering among the preachers. She was never reluctant to give her views, and this did not sit well with the ministers, who were used to having their word taken as gospel. Baker, brought up in a religious household that did not countenance subservience, would have none of that. As board member Reverend C. T. Vivian declared, "She wasn't church."[45]

Andrew Young, who followed Walker as executive director, and who was himself a minister, had an explanation of Baker's problems that came close to her own: King had a domineering mother and wasn't about to accept a surrogate one in his organization.[46] Baker said much the same thing, and also added the matter of class. King "was part of a middle-class background that was highly competitive on a level that to me means nothing." Prominent black Atlanta families measured their children's accomplishments against each other. Baker thought that King's background "had not provided him with any personal sense of struggle in the sense of getting through school, finding a place for himself in the church." She did not see him as a person who had fought his own way up and who might, therefore, recognize the importance of developing strengths in others. She felt that King, and others like him who had been provided with all of the advantages of a cossetted upbringing, could not accept the concepts of sharing and of developing the skills of others that she valued.

Some commentators see Baker as embittered by her experience with SCLC. King was one of the two civil rights leaders whom she criticized often, and sometimes vociferously (the other being Walter White). She sometimes referred to him sardonically as "the Great One," although in later years she expressed caution about some of her comments, saying that before they were put into print they "should be looked at carefully."

She was, though, more disappointed than bitter, because of what she viewed as a failure of leadership. Her disapproval was fundamental. She felt that many people, including King himself, failed to recognize the fact that "Martin did not make the movement; the movement made him." She was exasperated by the failure of SCLC to function as a "group-centered leadership, rather than a leadership-centered group," and appalled by its unwillingness (or inability) to organize a mass movement.[47] Furthermore, she knew that without the input of Rustin, Levison, and herself, the SCLC might never have come to be. This galled her because the SCLC failed to live up to its promise.

To put Baker's relationship with King in perspective, however, one wonders if there was not, in addition to a generational clash, also a clash of personalities. King was a decidedly social being. He liked to have fun, had a sense of humor, and took most things in his stride. Baker tended to be more serious, more focused. She did like to lift her glass of bourbon and enjoyed social gatherings with friends, but she was not able to unbend enough to take *organizational* matters lightly. She relaxed more with local people whose needs and desires she understood.

She enjoyed dinner parties, but they were only an excuse for talk. She occasionally gave dinners, but usually with a purpose, an organizational goal. Estelle Noble, who had met Baker when she was youth adviser to the NAACP, and Lee Simpson said that Baker didn't cook. Jackie concurred, though she said that Aunt Ella had to cook when she moved in with her. Jackie said that up to the time of her arrival, "Aunt Ella ate a lot of raw foods—even meat" (a practice that stemmed from her friendship with Josephine Schuyler). When Jackie arrived with her Southern tastes, Aunt Ella had to succumb and prepare fried chicken, though she always expressed an intense interest in gourmet fare, which was all the rage in certain circles in the 1960s and 1970s.

Baker found much of what she had hoped for in the young people of the 1960s movement. The students were not encumbered by strivings to be "in," to be accepted; they were not limited by a drive to get ahead, to gain a piece of the pie. More importantly, they brought their own daring and defiance vigorously into the battle for equal rights. She admired their confrontational stance and welcomed the inclusiveness of their thrust for the creation of the "beloved community."

CHAPTER SEVEN

Political Mama

The chief emphasis I tried to make was their right to make their own decision. . . . The only reason that I became relevant . . . was because I had lived through certain experiences and had had certain opportunities to gather information and organizational experience. . . . I have always felt that if there is any time in our existence that you have a right to make mistakes it should be when you're young, cause you have some time to live down some of the mistakes, or to offset them. I felt that what they [the students] were doing was certainly . . . creative [and] much more productive than anything that had happened in my life, and it shouldn't be stifled. . . . I must have sensed also that it was useless to try to put the brakes on, because it was unleashed enthusiasm . . . an overflow of a dam that had been penned up for years, and it had to run its course.

JUST AS ROSA PARKS DECIDED one day that she was not going to move to the back of the bus, the four North Carolina students who sat down at a whites-only Woolworth's lunch counter on February 1, 1960, also decided not to move. Thus began the new challenge to the system of legally supported racial segregation that had been in existence for decades. To Ella Baker it was a dream come true. Here was the beginning of the civil rights revolution which she had looked forward to since the days of the 1930s when she had ventured from neighborhood to neighborhood listening to speeches that carried the promise of change.

Within days the sit-ins spread across the South—where segregation was not simply custom, but the law—through North Carolina, to Maryland, Tennessee, Virginia, Alabama, Georgia, Kentucky, and South Carolina. Hundreds of students were arrested. They were taunted with racial epithets and often attacked by mobs of angry whites.

This upsurge was what Ella Baker had been waiting for. She received a call from an excited SCLC board member, Fred L. Shuttlesworth, who said that she must inform Martin of the amazing new development. Immediately grasping the momentousness of the event, she dutifully informed King and promptly set about the task of organizing this potential force into a cohesive one. She began to plan for a gathering of representatives from the protest areas, convincing the SCLC to put up $800 to cover the expenses of the meeting. She persuaded King to sign a call to "chart new goals and achieve a more unified sense of direction for training and action in Nonviolent Resistance."[1] To supplement the sit-in meeting that was scheduled for Easter weekend, April 15 to 17, in Raleigh, North Carolina, SCLC also planned nonviolence training for young people at three locations in the spring: Nashville, Mobile, and Shreveport.

Baker rushed out a follow-up letter to protesting students. Citing the courageous, dedicated, and thoughtful leadership manifested by the hundreds of Negro students who presented new challenges for the future, she urged that the "great potential for social change" called for a determination of the question, Where do we go from here?[2]

In preparation for the April meeting Baker went to Raleigh and reached an agreement with Shaw University on meeting rooms, meals, and accommodations. Since Shaw could only house about forty people, Baker contacted nearby St. Augustine College, the YMCA, and local residents whom she had met as a student there and during her travels for the NAACP. Baker arranged to stay with a Shaw alumna who had been in the class behind her, Effie Yeargan, a distant cousin of Max Yergin, a radical theorist whom Baker had met during her Shaw days and whom she had encountered again during her early days in Harlem. Yeargan was one of the founders of the Raleigh Citizens Association, which was organized to host the students, cosponsor the gathering, and provide whatever subsidiary housing was necessary.[3]

Having taken care of the logistics, Baker then went on to deal with policy. She began to press the issue of the independence of the students, which was to be the most important question at the meeting. In a memo to King and Abernathy, she eased into her agenda by remarking that on a trip to Raleigh-Durham she had had a chance meeting with Glenn Smiley of the Fellowship of Reconciliation and Douglas Moore, a young Durham minister. She pointed out that they "agreed that the meeting should be youth centered and that the adults attending would serve in an advisory capacity, and should mutually agree to 'speak only when asked to do so.' "[4] This was to become the central issue at the meeting, yet Baker's concerns were broader: She wanted an organization to develop.

She wrote Anne Braden, the codirector of the Southern Conference Educational Fund (SCEF), expressing the hope that "out of this meeting will come some workable machinery for maintaining affective [sic] communication between youth leaders in areas of recent and future protest activities, and a larger degree of coordinated strategy." She added that she hoped that "several work-teams of young persons can be financed for work in the South this summer. The need for developing more experienced young workers in the field of civil rights is obvious, I am sure. This may be only a dream of mine, but I think it can be made real."[5]

Determined to make the meeting a success, Baker set about the task of identifying the leaders of the various demonstrations. She scanned newspaper accounts, contacted people with whom she had worked, and wrote to heads of student bodies. She dispatched Reverend Moore on a tour of North Carolina and Virginia to urge demonstrators to send a representative. Lawson and CORE also contacted activists. In the end over two hundred delegates attended the Raleigh meeting, as well as observers from such organizations as FOR, CORE, the American Friends Service Committee, the National

Student Association, and the YWCA. Nineteen schools and colleges from the North were represented. Baker said that while the conference was too large to be a leadership training workshop, it became "a mountaintop experience of enthusiasm."[6]

Though the meeting was an exciting and productive one, there were problems. At the start a conflict arose over who would preside at the opening session. Baker suggested James Lawson, FOR's Southern regional secretary, who had recently been expelled from Vanderbilt University for his sit-in activities. Lawson was a leading advocate of nonviolence and had been training Nashville students in nonviolent techniques. King and Abernathy wanted Baker to open the conference, but she argued for Lawson, pointing out that he was closer in age to the students and that she was not "an advocate of nonviolence in the true sense." Baker prevailed. Her next contretemps was with the press, which she insisted be excluded from some sessions. She had, as she put it, "quite a run-in" with the reporters, but on this issue, too, she prevailed.

Soon thereafter, the major conflict came into play. This was the controversy that Baker had anticipated and had tried to prepare King for in her March memo. At issue was the question of the students' independence: Should the students set up a separate organization or become affiliated with an existing one? The leading contenders for the role of adult sponsor were SCLC and CORE. On Saturday morning Baker was summoned to a caucus. Present were King; his second in command, Ralph Abernathy; Wyatt Tee Walker, soon to become Baker's successor as director of the SCLC; and Lawrence Reddick, the SCLC historian.

The adult leaders did not seem to know where the conference was heading, so they asked Baker, who seemed to have more influence with the delegates than they did. She said that it was too soon to predict the outcome, but that it was more important to establish a temporary continuations committee "to permit the students to find their own sense of direction."

It soon became clear what the real purpose of the caucus was: to find out from her what the students might do—or more precisely, to figure out a way to coerce the students into becoming the youth arm of the SCLC. When the meeting participants began to divide up the delegations that each one would lobby, Baker dug in her heels, stating that she would have no part in dragooning delegations. Walker proposed in his calm, ministerial way that he could take care of Virginia. "Martin said he could talk to the Atlanta group and that he thought that Ralph [Abernathy] should take care of Alabama."[7]

So Baker walked out of the caucus. She was furious at the temper of the discussion and outraged by the ministers' plans to manipulate the students. The sit-ins were, to her, the beginning of a new approach in the fight for equality. She did not want to see it co-opted, corrupted, or changed. She felt that the students had something new to offer and to make the student movement a youth arm of an adult organization was a mistake. The adults had no understanding of the young people's vision. The young people were daring. They had something new to contribute. Up to now there had been no rebellion to match what had taken place after the first sit-in. She did not want this outpouring to be stifled.

Baker's departure signaled the beginning of a new phase for the civil rights movement. It was no longer to be controlled by a stodgy ministerial or bureaucratic presence. It was to be led by a new force.

The plenary session that followed was volatile. It became so tense that they resorted to, in Baker's words, "the old soothing syrup"[8] of "We Shall Overcome" to cool things down. Angry as she was over the plan to manipulate the students, she did nothing to prevent the maneuvering to secure votes in favor of affiliation—although she did speak out in the sessions for the young people's right to make their own decisions.

It could be claimed that SCLC had some grounds for seeking to adopt the young people. After all, it was SCLC money that had made the conference possible. It was the method of co-optation that aggravated Baker: She did not believe in arm-twisting. She did believe in the students, and in their promise.

It is doubtful that King exerted pressure on the students to affiliate with SCLC, but Ella Baker's stance was clear: Hope lay with the students. For her there was no illusion about what the ministers of SCLC could accomplish toward her goal of the development of a mass organization.

Charles McDew, an Orangeburg, South Carolina, student who was later to become SNCC chairman, said that Baker lobbied the students individually and advocated—at a closed meeting the students held without observers or other adults—the creation of an independent organization.[9] At the meeting's end the students had established the Temporary Student Nonviolent Coordinating Committee, made plans for continuations committee meetings, and adopted a statement of purpose, drafted by Lawson, that incorporated the principle of nonviolence, which "nurtures the atmosphere in which reconciliation and justice become actual possibilities."

> We affirm the philosophical or religious ideal of nonviolence as the foundation of our purpose, the presupposition of our faith, and the manner of our action. Nonviolence as it grows from Judaic-Christian traditions seeks a social order of justice permeated by love. Integration of human endeavor represents the crucial first step towards such a society.
>
> Through nonviolence, courage displaces fear; love transforms hate. Acceptance dissipates prejudice; hope ends despair. Peace dominates war; faith reconciles doubt. Mutual regard cancels enmity. Justice for all overthrows injustice. The redemptive community supersedes systems of gross social immorality.
>
> Love is the central motif of nonviolence. Love is the force by which God binds man to Himself and man to man. Such love goes to the extreme; it remains loving and forgiving even in the midst of hostility. It matches the capacity of evil to inflict suffering with an even more enduring capacity to absorb evil, all the while persisting in love.
>
> By appealing to conscience and standing on the moral nature of human existence, nonviolence nurtures the atmosphere in which reconciliation and justice become actual possibilities.[10]

At the mass meeting on Saturday night King delivered the main address and Baker spoke on the significance of the conference, sounding the theme with which she became identified. The lunch counter sit-ins were about larger issues, she said; they were "bigger than a hamburger."[11]

At the first meeting of the continuations committee in May 1960, Marion Barry, a Fisk University student who had participated in Lawson's nonviolent training sessions and in the Nashville sit-ins, was elected chair. By then the protest movement had spread across the South. There were hundreds of arrests, and violent confrontations had occurred in several cities. One of the reasons for the rapid spread of the demonstrations was the press attention they received, though Baker also felt that word of mouth was the strongest impetus: "A sister to a brother, members of the same fraternity, girlfriend to boyfriend, or simply calling up contacts, friends asking, 'What is happening on your campus?'" More importantly, the actions "were getting results."[12]

Baker felt strongly that the liberation movements in Africa and other parts of the world spurred on the U.S. civil rights movement. One of the most significant influences was the Sharpeville massacre of March 21, 1960. South African police fired into a crowd of eight thousand blacks who were staging a peaceful march; 69 people were killed and 180 were wounded. Here at home the failure to implement the 1954 *Brown* decision and the ineffectiveness of the Civil Rights Act of 1957 led to rising disappointment and "the developing climate of alienation of the young from the Establishment." She also pointed to the "additional impact on black youngsters of the rising independence of black people in Africa and other parts of the world."[13]

Baker had arranged for office space for the coordinating committee in a spare room at SCLC headquarters at 208 Auburn Avenue, and she got Jane Stembridge, a Union Theological Seminary student, to become the administrator. (They soon had to move out of the SCLC space, but Baker cajoled the landlord into renting them a tiny office across the street at a reduced rent.) Throughout this formative period SCLC lent its support to the fledgling organization. King and Baker attended all of the meetings, and SCLC gave encouragement as well as some financial aid.

During these early days some of Atlanta's "liberal" community criticized Baker for failing to keep the students sufficiently in check. Baker, however, felt that the students didn't need adult supervision, that "they had the right to make mistakes when they were young." Besides, she was exhilarated by the movement. To her it was "more productive than anything that had happened in [her] life." She felt strongly that it "shouldn't be stifled" and sensed, as others did not, that "it was useless to put the brakes on, because it was enthusiasm unleashed—an overflow of a dam that had been penned up for years and it had to run its course." Those who wanted to impose rules on the students wouldn't get anywhere because they simply could not communicate with them.[14]

Nashville sit-in leader John Lewis noted that although Baker was much older than the students, "in terms of ideas and philosophy and commitment she was one of the youngest persons in the movement."[15] SNCC worker Judy Richardson extended this judgment in an interview in 1993: "What was nice about Miss Baker is you never felt that she had a personal agenda that she was trying to put on. It was always about what is good for the organization, for black people, for whatever the larger issue was. [With] other adults you never really knew what else was hidden . . . what else they were trying to get through that they weren't talking about."[16]

In May, after the founding meeting of the Temporary Student Nonviolent Coordinating Committee, Baker organized a meeting in the chapel of Morris Brown College. Kenneth Kaunda, a leader of what was then known as Northern Rhodesia (Zambia), spoke, primarily to the students but also to some adults who had participated in the student movement. Then Baker addressed a workshop at Highlander Folk School on "The Place of the White Southerner in the Current Struggle," speaking on "What Can Be Done That Hasn't Been Done?" This meeting was one of the few at which Baker appeared in "movement attire," abandoning her neat business suit for trousers and a sleeveless blouse.

In the midst of helping the students set up the coordinating group, she was organizing the second State-wide Institute on Non-

Violent Resistance to Segregation[17] and preparing for her departure from SCLC on August 1, 1960. And as if this was not enough to occupy her, she was also soliciting clothing for the people of Fayette and Haywood counties in Tennessee who were being severely harassed for attempting to register to vote. Many had been evicted from plantations and were living in a tent city.

At the end of July Baker wrote to her many contacts in the South informing them of her impending departure from SCLC, saying: "My successor, the Reverend Wyatt Tee Walker, is a young man of vision, and I am confident that with him the program of the Conference will expand to meet the challenges that we face in the months and years ahead." She credited the demonstrating students for the inclusion of civil rights planks in both the Democratic and Republican party platforms. Baker had promoted the idea that the coordinating committee should send a delegation to each of the party conventions and had helped draft their testimony. She pointed out, however, that "planks and promises are only good when they are followed by action. That is why we must increase our determination to get all of our families, friends, and neighbors registered."

Then, as she so often did, she quoted from the Bible: "Now is our salvation nearer than when we first believed. Therefore, we must cast off the works of darkness and put on the armour of light." She continued: "The 'works of darkness' are ignorance, doubt and fear; but armed with truth and knowledge, faith and courage, we can and must follow the light of freedom to complete and certain victory." At the end she offered a small prayer: "May God grant you good health and increased courage to continue the fight for human justice and freedom for all mankind." There were also personal touches in the letter: she wrote that she cherished the fellowship shared and the cooperation received and spoke of her need for rest and a cataract operation, gave her New York address, and invited the addressees to visit her if in New York in August or September. After that, she assured them, she expected to be back in the Southern struggle.[18]

By this time, Robert Moses, who was to become one of the movement's most respected leaders, had arrived in Atlanta as an SCLC volunteer. A math teacher at Horace Mann High School in New York, he had been a volunteer in the Friends of SCLC office there, the brainchild of Rustin and Levison. Baker had not been apprised of Moses's impending arrival and no one had prepared work for him to do. Consequently, after a talk with Baker he began working in the SNCC office, where he became friends with Stembridge—perhaps in part because of their common bond as philosophy students. Moses credited Ella Baker and Jane Stembridge with getting him out of SCLC and into SNCC. "They knew I was disgruntled and gave me a way out," Moses said.[19]

Baker soon sent Moses off on a tour of Mississippi, Louisiana, and Alabama to convince demonstrators in protest areas to send delegates to the founding conference of SNCC, which was to be held at Atlanta University on October 14–15, 1960. Baker had returned to Atlanta from a trip to New York, where she had attended Jackie's wedding, to help the students prepare. There were few reporters present (myself among them), but the conference was a joyous occasion. When the delegates from Mississippi came in, they were greeted with a standing ovation. Mississippi was the toughest state, and the students from other areas, already battle-scarred, were paying tribute to the courage of the participants on the newest front.

The conference adopted the statement of purpose that had come out of the Raleigh meeting, dropped "temporary" from the name of the organization, formalized its relationship to the protest areas (meaning the places where sit-ins had taken place), and voted to publish the *Student Voice* monthly. SNCC (pronounced "Snick") was to be made up of one representative from each of sixteen states plus the District of Columbia. In addition, there was to be a staff made up of field secretaries and an expanded office staff. The constitution proclaimed: "SNCC shall serve as a channel of coordination and communication for the student movement. By direction of its Executive Committee through its staff it shall have authority to

Jacqueline pinning a corsage on Aunt Ella just before her marriage to Henry Brockington, September 17, 1960. (Courtesy of Jacqueline Brockington.)

initiate programs in areas where none presently exists, and to work closely with local protest groups in the intensification of the movement." In the formulation of the constitution it was decided to omit the phrase "in the South" from this paragraph, though SNCC remained a Southern-based movement. The constitution provided for voting members from other organizations, one representative each from the National Student Association, the National Student Christian Movement, and the National College and Youth Branch of the NAACP. There were to be observers from the American Friends Service Committee, American Civil Liberties Union, CORE, FOR, NAACP, SCLC, SCEF, National Student YWCA, the Southern Regional Council, and "any other group to be selected by the Student Nonviolent Coordinating Committee."[20]

Drawn by the excitement the movement engendered, many of these observers soon became SNCC staffers. Almost anyone who had contact with the rebelling students wanted to join in some way. Some promptly signed on for the duration at the going salary, $10.99 a week. Others went back North and joined support groups.

In the fluid days of the early 1960s, SNCC's structure was altered often. SNCC meetings were round-the-clock discussions of the organization's shape and function. Baker would sit in silence for much of the time, more often than not wearing a cotton face mask to protect her against the cigarette smoke. Like her mother, she suffered from respiratory troubles.

In these marathon meetings Baker used her old technique of asking questions. "I was not too sure that I had the answer," she recalled later. But often, her questions directed the discussions. Her technique was much like that of Nelson Mandela, who had learned it from his mentor, a tribal chieftain. Mandela wrote in his autobiography, *Long Walk to Freedom*, "I have always endeavored to listen to what each and every person in a discussion had to say before venturing my own opinion. Oftentimes, my own opinion will simply represent a consensus of what I heard in the discussion." Mandela always remembered the chieftain's axiom that a leader is like a shepherd: "He stays behind the flock, letting the most nimble go out ahead, whereupon the others follow, not realizing that all along they are being directed from behind."[21] This was, indeed, Baker's way.

Baker was a listener. Her practice was to hear everyone out and to accept ideas from even the youngest in the group—"if it was a good idea."[22] She taught the young people in SNCC that everyone had something to give, thus helping them learn to respect each other. SNCC chair Charles McDew recalled that she would pick out a kernel that was a good idea. "Somebody may have spoken for 8 hours, and 7 hours and 53 minutes was utter bullshit, but 7 minutes was good. She taught us to glean out the 7 minutes."[23]

This was a different way of working. Many adults tried telling the students how to behave, citing greater experience and knowledge, but this, Baker said, could not work for several reasons. In the first place, the young people were confident that there was something new about their movement, that it was innovative and successful to a far greater extent, achieving results more rapidly than earlier attempts had done. Then, too, Baker felt that the students were exhilarated by the speed with which their movement had grown. In a sense, they were leading the adults. She was convinced that despite King's growing prominence as a spokesman, SNCC was providing the cutting edge.

Baker's prescience was confirmed early in 1961 by two significant events: SNCC's move into the rural areas of Mississippi and the advent of the Freedom Rides.

At the urging of Baker, Bob Moses had made a second swing through Mississippi in 1961. There, at Baker's suggestion, he met with veteran activist Amzie Moore, whom Baker had known for several years. Inspired by Moore and C. S. Bryant in McComb, Moses laid out a plan for voter registration.

Taking two field secretaries with him, he set up headquarters in McComb, one of the poorest parts of the state. The group began working on voter registration. Their efforts soon drew national attention because of the violent reactions they encountered.

In the meantime CORE had started the Freedom Rides. Integrated groups of students, ministers, and priests boarded interstate buses to ride from Washington, D.C., to New Orleans with an intent to seek service in terminals along the route. In Alabama they were met by violent mobs. In Anniston, their bus was burned. In Birmingham, a white mob gathered and they were beaten as they disembarked; there were no police in sight. In Montgomery, law enforcement officers stood by idly, looking on as the riders were brutally beaten.

Attorney General Robert Kennedy called for a "cooling-off period," pressuring the students to stop the rides and focus on voter registration for the duration of a round of negotiations with bus company officials and local government representatives. So serious was the effort that draft deferments were offered to SNCC workers in exchange for concentrating on the vote. Largely through the attorney general's efforts, the Taconic and Field foundations and the Stern Family Fund provided money to the Southern Regional Council, which set up a tax-exempt arm, the Voter Education Project (VEP). Headed by Wiley Branton, a lawyer from Greenwood, Mississippi, VEP made grants to voter registration efforts, distributing over half a million dollars. SNCC received only $24,000 in 1962 and 1963.

The voter registration work led to the first major controversy in SNCC. The disagreement was over whether the organization should devote itself exclusively to direct action or to voter registration. This was the most serious of the organization's conflicts because it nearly caused a split—averted only by Baker's intervention. She was not about to watch her baby, her pride and joy, be destroyed by a doctrinal dispute. During a heated discussion at a meeting at the Highlander Center, Baker abandoned her custom of sitting on the sidelines and took an active part. She pointed out that direct action was a necessary adjunct to voter registration because the resistance to Negro voting attempts would be so strong that it would lead to protest demonstrations. They could do both, she said, and this essentially resolved the issue. SNCC proceeded to set up two sections, with Diane Nash, a Fisk student and a devoted adherent of Gandhian nonviolence, heading up direct action and Charles Jones, a young minister from Charlotte, North Carolina, as director of voter registration. As Baker observed later, however, "it became obvious there was no irreconcilable difference between the two tactics." Soon Jones and Nash would themselves decide that there was no need for the two posts.

By now SNCC felt the need for a strong executive secretary. The field secretaries voiced a need for someone to take charge, to give direction and hold the organization together. It was clear, however, that they did not want anyone to tell them what to do, to boss them around or cramp their style. Because they were confident that she had no interest in becoming a "Supreme Leader," they asked Baker to take the job. She declined, saying that she believed the post should be held by a younger person. Diane Nash and the direct action group urged James Forman to accept. He agreed, though somewhat reluctantly; he had come South to get into the action and did not look forward to an administrative job. Forman was from Chicago, but he had spent some years and many summers on his grandmother's farm in Mississippi. He was teaching in Chicago when the movement called him first to Fayette County, Tennessee, and then, in August 1961, to Monroe, North Carolina, where the national spotlight was turned on Robert F. Williams, a proponent of desegregation and of armed self-defense. Williams had been charged with kidnapping a white couple. He maintained that he was concerned about their safety and had offered them shelter when they drove into the black part of town during a period of high tension.

Baker, too, had been drawn to the Monroe confrontation. Here was a standoff between a black militant and the white power structure. The situation would appeal to any person who thought that the individual had a right to stand up and fight. Baker, however, did not go during the height of the crisis, when Monroe was swarming with representatives of the news media. As usual, she held back, waiting until she felt she could do useful work, after the headlinemakers had departed. "Usually you need people [later]," she said, "and not too many people go when the point of high focus has passed."[24]

She did visit in August 1962, to be of comfort to a woman whose only son had drowned. The kidnapping trial had been postponed, but Baker made the overnight trip because, as she wrote to Anne Braden, "there are some other developments which bear looking into." But her primary reason for going was because she felt the woman "ought to have somebody to be concerned. That was all."[25]

Forman arrived at SNCC at a crucial time. He was able to reconcile opposing forces by applying his gruff assessment that whatever was happening in local areas (known as "the field") was more important than whatever squabbles were taking place in the home office. He was able to maintain a sense of balance; in this he was in tune with Baker's drive to keep the organization focused.

If Baker was the mother of SNCC, Forman was the dad. Both were transplanted Northerners with Southern roots. Forman, though not close to Baker in age, was older than the other SNCC members, and both were forceful personalities. While Forman says of her in his book, *The Making of Black Revolutionaries:* "without her there would be no story of the Student Nonviolent Coordinating Committee," there was a subtle undercurrent of friction between them.

Yet in an interview in 1968 Baker praised Forman as "the guy who made [SNCC] into an organization . . . a fighting force." She said that he "had a sensitivity about people that almost amounted to his playing a father role." The students "felt he was young enough for them to relate to, and yet, at the same time to combine that sense of comradeship with a father image."[26]

Forman wielded enormous influence and did much to shape SNCC as it grew and changed. From the moment he stepped into the tiny SNCC office at 197½ Auburn Avenue until the day SNCC withered away, Forman was a formidable presence. While Baker and Forman agreed on many fundamental issues, their relationship was an ambivalent one. They agreed on the need for SNCC to be an organization with a structure; they disagreed on how to achieve this. Some of their differences stemmed from their ways of working. Baker, the elder stateswoman, would sit quietly in meetings without a word—sometimes for hours—breaking her silence with a meaningful question or pronouncement. Forman, on the other hand, would take charge immediately, making his proposals at the outset. Forman's proposals were often too grandiose for Baker's taste—like the 1965 purchase of a building for SNCC headquarters and a printing press. Baker was skeptical, too, of the ties to the Black Panthers that Forman and Stokely Carmichael pushed.

They did agree on the basic thrust of SNCC, the emphasis on developing the grass roots—although Forman did not have quite the same degree of confidence in the abilities of local leadership as Baker. But that may be too rash a judgment: perhaps Forman was just a man in a hurry. Certainly, he was less patient than Baker, who had been in the struggle so long. Baker, for her part, tried to adjust her goals to the timetable that Forman lived by. She respected his intensity, his revolutionary fervor, and his genius for organization; she simply wished that he would slow down.

They both felt that given SNCC's impetus it might be possible to build a revolutionary movement. Forman had a concept of building local organizational "cells" that would expand in concentric circles into a revolutionary force. Baker expressed somewhat the same idea to John Britton in 1968. Almost as an aside she referred to the Communist Party and "its cell groupings," commenting, "I don't think we had any more effective demonstration of organizing people for whatever purpose. . . . But the idea of getting small groups of people together, understanding what they wanted them to understand, and getting them organized for that—this is a good pattern."[27]

Baker agreed with Forman on the need to push the federal government for more action on civil rights, yet she probably would not have gone as far as he did. She backed SNCC's sit-in at the U.S. Department of Justice in protest of its inaction, and she was amused and somewhat admiring of Forman's rebuff to the powers on high. (When told that the White House was calling, Forman invariably would say, "Tell them I'm not in.")

Many conflicts arose in SNCC. Baker calmly sat through the long and heated debates, only intervening at crucial moments to help bring about a resolution. One such issue was the extent of participation in SNCC by Northerners. It was obvious to many Southern students, even as early as the April meeting in Raleigh, that Northern students were more politically sophisticated, more skilled verbally. To the Southern students they seemed to be "taking over," so from the beginning it was decided that SNCC should be a Southern-based, Southern-run organization. Yet, the problem of Northern participation kept coming up, reaching its peak in 1964, when the question of recruiting hundreds of volunteers from around the country for Mississippi Summer was under consideration.

One other debate was almost a constant: organizational structure. As always, Baker felt that an organization should have regular procedures, a clear idea of who was responsible for what and to whom: in other words, a chain of command. On this point she and Forman were united. By September 1961, Forman was executive secretary, succeeding Ed King. Convinced that King was not up to the job, Baker had persuaded him to return to college. (There was clearly a pragmatic side to Baker's nature, but it was tempered by her concern for the individual's well-being, as in this case: Push him out, but do it gently. Baker arranged for scholarship funds for King and maintained a correspondence with him over the next few years, cheering him on and forwarding money when it was needed. She had a genuine interest in helping him achieve his potential. By helping King further his studies, she helped him to grow.)

SNCC changed its structure often, partly in response to the growth of the movement, partly in response to changes in the movement's goals and direction. Between 1960 and 1965, SNCC's staff grew from sixteen to well over two hundred and its budget went from nearly nothing to over a million dollars. Such growth necessitated a change in structure to prevent chaos. By 1963, for instance, SNCC operated a fleet of about a hundred cars. Named the Sojourner Truth Motor Fleet, it had to be supervised; someone had to know where each car was, how long its lease would run, what its state of repair was. In sum, myriad details had to be handled. And this was only one of many items that cried out for a line of command.

In addition, since SNCC was based on local movements, it had to adapt quickly to changing conditions in each area. A wide range of issues had to be dealt with. Even as the fight for equal access to public accommodations (kneel-ins at churches, wade-ins at swimming pools, sleep-ins in hotel lobbies) was in motion, SNCC was already sponsoring a Christmas boycott of Atlanta stores and a struggle for black employment in Nashville and elsewhere. While there was some discernible progression from one phase of the movement to another, in actuality many forms of struggle were in progress simultaneously.

As the movement evolved, Baker's influence as a mentor was evident. Her professed aversion to the teaching profession did not prevent her from becoming a teacher—not in a formal sense, but there was no way that she could avoid this calling since she was intent on developing new leaders from among the local populace wherever she might find herself. Throughout her career she had seen that there were local people who were unhappy with their lot but did not know how to make changes. They had to be taught.

The designation "fundi" seemed to characterize her. *Fundi,* which I used as the film title for the documentary about her, is a Swahili word which denotes the person in a community who passes on the wisdom of the elders, the crafts, the knowledge. This is not done in an institutional way, a way which Baker would have rejected, but as an oral tradition, handed down from one generation to the next.

As SNCC developed, and the emphasis changed from civil rights to economic issues, there was always a need for education—workshops, study groups, training institutes. Many were set in motion by Baker, who felt strongly that a movement could not be based simply on oratory and action, but must be grounded in knowledge. When she worked for the NAACP, she had insisted on training, both for staff members and for local organizers, and she never let up on her drive to instill in organizers the need for facts to back up their rhetoric. She also recognized that the community needed educating, and this was the hard part. She helped to develop literature that could give the local community an understanding of the issues. Even middle-class, educated voters needed to be taught how their lives were linked with those who were less advantaged.

Baker had a profound influence on SNCC in this regard, but her impact in other areas was no less significant, as the minutes of SNCC staff meetings clearly show. For example, from the minutes of the June 9–11, 1961, meeting in Louisville, Kentucky: "After discussion on [the Mississippi Project] by Miss Ella Baker, it was decided that the financial and personnel problems were too great for immediate summer commencement of this program. It was moved to table this matter until the July meeting."[28]

But an even more powerful indication are the recollections of Charles McDew, the second chairman of SNCC: "I never told this to a soul. . . . Ella made me chairman. The meeting had been very long and you could tell there was this fight [for the chairmanship] going on between the forces in Atlanta and the forces in Nashville and the forces from Virginia, and Miss Baker said, 'Would you want to be chairman?' I said, no-o-o, not for love or money, and she said, 'Don't you understand [that] you're the only one here who doesn't want to be chairman?' She asked me if they were to elect me, would I be willing to be chairman, and I said, 'Well, I'll think about it.' The next day she asked if I had thought about it. She said, 'If you're interested in seeing that you all get something done, then you should be chairman. You owe it to yourself and the rest of us to be chairman.' We were clearly at an impasse because of all that maneuvering, and Miss Baker said, 'You are the only one here without a constituency. I mean if you want to help us, then you should accept being chairman.' I believe that she talked to other people, but I hadn't talked to a soul except Miss Baker, and, hell, I was convinced. I know Miss Baker made me chairman of SNCC, period."[29] McDew served for the next two years.

McDew recalled that, as chair, he broke the tie in the vote on whether to continue with direct action or concentrate on voter registration. "That was one of the times she lobbied me. She said, 'If you go to Mississippi and see Mr. Steptoe, Mr. Turnbow, or Amzie [local leaders], you will see that you can't do voter registration without direct action.' "[30]

Meanwhile, Harry Belafonte, an early supporter of the students, had invited sit-in leaders to meet with him in Washington in late June 1961 to discuss voter registration. Out of the meeting rose a vision of a student movement of 100,000 to 200,000, and a consensus was reached that "the voter registration project should be given top priority by SNCC while other direct action projects such as sit-ins, etc. be simultaniously steped [*sic*] up."[31] In October a temporary executive committee was appointed at an SNCC staff meeting, consisting of Baker, Belafonte, McDew, Connie Curry, and two members each from the voter registration and direct action staffs. It was mandated to "work deliberately to expand and democratize the organization of SNCC, to seek the development of a functioning communications system which will clarify the nature of the movement to the country, and to provide students with stimulus and strategic information."[32] This committee was given broad powers to define the functions of SNCC officers and staff, but it functioned only for a month. At the next staff meeting, in November, a pared-down executive committee was created. Forman had begun to establish order.

BAKER'S TRAVEL SCHEDULE for the summer of 1961 seemed as heavy as in her NAACP days. She went to Jackson, Mississippi, to work with Bob Moses for 5 days, then to Berkeley to attend a SLATE conference. At the beginning of August she went to Columbus, Ohio, to attend the NSA's fifth Southern Students Human Relations Seminar. From there she made a stop in Cincinnati to visit Fred Shuttlesworth's wife, Ruby, who was a great friend and had been ill. She also spent time in Raleigh, North Carolina, and Jackson, Tennessee, helping to organize voter registration campaigns.

In the midst of this she was asked to become the guardian of Brenda Travis, a McComb high school student who was being held in a reform school after she had participated in voter registration demonstrations. Baker took over as her temporary guardian and arranged for her to go to summer camp in Michigan, to which she took Brenda, and boarding school in North Carolina.

In 1961, Charles Sherrod and Charles Jones went to Albany, Georgia, to do voter registration; they spent some weeks talking with the local people in preparation for the drive. Then, on November 1, 1961, the first of the Albany sit-ins took place. Nine students sat in at the bus terminal, and on December 10 a group from the Atlanta SNCC office took a "freedom ride" on the train to the Albany railroad station and were arrested. This touched off mammoth demonstrations, which increased over the next few months. The Albany Movement was formed soon after, with William G. Anderson as president and Slater King as vice president. By the time that Baker went to Albany in mid-December more than seven hundred people had been arrested. In typical fashion Baker, away from the television cameras and news reporters, was busily noting down the needs of those about to demonstrate and go to jail. The questions she was asking ranged from "Do you have a toothbrush?" to "Have you informed your parents where you are?" to "Have you thought through the question of jail-no-bail?"

These were for her the essentials, what in those days was called the "nitty-gritty," the guts of the issue, the core of the problem. This was what she dealt with.

CHAPTER EIGHT

On the Way to Freedom Land

In a conference in Texas . . . [Bob Zellner said to me], "You don't make us feel like damn fools." . . . There was [a] need for recognition and approval . . . and there were a lot of adults who did not approve. . . . Not only did I approve [of] what they were doing, but I didn't compete with them. . . . This was why in a period of crisis they would turn to [me] and would listen, and felt that I wasn't gonna do anybody in.

"I ASKED MY MOTHER, come go with me, I'm on my way, praise Lord, I'm on my way." The hymn came wafting out of the small chapel. The mass meeting was warming up.

Baker had taken part in innumerable such meetings, but this was my first in an isolated rural community.

We had driven to the remote church deep in the countryside of Southwest Georgia in a broken-down school bus. We hadn't been sure that we would make it, since the bus had stopped dead on a lonely country road, but the experienced SNCC worker, Charles Sherrod, had coaxed it back to life again. Now here we were and there was the congregation enthusiastically belting out "I'm on my way, O Lord, I'm on my way, to Freedom Land." We had arrived at Piney Grove Church, where the shades had been lowered because motorcycles were circling the building.

The Reverend Agnew James of Lee County was chairman. He began the service with "Guide my feet, while I run this race." The Reverend Wells read the scripture to a chorus of amens: "Blessed is the man that walketh not in the counsel of the ungodly, nor standeth in the way of sinners, nor sitteth in the seat of the scornful." Then Reverend James got down to the business of the night. "It seems like we're losing ground; according to the highest court in Georgia, we're not getting our rights. That's why you should go down and register. We got twenty from Dougherty. This means you better get twenty-five to match us. They kills the minds of the people in the rural areas," Reverend James continued. "I've been boycotted and they say it's because I'm the head. They can boycott and double-boycott—I am going to stay right here and work and fight and not give up. I'm not suffering for anything; they are just telling me that I am. That's all. They can put every stone in my path—they can put a mountain there—and then I'm going to peek around it and still tell you to go register."[1]

This was the spirit in rural Southwest Georgia, the area where counties were dubbed by movement workers with such names as Terrible Terrell and Bad Baker. The Piney Grove gathering was one of many weekly, biweekly, sometimes nightly mass meetings held throughout the area. By this time music had infused the movement—not just "We Shall Overcome," but "This Little Light of Mine" and "We Are Soldiers in the Army," or "Hold Up the Blood-Stained Banner," which had been changed to "Hold Up the Freedom Banner." The Freedom Singers, an a capella group of SNCC folksingers, was performing around the South and at Northern fund-raising events, singing old gospel hymns and new movement songs they had written. Music banished fear. If we had thought about it, we would not have stood before an open church window silhouetted for the night riders outside in the dark, but in the presence of music we simply did not remember to be afraid. When the mob surrounded the First Baptist Church in Montgomery, the people supporting the Freedom Riders sang the traditional hymn "Leaning on the Everlasting Arms." When the students were ready to go to Rich's Department Store in downtown Atlanta, they sang "This may be the last time, the last time, brother. I don't know." I was with them as they made last-minute plans, checked their walkie-talkies, and sang their songs. All dressed up in their Sunday best, they didn't look like soldiers about to go into battle; nevertheless, they were prepared to face death that sunny day in "the city too busy to hate." They were all quickly, quietly, efficiently arrested by Chief L. C. Little, the Reverend Martin Luther King Jr. among them.

The music helped, but it was the courage of the local people that enabled people to conquer their fear. Aunt Mama Dolly, a tiny, gray-haired woman of about 70 who lived alone on an isolated farm in Lee County, had a boarder, Penny Patch, a young, white SNCC worker. Aunt Mama Dolly went to the door holding a shotgun if a white man appeared on her property. Hartman Turnbow of Mileston, Mississippi, also wielded a shotgun to protect his family and the nonviolent SNCC workers. Ella Baker knew them all.

Southwest Georgia was nearly on a par with Mississippi. Out of 4,533 white residents in Terrell County, for example, 2,894 were registered; only 51 of the 8,209 Negro residents were registered. Claude Sitton wrote in the *New York Times* of a mass meeting in a church in the small town of Sasser, Georgia, that was invaded by the county sheriff and his deputies, who threatened the local people and the white SNCC workers while a white mob gathered outside.[2] Baker had established a relationship with Sitton at the Raleigh meeting in 1960. Sitton was beginning to understand the movement, which came to him full force at the Sasser meeting. The incident at Sasser pushed several reporters out of their "objectivity." It was a turnaround for the national press.

The October 1962 *Student Voice* reported on conditions in Southwest Georgia, listing the following incidents:

Ralph Allen, a white student from Massachusetts, and Charles Sherrod were arrested for vagrancy when they appeared at the Terrell County courthouse with a group of potential registrants.

Allen and Joseph Pitts of Albany, Georgia, were beaten in Dawson, but were unable to get warrants for arrest of their assailants.

Penny Patch was threatened by local police in Lee County, who said they would "throw her in the swamp."

Four Negro churches were burned to the ground in August and several homes were shot at.

Three SNCC workers were wounded when shots were fired into the home of Mrs. Carolyn Daniels, a movement stalwart.

SNCC field secretary Jack Chatfield was shot twice in the arm.

James Mays, a Lee County teacher who had been fired from his job for participation in the voter drive, reported twenty-four bullet holes in his house.[3]

By 1962, Baker, who still dressed as she had during her days with the NAACP in a stylish suit, crisp blouse, and hat, was traveling around the South to protest areas, SNCC meetings, colleges, and workshops in her new job as human relations consultant to the National Student Young Women's Christian Association.

She had stipulated when she accepted the position that she could only work part-time because she wanted to be free to work with SNCC. She and coworkers Roberta Yancey, Sandra Cason, and Mary King traveled to white and black colleges attempting to break down racial divisions. All three of her staff eventually joined SNCC as field secretaries.

Baker felt that white students had a strong desire to become involved and that they were hampered by college administrators. "To establish and implement a policy of racial inclusiveness in this region has required a consistent and persistent drive," she said. Despite the difficulties, the first statewide, interracial meeting of Y-affiliated college students was held in Columbia, South Carolina, on February 5, 1961. Called "What Next, Joe College?" the meeting was designed to help prepare white students for integration. Later, two conferences were held at Highlander on the role of the white student. Baker was involved in both. At these and other meetings Baker encouraged white students to rally around the issue of

A 1960s Student Nonviolent Coordinating Committee gathering at the home of playwright Lorraine Hansberry. From the left: unidentified woman, Victor Rabinowitz, unidentified man, Don Harris, Avon Rollins, Lorraine Hansberry, Theo Bikel, Nina Simone, James Forman (partially hidden), Marion Barry, John Lewis, Robert Whitfield, Doris Derby, Ella Baker. (Courtesy of Jewell Gresham Nemiroff, executrix, the estate of Robert Nemiroff.)

academic freedom, "to do for white Southern schools what the Negro students had done for civil rights." Because both parental and college administration strictures effectively prevented the white students from coming out against the system of segregation openly, she focused on "the question of their own handicaps" and defended their right to hear other points of view and to discuss things that were relevant to the outside world. The white students were agonizing about their desire to be a part of what was happening, but they were unable "to cut loose from the umbilical cord either at home or at the university."[4]

But Baker always had a hands-on approach, so she tried to reach the students as individuals, recognizing the guilt that some experienced at not being able to participate more actively. In her constant pursuit of the possible, she pointed out that picketing and demonstrations were not the only ways in which concern could be translated into action. "It is better to concentrate on what can be done than to despair about what cannot be done," she said. A letter from a white student at Duke University spells out the need felt by many young people: "First of all my visit with you gave a new perspective which has given me new peace. I think I realized something new that happened when you were with our study group: that is, that I was released from the worry over the vast amount you can't do, you are able to work really at what you can do. Also, I am so glad you caught me up to realize that human relations with those closest to us is important too."[5]

Some of the white students were prepared to get into the movement even if only in a small way. Baker was invited, for example, to be the first Negro ever to speak at a convocation at Southwest University in Memphis. But her assessment of the experience was that she "let the kids down," because they had planned a daring action. "They were going to steal the key to the guest house and sneak me in." Since they hadn't told her they were prepared to house her, she had made arrangements to stay in a downtown black hotel.[6]

THE YEARS 1961 TO 1963 were hard years for the young movement workers entrenched in the hard-core areas where resistance was fiercest. The Ku Klux Klan was on the rise and White Citizens Councils were active. In Americus, Georgia, three SNCC workers were charged with sedition; in Baton Rouge, Louisiana, three were charged with criminal anarchy. In Albany, Georgia, nine movement workers were indicted, three for conspiracy to obstruct justice and six for perjury; this time it was not local officials who brought charges but the federal government. Aside from a few voting rights suits, this was the first time that the federal government had filed suit under the Civil Rights Act of 1957. It was also the first time that the government filed a criminal action.

By early 1963 SNCC was active in four counties in Southwest Georgia; in Orangeburg, South Carolina; in three agricultural counties around Selma, Alabama; in Pine Bluff, Arkansas; and in six counties in Mississippi—and it was hard-pressed for funds.

SNCC had established a WATS (Wide Area Telephone Service charging a flat monthly fee) line so that field secretaries and organizers could make inexpensive calls to the central office to keep the office informed of events in the field, but primarily to act as a security check. Whenever organizers traveled anywhere, they had to phone in their time of departure, destination, and expected arrival time and to report in immediately upon arrival. From these reports one gets a picture of what kind of conditions these young people were operating under. For example:

> *Greenwood, Mississippi:* Since February 20, four Negro businesses on the same street as the SNCC office have been destroyed by fire; SNCC field secretary Sam Block was sentenced to 6 months in jail on a charge of "circulating breach of the peace," later changed to "issuing statements calculated to breach the peace"; staff worker James Travis was shot in the head while driving a car near Greenwood; four other SNCC workers were cut by glass when their car's windshield was shattered by gunshots from a passing car.

> *Ruleville, Mississippi:* Williams Chapel was fire-bombed at 2 A.M.; the fourth in the past 10 days in Mississippi. The chapel is across from the Hamer house and had been the scene of a voter registration meeting six hours earlier. Fannie Lou Hamer was a sharecropper who led the voter registration drive in Ruleville. The burning followed seven incidents of bottle throwing at homes and at summer volunteers. . . . Previous burnings in the past 10 days: June 16, Philadelphia; June 21, Brandon in Rankin County; June 23, Moss Point.[7]

In the summer of 1963 urban areas erupted. Blacks in Birmingham, which had been the scene of house and church bombings, spilled into the streets in response, overturning and burning cars and smashing store windows. The police turned high-powered fire hoses on the protesting youngsters, sweeping them down the streets in front of television cameras.

Baker, who received these reports in printed form, but most often by telephone, knew all of those attacked. She traveled to wherever there were confrontations and marshaled forces for the defense of her "children"—the jailed, beaten, humiliated.

BAKER, WHO HAD MOVED BACK TO NEW YORK, became an active fund-raiser, working with the New York Friends of SNCC office while continuing in her role as adviser.

She was a main organizer of a Carnegie Hall benefit concert on the third anniversary of the sit-ins, February 1, 1963. She and I worked out of the SNCC office at 5 Beekman Street, loaned to us by FOR. The working committee included the actor Ossie Davis; Art D'Lugoff, the impresario, and his brother Burt, a doctor; Robert Nemerov; and Theodore Bikel, who gathered a star-studded list of invitors, including James Baldwin, Harry Belafonte, Diahann Carroll, Jules Feiffer, Viveca Lindfors, Pete Seeger, Nina Simone, and Shelley Winters. The cast included Tony Bennett, Ossie Davis, Ruby Dee, Charlie Mingus, Thelonious Monk, the Herbie Mann Sextet, and the Freedom Singers. The event was exhilarating, producing an emotional high when all of the SNCC field workers in attendance gathered onstage to wild applause. Baker's report of the concert to SNCC headquarters stated: "That 'A Salute to Southern Students' was a sell-out with over a thousand persons turned away and with net returns of more than $8,000 is certainly in the nature of a miracle." Work for the concert revealed one of Baker's characteristics: she was stubborn. Often at 10 or 11 P.M. I would beg her not to carry home the day's receipts in her battered black handbag on the subway up to Harlem, but she persisted and she prevailed.

This was the first of major fund-raising events in New York. It was followed by a reading in Town Hall in 1965 of a script by Warren Miller based on reports from the field and starring Alan Alda, Ossie Davis, Ruby Dee, Al Freeman, Jr., Gloria Foster, Julie Harris, Rita Moreno, and others. Baker protégé Roberta Yancey organized two elegant $100-a-plate dinners out of the New York Friends of SNCC office. Arthur and Mathilda Krim, Frances Dole, and other supporters hosted large fund-raising parties. SNCC leaders Charles McDew, James Forman, and Robert Zellner "starred" at such events, speaking in the unreal atmosphere of New York's Upper Eastside of burnings, bombings, and killings taking place even as the canapés were passed. This was SNCC's venture into the world of fund-raising, allowing them to capture some of the territory that had formerly been exclusively SCLC's.

By now Baker had left the Y and was working as a part-time consultant for the Southern Conference Educational Fund. SCEF was the successor of the interracial Southern Conference for Human Welfare, which had been founded in 1938 as a coalition of liberal, labor, and New Deal proponents of change. SCEF's primary goal was to promote integration by working with Southern whites, but it worked closely with both SCLC and SNCC. SCEF had made a grant of $5,000 to SNCC to hire Robert Zellner, a white college student, to work on white campuses. For a time its codirector, Anne Braden, was one of SNCC's adult advisers.

Baker was more comfortable with SCEF and found in their board meetings "a sense of mutuality."[8] The activists were more like-minded, more concerned with people, less hierarchical, and more democratic than those in most other organizations she had worked for. She felt that SCEF was in tune with what SNCC was trying to do, and that SCEF people had a better understanding of what was happening and, more importantly, of what needed to happen. She amended that statement with the comment "or what we thought needed to happen." SCEF had an honest respect for people, unlike the Y, which had a "syrupy respect for people," and the ministers, who had no respect for people at all.

For example, after a bomb exploded in the offices of the Shreveport, Louisiana, Christian Movement, an SCLC affiliate, SCEF responded immediately. "Jim [Dombroski] was the first person to call and offer to raise funds to offset whatever losses were involved, and this was not true of the head of the organization to which Simpkins's organization . . . belonged." Jim and Carl Braden went to Shreveport to help draft a statement urging the federal government to respond to the outrage. "They could have written the statement and gotten it ready in a short time, but they did not. They worked with Simpkins, and worked at his pace. All of us were there. They didn't push. . . . They subjected their time schedule to his time schedule and his committee's capacity to move. [They] didn't try to take the leadership away from him at all, even though in terms of time saving it would of perhaps been more efficient."[9] This is a subtlety in terms of organizing, an Ella Baker specialty. Many organizers would simply have taken over and done the job, quickly and efficiently. Ella Baker's way was to slowly guide the local leader to the goal, or to just wait out his or her own perception of how to get there. This, to her mind, was also SCEF's way.

In her work for SCEF Baker was primarily involved with organizing educational conferences and workshops, for instance, the "Conference on Time for Action in the Mid-South," held at Virginia State College in Norfolk in April 1963. One of the biggest jobs she undertook for SCEF was the planning of a civil liberties conference held on June 28–30, 1963, in Atlanta. The workshop-cum-retreat brought together representatives of grassroots groups to discuss the interrelationship of civil liberties and civil rights. Together with Carl Braden, the codirector of SCEF, Baker helped organize a mock civil rights commission hearing, held in Washington, D.C. She and SCEF coworker John Salter also toured midwest and western states to encourage pressure on Congress in support of the pending civil rights bill. During all of this, however, her main concern was SNCC.

In April 1963 both she and Anne Braden attended SNCC's staff meeting. Once again SNCC revised its constitution re-adopting its original statement of purpose affirming its commitment to "the philosophical or religious ideal of nonviolence as the foundation of our purpose, the pre-supposition of our faith, and the manner of our action." The structure was changed, giving more power to a fifteen-person executive committee and to the executive secretary. This structure was altered in subsequent meetings of the executive committee as SNCC's staff and budget grew and its activities became more diverse.

Baker, who characterized the student movement as "the most authentic of revolutionary thrusts," emphasized at the April meeting the necessity of protecting their movement by fighting for their civil liberties. She told the students that they must be cognizant of the fact that "opposition to the civil rights struggle more and more will be conducted under the cloak of national security."[10]

By the end of 1963 the issues had become extremely complex. Urban eruptions were forcing the movement to focus on economic problems: unemployment, housing conditions, and widespread poverty. At the year-end meeting SNCC adviser Howard Zinn pointed to the wide variety of questions facing the movement, and Baker, saying that too much emphasis was placed on action rather than on planning, suggested that discussion should center around two or three aspects of the general problems raised by Zinn. Baker expressed the general feeling that SNCC should develop a formal program of economic education for its staff.

A subsidiary question was raised by Bob Moses, who urged that a tax-exempt arm of SNCC be established. As a result, Baker set up the Fund for Educational and Legal Defense (FELD). The fund was administered by Baker, Carita Bernsohn, Michael Standard, a lawyer long associated with New York Friends of SNCC, and myself. FELD provided scholarships for a number of SNCC workers and remained active until the late 1970s.

But it was the question of civil liberties that preoccupied those at the December meeting, a question that had plagued the movement since its beginning. Baker had long stressed the connection between civil rights and civil liberties and had long been active in the struggle to bring the civil liberties question into the movement. She served on the board of the Committee to Abolish HUAC (the House Committee on Un-American Activities) and spoke at events it held around the country.

SNCC had always staunchly resisted red-baiting, maintaining that workers' and supporters' political affiliations would be ignored as long as they adhered to SNCC's goals. The leaders of other civil rights organizations often criticized SNCC's position on civil liberties. While relations among the civil rights organizations appeared to be cordial on the surface, they were showing signs of wear. From the beginning there had been tension between CORE and SNCC on the one hand and the NAACP and, to a lesser extent, SCLC on the other. Irritations were growing around fund-raising, credit for actions, and media attention. For example, SNCC people felt that the older organizations were raising money based on SNCC's actions. The NAACP felt that it had been preeminent in the fights around voter rights and public accommodations, and that this younger organization was moving into their territory without giving them credit. In addition, there were differences over attitudes toward the federal government. SNCC felt that the NAACP was too cautious in its criticism of the government, whereas the NAACP felt that SNCC was too brash and injudicious. The NAACP also did a bit of red-baiting, insinuating that SNCC was influenced by the Communist Party.

Because of the need for better coordination, the Civil Rights Leadership Conference was formed. Representatives at one of the early meetings in 1962 included Forman and McDew, Roy Wilkins and John Morsell from the NAACP, Jack Greenberg of the Inc. Fund, Whitney Young of the Urban League, and King and Walker of SCLC. Even the American Friends Service Committee was represented, but at Wilkins's insistence, CORE was left out. As Forman reported to an SNCC regional meeting in Atlanta, the discussion proceeded peacefully until it turned to SNCC, which seemed to be "a thorn in the flesh to many of the groups."[11] Wilkins was concerned that other organizations were displacing local NAACP chapters. He was critical of direct action and felt that the sit-in at the Justice Department was wrong, since, in his view, the department was the movement's only friend in Washington.

Friction over this issue and others lasted throughout the 1960s. Baker felt that the role of SNCC, and other civil rights groups, was to challenge the federal government, to try to force it to take more forthright action.

From its earliest days SNCC people had been ambivalent toward the federal government. On the one hand, workers in the rural areas thought that their contacts with the U.S. Department of Justice might give them some protection; on the other hand, they knew that the FBI men—white Southerners, taking notes—were not on their side. Yet they felt that they should keep appealing to the federal government for support. What they sought was a definitive statement from Washington, not only condemning the violence but also affirming in resounding terms the rights of the deprived. SNCC workers also felt that if they could expose federal inaction to public scrutiny, it might force the government to enact more stringent civil rights laws and strengthen enforcement.

The fight for civil rights is a political football, and the role of the federal government has always been a shameful one, beset by political considerations. In 1963 I covered the annual NAACP convention and accompanied a delegation to Washington to petition President Kennedy to fight for a civil rights bill. Kennedy refused, saying that this was not the time, then personally ushered us into the Lincoln bedroom as a sort of sop.

Just prior to the 1963 March on Washington, Aubrey Williams, who had been a member of President Roosevelt's New Deal team, wrote to King about an earlier march that was planned for D.C., A. Philip Randolph's threatened 1942 march against unfair employment practices. Roosevelt had sent Williams to New York to try to persuade Randolph to call off his march. Williams called a meeting of Walter White, Randolph, Eleanor Roosevelt, and Anna Rosenberg of the War Manpower Commission, in New York Mayor Fiorello La Guardia's office. They telephoned the president, who pleaded that "such a march would turn the people against the Negro," but agreed to a meeting in Washington, at which Randolph made an eloquent argument for a Fair Employment Practices Commission. Roosevelt finally directed Williams, La Guardia, Robert Jackson, who had been attorney general but was then a justice on the U.S. Supreme Court, and Anna Rosenberg to draw up the FEPC order and, after weeks of delay, finally signed it. Williams ended his letter with these words: "Remember, you get nothing for free."[12]

Baker had used these very words in a 1959 column in the *Pittsburgh Courier,* pointing out that the "capacity to try again implies a deep faith in the Federal Government and constitutional democracy. But just how long can Negro citizens retain this faith as they daily watch the power structure of the South openly defy the government and select the laws it wishes to obey while ignoring others? Both political parties must be made to face this question, and the only way to do it is to beat them at the old game of playing politics with civil rights. Their forward passes and field goals must be blocked by the strategic use of the Negro vote, North and South. Can Negro leadership achieve a unified front and do this for the 1960 elections? Or, will a few appointive jobs and the pious claims of the inept, liberal 'friends' in Congress that they have done their best to pass effective legislation keep us from facing and acting on the facts realistically?"[13]

Despite the urgent pleas from civil rights leaders for a strong moral demand for the rights of black people, the federal government throughout the early 1960s steadfastly maintained their adherence to what they felt were political necessities. The federal government instituted several voting suits, but the Kennedy administration focused primarily on personal communications. Robert Kennedy, the attorney general, took to the telephone, talking to Greyhound during the Freedom Rides, to Governor John Patterson of Alabama during the siege of the Montgomery First Baptist Church, and to King whenever he felt there was a crisis. President Kennedy even called Coretta King when her husband was in jail in Birmingham.

The main purpose of the Kennedys' intervention was to seek "cooling-off" periods. The movement was embarrassing the U.S.

government. The answer to the violence of white racist citizens, law enforcement, and other government officials—high-powered fire hoses turned against demonstrators in Birmingham, ferocious German shepherds turned on marchers in Greenwood, fire-bombings of homes and churches, and murder—was to get the demonstrators to call a halt. The attorney general failed to deal with the charges of sedition against nine Albany SNCC workers in Americus, Georgia, but indicted three SNCC workers. This was typical of the federal government's response.

A low point had been reached on the night when federal troops were dispatched to secure the area around the University of Mississippi in 1962, when James Meredith was about to enter its hallowed halls. In his nationwide televised broadcast President Kennedy spoke about the prowess of Mississippi's football team and invoked the hallowed tradition of sports fairness.

The speech was an attempt to tie race relations to the administration's fight against communism, but almost as importantly, the government tried to balance the moral issue of civil rights against politics as usual.

Baker wrote in her "Shuttlesworth Says" column: "The unholy alliance between Southern Democrats and the Republicans of the House has successfully killed any chances of getting effective civil rights legislation in the first session of the 86th Congress."[14] From 1952 to 1965, any sop to civil rights proponents by the Democratic Party was aimed at getting the most that could be had from the Negro vote while at the same time maintaining its ties with the solid South. The challenge was soon to come. Back in Mississippi SNCC had been working in the Council of Federated Organizations (COFO, made up of CORE, SNCC, and the NAACP) to motivate local Negroes to organize in a way that could not be ignored and to make clear their assertion that they were a part of the "democratic process."

Ella Baker was to play a pivotal role.

Grassroots Politics

*When the [Mississippi Freedom Democratic Party] had reached
the point of wanting to make this national thrust along the lines of
challenging the convention delegates . . . the move was to form a
national committee which would direct strategy. I resisted this. . . .
I felt we who were outside of Mississippi could be supportive, but
we should not be the ones to determine what moves were to be
made. We shouldn't be spokesmen. This was the major thing. . . .
It was highly important, number one, for the people of Mississippi
to speak for themselves. . . . Number two, that there was an area
of need: namely reaching other Democrats to take a position in the
convention or to be supportive prior to the convention.*

"UNTIL THE KILLING OF BLACK MOTHERS' SONS becomes as important to the rest of the country as the killing of white mothers'
sons, we who believe in freedom cannot rest," Ella Baker challenged
in a ringing speech to the state convention of the Mississippi Freedom Democratic Party (MFDP) in Jackson on a sweltering August
day in 1964.

Baker's speech followed one by Joseph Rauh, the attorney for
the MFDP. After outlining the position of the party's quest for seating at the upcoming Democratic Party national convention, he made
a regrettable, but typical, gaffe by expressing his admiration for
"you people," a phrase that makes the hackles of black people rise.

Fiery, indeed, was Baker's address. She spoke of the MFDP as
a "demonstration of the people of Mississippi that they are determined to be a part of the body politic of Mississippi." "We are here,"

she said, "to demonstrate the right of the governed to elect those who govern, *here, in this* state." She pointed out that the Southern states functioned as an oligarchy and that the rest of the country went along with it. "It has never been true that the Negro people were satisfied. It was never true even in the darkest days of slavery."[1] Shouts of "Freedom! Freedom!" rang through the Masonic Temple hall.

This, the state convention, was a prelude to the party's attempt to unseat the regular Mississippi Democratic Party delegation to the national convention. It had all the earmarks of a political convention. The path leading to it had been paved by the Freedom Vote of 1963, in which over 90,000 Negroes participated, and by county-by-county meetings that were replicas of Democratic Party meetings held throughout the country. The difference was that this was an expression of the disenfranchisement of Negroes; this was a statement of the desire of black people to take part in the democratic process.

Baker said: "It is important that you go to the convention whether you are seated or not. It is even more important that you develop a political machinery in this state. The Mississippi Freedom Democratic Party will not end at the convention. This is only the beginning. You are waging a war against the closed society of Mississippi. You have not let physical fear immobilize you."

When she ended with the words, "But we have sense enough to know who is using us and who is abusing us," the delegates jumped to their feet with a prolonged ovation and then began to sing:

"Ain't gonna let nobody turn me round,
Turn me round, turn me round.
Ain't gonna let nobody turn me round.
Gonna keep on a-walkin', keep on a-talkin',
Marchin' up to Freedom Land."

In true convention style, delegates took up county signs and marched around the bunting-draped hall in a singing, clapping fifteen-minute demonstration. The MFDP was on its way.

The party was made up of people who, in their own vernacular, spoke of going down to "reddish" at the "circus" clerk's office, who said that they were fighting for their "silver" rights.[2] These were the people who had put their lives on the line. They had taken the young SNCC workers into their homes, they had gone down to the courthouse to register to vote, they had defied the powers that be. Despite bombings, threats, economic boycotts, and an array of other intimidations, they had stood fast.

The concept of a Freedom Vote and of the MFDP itself had grown slowly during 1962 and 1963, when SNCC was debating where its concentration should be. The idea of trying to express the desire of black people to take part in the democratic process had grown naturally out of the exclusion that black people felt, but it flourished because of the movement, which had already birthed a sense of empowerment. Yes, they could break down the barriers of segregated water fountains and lunch counters—so why not win the right to vote, to have a voice in who became sheriff or mayor or town council member?

In some sense, the movement had its own momentum, and it propelled the young SNCC workers to new decisions, new directions, and new visions. All along the way Baker kept them focused on the need for education—they must have knowledge of how to use the system—but primarily she emphasized the need to develop local leaders and local movements. Perhaps it was she who was really responsible for the birth of the MFDP, because she had stressed so heavily the need to nurture local leadership; in any case, the MFDP did indeed come into being as a locally born organization.

The MFDP was organized after the enthusiastic response to the Freedom Ballot, or Freedom Vote. Hundreds of local people took part in canvassing and organizing the mock election. In the spring of 1964, COFO voted to establish the MFDP, to challenge the seating of the state Democratic Party delegates at the national convention in August, and to run its own candidates in each of the five congressional districts. The new party became part of the Mississippi Freedom Summer program of 1964, along with the Freedom Schools and community centers that were established throughout the state and the continued struggle to register black voters.

The wisdom of inviting hundreds of Northern volunteer workers, particularly white workers, to take part in Freedom Summer was debated endlessly at SNCC meetings. Baker played a decisive role in the planning, and took part in the extended debate. The executive committee meeting at the end of December 1963 debated the issue, which was being actively pushed by Allard Lowenstein, who had brought a hundred students from Yale and Stanford into Mississippi the previous summer. Moses pointed out that COFO had already rejected the idea. If SNCC proposed bringing in volunteers, particularly white volunteers from the North, the question would have to be rediscussed by COFO. Those in favor of "invading" the state argued that such action might force the federal government to take a moral stand on civil rights and move to protect civil rights workers; also, the more workers there were, the more Negroes would be registered. But would large numbers of white students working in the state provoke such a degree of violence that the situation would be intolerable?

At the April executive committee meeting Moses said that he had sent a letter to "Friends of Freedom in Mississippi"—Roy Wilkins, James Farmer, Martin Luther King Jr., James Forman, A. Philip Randolph, Bayard Rustin, John Lewis, Harry Belafonte, James Baldwin, Dick Gregory, Ossie Davis, Marlon Brando, Aaron Henry, Ed King, Robert Spike, Jesse Gray, Larry Landry, Clyde Ferguson, Noel Day, and Ella Baker—urging that pressure be exerted on the federal government to guarantee protection.

> I am writing on request of the Executive Committee of the Student Nonviolent Coordinating Committee and in my function as Program Director of the Council of Federated Organizations (COFO). . . . It is our conviction that only a massive effort by the country backed by the full power of the President can offer some hope for even minimal change in Mississippi. . . . Violence is prevalent throughout the state, at least six Negroes have been killed by whites in the past three months . . . the responsibility for main-

taining law and guaranteeing, at the same time, the right to peaceful protest, must rest in the final analysis in the case of Mississippi with the President of the United States.[3]

In an early June 1964 meeting SNCC staff discussed the prospects for Mississippi Summer. After long debate Baker said, "The conversations sound as though this is the first discussion of white involvement. The problem is basically one of insecurity. Perhaps we have an inflated ego. Are we prepared to take the revolution one step further?" She stressed that the struggle could not grow without an examination of SNCC's goals.[4]

The debate continued. What would happen to SNCC with an infusion of hundreds of Northern white students? How could SNCC with its rudimentary organizational structure manage even to keep track of hundreds of volunteers? How could they be housed and fed? Essentially, the underlying, somewhat cynical question was, Is it worth it? If the white sons and daughters of prominent people in the North were subjected to the same abuse and terror, and even death, as the Southern Negro student or sharecropper, would the nation take notice and make some changes? It seemed to be a hard-nosed decision for the idealistic revolutionaries of SNCC, but it was a reality. SNCC was willing to put on the line not only their own lives but the lives of the volunteers as well.

But no one expected tragedy to occur as early as it did. In June 1964, while the orientation session at Oxford, Ohio, was taking place, three movement workers disappeared in Mississippi: James Chaney, Andrew Goodman, and Michael Schwerner. All of the workers were alarmed. Shortly after I arrived in the Meridian, Mississippi, office, where the three workers had last been seen, an anonymous call came in threatening our lives. We all took it seriously. A second call illustrated how strange the Southland really was. A male voice inquired: "Are you one of those white, Northern bastards?" The COFO worker replied: "No, I'm Negro." The caller paused briefly, then said, "Oh, excuse me," and hung up.

It was a grim time. Every threat was taken seriously. We knew in our hearts that three comrades were already dead. We felt that there were more deaths to come. But we were determined to find out what had happened to them.

Throughout the long summer we met, always with the presumed deaths hovering over us. One night at the Sun and Sands Motel where we were staying (the only integrated motel in Jackson, Mississippi), a number of us talked about how we could find out what had happened to our comrades. To foil any wiretappers we talked with all the faucets in the shower and sink running and with the television going full blast. We talked about the failure of the FBI to find out what had happened to our coworkers, we talked about leads that movement workers had uncovered, and we talked about leads that the FBI either had not followed up on or had not divulged. We were talking about scary stuff, and I for one was scared. After the meeting I went up to my room but found that I could not stay there, not with all that expanse of glass window beside my bed, so I somewhat sheepishly telephoned SNCC supporter Michael Standard in the room below mine and pleaded with him to come get me and let me sleep in his room. I was that scared.

A few days later I was back in Meridian, in Neshoba County where the disappearances had taken place. A young punk leaned into the car and said, "Y'all come on up to Philadelphia. We'll show you what fer." As if that wasn't enough, when I sat in the courtroom with hostile locals surrounding us, my press credentials were ignored. I was told to move out of the press section. Then everyone was ordered out of the hotel where the lawyers, Bill Kuntsler and others, were staying because I was present! (Bill protested that he had just sent out his pants to be pressed, but to no avail.)

The federal government did send in a number of agents and made an intensive search of the rivers and coves of Mississippi, turning up a number of bodies of murdered black men, all unreported. But it was the movement's own investigation that finally directed federal investigators to the dam where the bodies of the three civil rights workers were buried and, eventually, to the arrest of the law enforcement officers involved in the murders. Sheriff Lawrence Rainey, Deputy Sheriff Cecil Price, and seventeen others were arrested in December 1964. Three years later, eight were convicted of conspiracy. Eleven were acquitted. None were charged with murder.

Over the summer civil rights workers had kept working. One day I went out to get a hamburger from a restaurant next door to the COFO office. When I came back I was met by Rita Schwerner, the wife of one of the missing civil rights workers, who said: "Chuck McDew hasn't called in." We all went into a tailspin—when someone didn't call in as required, we expected disaster. It was poignant—eerie—to get the message from Rita, who was still awaiting news of her husband's fate. Chuck eventually called in. He was still alive.

In the meantime the work around the MFDP continued. To Baker, the MFDP was an expression of one of her most cherished hopes: local people who had developed into leaders were about to take on the establishment. At its 1960 convention the regular Mississippi Democratic Party had proclaimed its belief in the Constitution and the Bill of Rights, but it affirmed its adherence to states' rights and stated: "We are opposed to any legislation, federal or state, setting up what is known as a Fair Employment Practice Commission. . . . We believe in the segregation of the races, and are unalterably opposed to the repeal or modification of the segregation laws of this State, and we condemn integration and the practice of non-segregation. We unalterably oppose any and all efforts to repeal the miscegnation [*sic*] laws."[5] It was this stance that the MFDP challenged.

The state legislature meanwhile had enacted a series of laws designed to thwart the movement's efforts: House Bill 64 authorized cities to restrain movements of groups and individuals. House Bill 546 prohibited the unlawful picketing of all public buildings, streets, sidewalks, and other places belonging to the city, county, and state; Senate Bill 1517 increased penalties assessed by city courts. Senate Bill 1526 authorized municipalities to "pool" personnel, manpower, and equipment. Senate Bill 1545 provided a maximum penalty of $500 and/or 6 months in jail for printing and circulating material promoting a boycott.[6] In addition, the State Sovereignty Commission had suggested the use of other laws that related to the refusal to disperse, to boycotts, and to making false statements to federal authorities.

Alarming as these new laws were, the preparations made by the city of Jackson were even more threatening. Mayor Allen Thompson told *Newsweek* magazine in February: "They [the civil rights workers] are not bluffing and we are not bluffing. We're going to be ready for them. . . . They won't have a chance."[7] Jackson increased its riot-trained police force from 390 to 450, purchased 200 shotguns, and stocked up on tear gas and gas masks. The city was also the proud new owner of a heavily armed 13,000-pound, twelve-man tank.

Baker, who was coordinator of the New York Ad Hoc Committee in Support of the Mississippi Freedom Democratic Party, continued her work with the party. Immediately after her speech at the state convention, she moved to Washington to prepare for the forthcoming Democratic Party convention. She told the *Washington Post*: "Our party provides the people of Mississippi with their only choice. Not only are Negroes being denied the right to vote there, but the National Democratic party is being denied the right to be fairly represented."[8] She undertook the job of getting as many state delegations to support the seating of the MFDP as she possibly could. In this effort she had the unfailing aid of Representative Edith Green and Senator Wayne Morse, both of Oregon. In recalling those days Eleanor Holmes Norton explained that Baker turned over to her the task of pursuing the delegations because, she said, "I guess she was just too tired to do it."

Tired though she may have been, Baker remained key in the attempt to get delegations lined up to support the MFDP challenge, firing off letter after letter to convention delegates urging their support. On July 2, 1964, she sent the following telegram to the chairman of the Oregon Democratic Party:

> The Mississippi Freedom Democratic Party, which is open to all citizens regardless of race, creed, or color, will democratically elect a delegation to go to the national Democratic convention and ask to be seated in place of the Dixiecratic delegation which will be sent by the traditional party. We ask your help in putting the

Oregon Democratic convention on record as supporting the seating of the Mississippi Freedom Democratic delegation. Michigan, Wisconsin, Minnesota, Massachusetts have all gone on record at their state conventions as backing the seating of our delegation. The Democratic State Executive Committee of New York and California have also called for the ouster of the Mississippi Dixiecrats and the seating of the Freedom delegation. Governor Brown, on learning of the Central Committee action in California, said he could not be more pleased. He said the traditional Mississippi Party was so far out of tune with the national Democratic party that it should not be allowed near the convention hall. The liberal democratic tradition of your state party should necessitate a resolution by your convention to work for the seating of the Freedom Democratic Party. Help us make Mississippi and the country more democratic.[9]

On June 8, Baker made a presentation to the Governor's Conference in Cleveland outlining the reasons for the MFDP challenge. She pointed out that the 1963 campaign literature of Mississippi's Governor Paul B. Johnson stated that the Mississippi Democratic Party "is entirely independent and free of the influence of domination of any national party" and it "long ago separated itself from the National Democratic Party, and . . . has fought consistently everything both national parties stand for." She went on: "We need hundreds of Democrats . . . to instruct their delegates, petition their representatives, party leaders and the President to face up to the fact that only a renegade democratic party exists in Mississippi which enjoys the benefits of national affiliation but spurns all responsibilities and can only continue to bring disgrace to the National Democratic Party."[10]

Meanwhile, the SNCC office continued to compile a list of violent incidents in Mississippi:

June 16, Philadelphia: Mt. Zion Baptist Church burns to ground. Fire starts soon after Negro mass meeting adjourns.

June 21, Brandon: Molotov cocktail explodes in basement of Sweet Rest Church of Christ Holiness.

June 21, McComb: Homes of two civil rights workers planning to house summer volunteers bombed. One damaged extensively. Seven dynamite sticks left on lawn of third home.

June 23, Moss Point: Knights of Pythias Hall firebombed. Used for voter rallies.

June 25, Ruleville: Williams Chapel firebombed. Damage slight.

June 26, Clinton: Church of Holy Ghost arson. Kerosene spilled on floor and lit after local white pastor speaks to Negro Bible class.

July 3, So So: "The Greasy Spoon," a Negro grocery and teen spot, is bombed. Damage minor.

July 6, Jackson: McCraven-Hill Missionary Baptist Church damaged by kerosene fire.

July 6, Raleigh: Methodist and Baptist churches burned to ground.

July 7, Vicksburg: Bovina Community Center burns.

July 8, McComb: SNCC Freedom House bombed. Two workers injured.

July 11, Canton: Small firebomb thrown onto Freedom House lawn.

July 11, Vicksburg: Amateur bomb thrown through window of Negro cafe; no damage other than broken window.

July 11, Browning: Pleasant Plan Missionary Baptist Church burns to ground. Whites tried to buy it, Negroes wouldn't sell.

July 12, Natchez: Jerusalem Baptist and Bethel Methodist churches burned to ground. Home of Negro contractor firebombed.

July 14, Laurel: Gas bomb thrown at local Negro's home.[11]

And it went on like that throughout the summer. Yet the MFDP kept working, garnering support for its challenge, and Baker and her team in Washington continued to pressure delegations across the country for support. In many private meetings Democratic Party officials and their supporters sought to convince the MFDP delegation that for the good of the country it would be wise to compromise. The Democrats wanted smooth sailing for the nominations of Lyndon Johnson and Hubert Humphrey, and the FDP stood in the way. Martin Luther King Jr., Bob Moses, and Ella Baker held out for the right of the MFDP delegation to make its own decisions. Johnson sent Humphrey out to meet with the FDP's potential supporters, to persuade them of the necessity of closing ranks around the president. Johnson also asked for FBI help, which came in the form of a wiretap on King's suite, the placement of informants in the MFDP, and agents posing as NBC correspondents who gathered information through news "interviews."[12] Bayard Rustin, who had been doing yeoman service trying to get administration officials and MFDP representatives, particularly Dr. King, together was reported by the FBI to have said that things might be worked out "if we can get around Ella Baker."[13] While Baker and Bayard had been close allies for many years, their paths had diverged in the early 1960s, when Baker saw in the feisty SNCC workers the possibility of real mass organizing work and Rustin was moving from "protest to politics," as he wrote in an article in 1965. Rustin apparently felt that Baker would opt for the empowerment of the local Mississippians whatever the cost to the Democratic Party, while he was inclined to the politics of compromise, to realpolitik. As Baker put it, "Rustin's position had shifted into the camp of Humphrey, the Save-the-Country camp."[14]

As the convention opened the maneuvering continued. MFDP delegates and their supporters were busy outside the convention hall garnering much press attention. Fannie Lou Hamer made headlines, both before and after her appearance before the Credentials Committee. Hamer told the committee that she had been thrown off the plantation where she worked as timekeeper, and where she had worked in other capacities for over eighteen years. She also spoke of the night when she was in jail in Winona, Mississippi, and had been beaten by two prisoners on orders of the police. Tears streaming down her broad face, she cried: "Is this America? Is this the land of the free; is this the home of the brave?"[15]

Four days before the convention opened, the MFDP had been promised the eleven votes needed in the Credentials Committee to force a floor vote on seating the MFDP delegation. President Johnson, who was adamantly opposed to a floor fight, pulled out all the stops. MFDP support dropped to eight. There were all kinds of dirty tricks. For example, on the day that Baker was visiting the Nebraska delegation the chairperson delayed the meeting pending the arrival of the governor. He finally came and promptly announced that the MFDP had accepted a compromise. When Baker spoke, she expressed her chagrin "at the great loss . . . of the people who were at the convention who had had no opportunity to participate in any decision-making." The announcement of the acceptance of a compromise, however, was premature.

At a meeting of MFDP workers in King's suite, Joe Rauh argued that "the great heart of the Negro people had demonstrated its capacity for forgiveness and understanding." He urged that the same capacity should operate in this situation; otherwise the Democrats might lose the election. Baker got up at that point and said that those who claimed to support the MFDP would remain with it when the going got rough as well as when it was easy. She said that to call upon the MFDP to be understanding of Mr. Humphrey's desire to win was saying, "Forget what *you* need. Support *his* winning." She drily commented: "They never invited me back."[16]

Many seasoned politicians were disheartened by the events. Edith Green told Baker that she was so disgusted with what had taken place that she was not certain she wanted to continue in politics.[17] Even the right-wing columnists Evans and Novak, who consistently charged that SNCC was a Communist front, wrote: "To many delegates, this wasn't a Democratic convention at all. They will be leaving here vaguely frustrated and unfulfilled—the price President Johnson is paying for his rigid suppression of rebellion at Atlantic City."[18]

The president assigned Hubert Humphrey the task of thwarting the MFDP, threatening him with the loss of the vice presidential nomination if he didn't succeed. Humphrey's allies rallied. Walter Reuther left an important negotiation session with General Motors at the president's insistence to fly to Atlantic City to exert his influence. There, among other threats, he told King he would cut off UAW donations to SCLC if King failed to back the president.[19]

The maneuvering of Humphrey and his allies finally succeeded in keeping the question of which delegation was to be seated off the floor. They formulated a "compromise" that they hoped would appease the Freedom Democrats. The MFDP was offered two at-large seats and the promise that in the future no delegation would be seated that was not racially balanced. The MFDP was angered by the way in which the compromise was adopted. The Credentials Committee announced that the compromise had been accepted, while Aaron Henry, Ed King, and Bob Moses were still discussing the proposal with Humphrey, Reuther, King, Rustin, and others. By then, MFDP support for bringing in a minority proposal had dropped from eleven to eight. This had been achieved by outright threats to FDP supporters such as: loss of jobs, denial of a judgeship appointment.[20] The MFDP delegation was profoundly upset by the compromise, which not only proposed that only two delegates should be seated but even named the two: a white, the Reverend Ed King, and a black, Dr. Aaron Henry, party chair. This was the ultimate insult.

In the face of the loss of support, the FDP held an 8-hour caucus addressed by Martin Luther King Jr., James Forman, Bob Moses, Fannie Lou Hamer, and Baker. There is no verbatim record of what Baker said at the meeting, but Mrs. Annie Devine, a founding member of the MFDP, recalled Baker's advice as being "make your own mind up and do what your mind tells you."

The delegation voted to reject the compromise despite the urging of Rustin, King, Rauh, and Aaron Henry. In the end King and Henry accepted the decision and backed the delegation's stance. King's position for acceptance had never been unequivocal. At one

One of many rallies outside the convention hall at the 1964 Democratic National Convention. Ella Baker, far right. From left: Unidentified, Fannie Lou Hamer, Eleanor Holmes Norton; rear, Stokely Carmichael. (© George Ballis.)

point he said that as a Negro leader he would advise acceptance, but if he were a Mississippian he would advise rejection.

All except three of the regular Mississippi delegation left the convention rather than sign the oath of loyalty to the national candidates, so many of the MFDP delegates managed through the help of friends to enter the hall and take the seats vacated by the state party regulars. In the meantime the national media focused on the continuous demonstration the MFDP and its supporters held outside the convention hall, with vibrant singing led by Fannie Lou Hamer and Bernice Reagon and speeches by civil rights leaders.

In a speech at a *National Guardian* dinner held that fall Bob Moses summed up the events: "We told them: You say we're not legal because we don't abide by Mississippi's laws, but the laws of Mississippi are illegal. They're outlaws down there."[21]

Baker had never actually thought that the MFDP delegation would be seated at the convention. She regarded the effort as a learning process. She believed that if the issue had been brought to the convention floor and people had had the opportunity to vote, the MFDP could have been seated. "But I knew enough about political chicanery to know that if a vote is likely to go against the powers that be, they try to find ways of keeping that thing from coming to a vote. And so, this is what they did."[22]

Did the disenfranchised Negroes of Mississippi think they would prevail? Some did and most did not. But they demonstrated for all the nation to see that despite their moral claim (which almost no one denied), and despite the illegality of the state of Mississippi's position, the MFDP had been denied seating at the convention because of political expediency. "What the Administration wanted was a loyalty oath from the 'regular' Mississippi delegation," Moses explained in his *Guardian* speech, "and they were willing to use us as pressure to get that loyalty oath. They wanted some way to move the Southerners more into line. . . . Now the Administration presumably would like to use the congressional challenge to tighten up on seniority. That is, not to oust people from seniority but to make those people who are in seniority posts push through legislation. They've got a lever on them. So they're willing to use us."[23]

The following year, the MFDP challenged the seating of the five Mississippi congressmen. It was doomed to failure, of course, and the five MFDP candidates knew it. But the MFDP did achieve two monumental goals: it organized the African American population of Mississippi into a cohesive force, and it forced Democratic Party politics into a more democratic framework. The MFDP's challenge eventually led to a change in the Democratic Party's rules, which required all delegations to its convention to support the national platform and to include racial representation in proportion to the state's population. And from 1972 on women were to represent 50 percent of the delegates!

While there was intense concentration on the MFDP challenge, the COFO staff and its volunteers kept working in Mississippi. Over the summer they established forty-one Freedom Schools in twenty communities, with 175 teachers and 2,165 students. They built thirteen community centers and continued to conduct voter registration throughout the state.

"The Summer Project left behind new rays of hope in Mississippi," Anne Braden wrote in 1965. "It did something profound to the people who came from the outside too. The Mississippi movement was not callously using them as cannon fodder. Those who came knew they were risking their lives and wanted to do it. For some it was the beginning of a lifetime commitment; for almost all it was an experience that would forever make their lives more meaningful. SNCC, which conceived the project, sensed something most of the nation did not previously seem to know—that a sizable number of young Americans yearn for something meaningful to which they can relate their lives."[24]

As fall approached, the violence increased. In McComb eleven homes and churches were bombed between August 28 and September 21. Meanwhile the National Council of Churches in New York tried to resolve the recurring problem of rivalries among the leading civil rights organizations. At a meeting mediated by Robert Spike of the NCC, NAACP officials criticized Moses for his lack of cooperativeness and high-handedness. SNCC staffers Courtlandt Cox and Mendy Samstein defended Moses and said that decisions were made by local people. Joseph Rauh and Allard Lowenstein began sniping at the National Lawyers Guild, maintaining that it was a Communist front organization. Participants finally agreed to hold another meeting with both Moses and Jim Forman in attendance, but leaders of other civil rights organizations never did accept the idea that Moses did not make MFDP and COFO decisions. Their style of leadership simply could not conceive of local leaders making decisions.

COFO outlined a program for 1964–1965 that encompassed voter registration, Freedom Schools, community centers, a literacy program, and medical, legal, and educational programs. But SNCC was ready to move on to projects in other areas: southwest Georgia, Arkansas, and, as a priority, rural Alabama. In 1965, Selma, Alabama, became the center of confrontation.

CHAPTER TEN

In Her Image

The struggle is eternal. The tribe increases. Somebody else carries on.

On JANUARY 19, 1965, sixty people were arrested in Selma, Alabama, for refusing to enter the courthouse via the backdoor. Among the group were John Lewis, SCLC's Hosea Williams, and Amelia Boynton, the leader of the Selma Voters League, who was dragged by the collar from the courthouse steps by Dallas County Sheriff Jim Clark. One hundred fifty-six more arrests took place the following day. The Dallas County voter registration campaign was heating up. Elsewhere in the South it was much the same. The WATS line reports give the following picture:

Vicksburg, Miss., January 17: A Jitney Jungle Supermarket here closed down its lunch counter, putting 13 Negro employees out of work, after Negroes sought service. . . . The owner, Peter Nosser Sr., said he couldn't serve Negroes because his brother is the mayor of Vicksburg. (Mayor John Nosser is a Mississippi "moderate." His house and several supermarkets owned by his family were recently bombed by the Klan because he hired Negroes, and now he is scared.)

Moultrie, Ga., February 16: 216 students . . . were arrested today as they demonstrated in front of the courthouse in protest of the bad conditions at Bryant HS. The boycott of Bryant HS is continuing, as is the Freedom School.

Laurel, Miss., February 16: COFO office burned. The fire was apparently part of a continuing attempt to intimidate the local Negro citizen, Cleveland Golden, who has rented the building to COFO since November. On Christmas Eve, a restaurant he owned was burned. In January fire was set to a hotel owned by Mr. Golden, who was inside at the time and jumped out of the window, breaking his leg.

Marion, Ala., February 19: As about 300–400 people gathered at the door of the Zion Methodist Church state troopers converged on them and began to beat them with billy clubs. . . . Jimmy Lee Jackson, 26, was shot twice in the stomach and is in critical condition. He was also beaten about the head. A CBS team was thrown in jail and their cameras were smashed; one guy from UPI is in the hospital.[1]

Emotions were high at the February SNCC coordinating committee meeting at Gammon Theological Seminary in Atlanta. The debate over its structure and future continued. Many of the "veterans" were suffering from battle fatigue, and the pressures of Freedom Summer had increased tensions within the organization. Gammon, with its rolling lawns and peaceful atmosphere, did nothing to calm the frayed nerves of the youngsters, who had been scarred by the summer's deaths, bombings, and church burnings. Only Baker remained calm. The debate, sometimes rancorous, again centered on the question of how much responsibility should belong to local people. In the course of the long hours of discussion, those who urged a formalized structure for SNCC were often overwhelmed by the heartfelt emotional pleas of those who sought less rigidity. They were the "Freedom High" faction, almost certainly inspired by Bob Moses, who had a good deal of faith in local people and an antipathy toward the establishment of entrenched national organizations. (Not wanting to be used as a media figure to enhance the status of the organization in fund-raising campaigns, Moses announced that he was dropping his patronymic and reverting to his mother's name— his middle name—Parris. The following year he left the country and after some travels spent over six years teaching in Tanzania.)

The discussion at the meeting was a wide-ranging one, but at its core was the relationship of the local people to the SNCC staff. Many argued that "we" did not know anything, that only the share-cropper or plantation worker could say what the problems and solutions were. "We" were outsiders and could only learn from the people. Those who wanted more structure—the "Forman faction"—argued that the organization was too large to function without defining jobs, functions, and responsibilities. They felt that there should be lines of command, accountability, and rules of procedure.

At one point in the debate a scuffle broke out, and I began to weep. I was overwhelmed by the apparent breakdown of the concept of the beloved community. Baker, seated next to me, immediately stood and began to sing: "We shall overcome, we shall overcome, we shall overcome one day. Deep in our hearts, we do believe, we shall overcome one day." She had them on their feet and singing vigorously in an instant. In truth, she felt that singing "We Shall Overcome" was a sort of opiate—but she used it, and it worked. Perhaps Baker's reaction was instinctive, perhaps calculated, but it worked. We became a band of brothers and sisters, a circle of trust, once more.

The February 23, 1965, report of the meeting said: "The meeting at Gammon Theological Seminary closed with the singing of 'We Shall Overcome' and the dedication of the SNCC people there assembled that the resources of the organization and the skills of its field secretaries must be put to a constant struggle in behalf of poor people. For despite the gains that the student movement has [succeeded] in making, people are still poor, voteless, without jobs, suffering from police brutality, inadequate housing and a denial of dignity. . . .

"Since October we have been grappling with many problems in our organization and within the society at large," the report continued. "We have been struggling to find better ways to effect our concept of allowing people in the communities to participate more in making decisions affecting their lives."[2] There is no doubt that Baker was the chief influence in the decision to emphasize and develop local leadership.

Baker's presence was distinctly felt. She was most obviously influential when she spoke up at meetings or counseled the leadership. Most SNCC staffers felt the need for her input. Lurking in the background was the idea that Miss Baker might not approve of this or that decision. Someone nearly always checked with her. As Chuck McDew expressed it: "Her philosophy became our philosophy. . . . Miss Baker sort of shaped us in her image."

Baker's influence was pragmatic. When membership on the coordinating committee was extended to include all staff members as voting delegates as well as "members of student and community groups across the south," and representatives of Friends of SNCC groups, Baker argued that decision making by three hundred people would be unwieldy and urged that smaller committees be chosen to deal with specific areas. An expanded executive committee was chosen, ostensibly to give "people who have less visibility in the organization . . . more responsibility," but primarily to put control of policy decisions in the hands of staff. Once again Baker and Howard Zinn were reappointed advisers; a secretariat made up of John Lewis, James Forman, and Cleveland Sellers, the newly elected program secretary, was formed "to assist in the day-to-day running of the organization."[3] Stressing two of the areas that Baker continually put forth, namely, the need for staff to have concrete knowledge and the importance of developing local leaders, the meeting voted to expand educational programs and political organizing. The MFDP had begun organizing in new Mississippi communities, and people in other states expressed interest in replicating their efforts. SNCC expanded its campus travelers' program, with seven staff members organizing on both white and Negro campuses under the leadership of Ed Hamlet.

SNCC had been organizing in Selma, Alabama, since early 1963. It now decided to expand its Alabama staff to thirty-five and begin work in ten rural counties. Lowndes County took the lead. Using the black panther as its party symbol, the Lowndes County Freedom Organization pushed voter registration and nominated candidates for local elections. LCFO chair John Hulett, who was elected sheriff in 1970, explained the black panther symbol this way: "The black panther is an animal that when it is pressured it moves back until it is cornered, then it comes out fighting for life or death. We felt we had been pushed back long enough and that it was time for Negroes to come out and take over." (Two years later the symbol assumed new importance when it was adopted nationally by the Black Panther Party.)

Selma had been heating up during the spring. After Martin Luther King Jr. led a march there on February 1, there were huge demonstrations and more than a thousand arrests. The situation escalated after 26-year-old Jimmy Lee Jackson was killed by a state police officer, and the SCLC announced a march from Selma to the state capital at Montgomery. SNCC opposed the march on the grounds that the danger to local people was too great, but it did agree to provide support services, and the executive committee agreed to allow SNCC staff to participate as individuals.

Major John Cloud of the state police, and Sheriff Jim Clark and his deputies, met the marchers at the Pettus Bridge in Selma and ordered them to turn back. When the marchers refused, they were brutally attacked by mounted police in a now infamous confrontation. King was not present, but he did agree to lead a second attempt to cross the bridge. But after a conference with Attorney General Nicholas DeB. Katzenbach, King made an agreement with the authorities to turn the second march back when ordered to do so. SNCC staffers were furious. In the aftermath of the march a white minister, Jonathan Reeb, was killed and there was a national outpouring of sympathy. The president even sent a plane for Mrs. Reeb. SNCC workers were enraged; no such gestures had been made for the family of Jimmy Lee Jackson.

Forman and other SNCC staffers mobilized hundreds of students to demonstrate at the state capital building in Montgomery. SCLC leaders attempted to halt the demonstrations, but the students persisted. After they were attacked by mounted police on March 15, they returned to the state capital, where Forman made a rousing speech: "If we can't sit at the table of democracy, we'll knock the fucking legs off." Forman regretted using such strong language, but later wrote that "the charge by the posse earlier that day . . . was still in my mind [and] it was difficult not to speak out in anger."[4] After several negotiating sessions the Selma-to-Montgomery march finally took place, peacefully, on March 25. That night a white volunteer from Detroit, Viola Liuzzo, was shot and killed as she drove marchers back from Montgomery to Selma.

Forman was among the SNCC staffers criticized for acting on their own. He had spent over $5,000 on support materials for the march and had organized the students for the Montgomery demonstrations without going through channels. Mrs. Hazel Palmer, a local MFDP leader from Jackson, Mississippi, said in Forman's defense: "I heard local people saying 'we should have gone across that bridge.' What should Forman and Lewis have done? Wait and sit down with a committee [to decide] what they should do each step of the way?"[5]

By the spring of 1965, SNCC, though expanding its organizing efforts, seemed to be in some disarray. In trying to get their house in order they were now ready to take Baker's advice, tendered months before, to establish some personnel guidelines. At the spring executive committee meeting many staffers complained about "floaters," workers who left their projects to go wherever they wished. Among those criticized were Bob and Dona Moses, who had pulled out of Mississippi and turned up in Birmingham without reporting to Alabama project director Silas Norman. True to their tradition, SNCC organizers tried to be judicious in their deliberations, but many of their problems were prickly ones, for example, whether to keep recalcitrant staffers on the payroll. Fay Bellamy wanted to know: "Where on earth did the idea come from of being able to hire but not fire?"[6] Baker pointed out that there were many reasons for staff members' moves from one locale to another. Chief among them was "battle fatigue," but there was also a sense that once a community was organized there was nothing left for them to do. Some veteran staffers, with Baker and Zinn in agreement, kept pushing for a comprehensive program, citing its lack as a reason for staff members, "floating." It was agreed that whatever rules were finally devised by the personnel committee, they would apply to all. The crisis finally passed with the pressure of the increased organizing efforts in the rural counties.

In the meantime there was continued pressure on the federal government, with some response. In 1961 the Justice Department had brought suit in Dallas County around the use of the literacy test, but to no avail. According to an SNCC report, dated February 25, 1965, "the lines of applicants continue to queue up so that Negro citizens may have their brief, futile encounter with the Dallas County Board of Registration."[7] Now the government contended that the tests were in violation of the Civil Rights Act, which had been drafted by the Kennedy administration and passed into law under Lyndon Johnson on July 2, 1964. The federal government was at last on the verge of accepting the call to take a moral stance. Not least among the reasons was the renewed vigor of demonstrations and the vow of Governor George C. Wallace to oppose admission of blacks to the University of Alabama. On May 24, Attorney General Robert Kennedy met with a number of black intellectuals in New York, among them James Baldwin, Harry Belafonte, Lorraine Hansberry, and Kenneth Clark. Kennedy was stunned by their outspoken and angry attacks on him and on the government's lack of leadership in the fight for equality. According to historian David Garrow, "Kennedy left the session furious at the lack of appreciation . . . for the government's efforts concerning civil rights," but sensitized "more deeply than ever to the fact that what the federal government had done still fell short of what was morally necessary."[8]

The following year, the Voting Rights Act was passed. As he signed the bill, on March 8, 1965, Johnson endorsed the Selma demonstrations, saying that they "have awakened the conscience of this nation" and then pronouncing, melodramatically, "We shall overcome."

The Voting Rights Act spurred voter registration in the Mississippi Delta. The Justice Department brought suit against the Sunflower County registrar, who was enjoined from making distinctions between potential voters based on race. The court ruled that registration must be based on age, residence, and literacy. With a population that was 68 percent Negro, 3,000 blacks were registered to vote out of the 14,000 eligible; 8,000 of the 9,000 eligible white voters were registered. Despite the ruling, registration of blacks retained its slow pace, so the MFDP brought suit and won, overturning the town of Sunflower's municipal elections of 1965.

Though she had moved back to New York, Baker worked with the National Committee for Free Elections in Sunflower and with the people organizing in the county. On one trip to Sunflower, she counted the houses in the white section to get an idea of the relationship of residences to voting rolls. There were about 60 houses and about 120 whites registered. The town of fewer than 700 inhabitants was three-quarters black.

Baker attended an executive committee meeting of the MFDP in Jackson, which had been called by Annie Devine and Victoria Gray, two of MFDP's congressional candidates. There the statewide importance of the Sunflower decision was discussed. She and Mrs. Gray decided to go to Sunflower to assess what Baker termed the "strains" in the community. They were joined by Harry Bowie, an Episcopal minister working in McComb for the Delta Ministry, and a local MFDP leader, Johnnie Mae Walker. Baker felt that one of the problems was that the MFDP county chair was "a 19-year-old young fella," Otis Brown, who had replaced an elderly resident, Mrs. King. Deciding that a reconciliation was needed, the group went to visit Mrs. King. Baker's companions left her to talk with Mrs. King alone, feeling that she would more readily unburden herself to Baker, since, as Baker put it, "I was more of her contemporary." Mrs. King was miffed at having been ousted from office, but Baker succeeded in convincing her to continue playing an active role. In addition to smoothing ruffled feathers, the group met with Sunflower activists and encouraged them to do their homework by using one of Baker's old techniques: asking questions. Are the aldermen elected by districts or on a citywide basis? How big are the districts? And so forth. The questions pointed to the need for solid information.

One of the things that surprised Baker was that even after the searing experience of Mississippi Freedom Summer, the local people were anxious to have outside organizers come in, including whites. They said, realistically, that there were blacks who would accept a statement from whites that they would not accept from Negroes. But they had a caveat: they did not want people coming in who had their own agenda. According to Baker, "they needed people who could unify the dissident strains rather than people who would help to widen any gaps that existed." Consonant with her usual generous bow to youth, and articulated in her customary gentle way, Baker described Otis Brown as a young man who "has much more insight than many of the older people, but who still is a young person who perhaps hasn't thought through some things." For example, Brown's idea that clothes and food should be given out on election day was shot down by older workers, who pointed out that if they started the practice of buying allegiance, opponents of Negro voting could always afford to spend more. Baker, of course, agreed, but she said, "Our real job was to accept the fact that these people could learn and understand as we had come to learn and understand."[9]

Later, reflecting on that struggle, Baker pointed out that "none of us who had the positions we now hold had those positions all of our lives, that some of us had just gotten to understand these things in the last couple of years." She reasoned that if some were able to understand, then others could understand, if time were taken to explain. She believed that this could be much more productive than trying to play the game of offering the highest stakes economically.

But as important as this was, Baker's analysis of the Sunflower community was even more significant. She analyzed by asking questions: How did the people live? Were they on relief? Were they getting surplus food? How much illness was in the home? Baker said: "There were some serious illnesses, I think. Where I stayed there was a five-year-old boy who they thought had asthma, but it seemed to me from the little reading I had done that it might be cystic fibrosis."[10] She felt that the medical problems of the community might become the basis for a political platform. Exposing conditions in

Senator James O. Eastland's home county could provide an issue that might be used against him, she said.

Out of this grew an idea. In January 1965, SNCC had been instrumental in organizing the Mississippi Freedom Labor Union, making the first connections between civil rights and economic rights. This decision was a major breakthrough. At last the question of economics, and class, could come to the fore. By the spring of 1965, the union had over 1,300 members; 350 members, mostly cotton workers, were out on strike.

The MFLU staged several strikes that resulted in wage increases. When fifteen MFLU workers staged a walkout at Senator Eastland's plantation in Sunflower County, it was a very important psychological victory. Many families, evicted from plantations because of union activity, lived for several months in a tent city near Tribbett, Mississippi. Pressing for federal aid, seventy people moved into an empty barracks at the Greenville air force base. Citing the lack of running water and fire protection, the federal government evicted them. One of the strike leaders, Isaac Foster of Tribbett, commented: ". . . the federal government can't tell me that was the reason we was put out, because all over Mississippi houses don't have running water or fire protection."[11] This statement, by a local leader of a sharecroppers' union on the sixth anniversary of the sit-ins, indicates how far the movement had come since the early days when youngsters sat in at lunch counters. Then the demands had been for equal access to public accommodations. Now the movement was turning to the question of economic justice.

SNCC also formed the Poor People's Corporation to provide loans to self-help organizations and cooperatively run businesses. About three hundred people attended its first meeting on August 29, 1965. By then five businesses were in the development stage and one, the Madison County Sewing Firm of Canton, Mississippi, was already producing clothing. Others in the planning stage were leather and woodworking cooperatives and a second clothing co-op. Soon a distribution outlet named Liberty House was formed, with a store in New York's Greenwich Village (run by Yippie leader Abbie Hoffman) and a catalogue operation.

This was exactly what Baker had hoped and fought for as a long-time advocate of education, particularly economic education. She did not formulate the ideas concretely, but merely pushed for education, an understanding of the economics of segregation, and the relationship of the federal government to the economic needs of local people.

Now living in her Lenox Terrace apartment at 10 West 135 Street, Baker often went South to fulfill speaking engagements and attend SNCC meetings. In New York she engaged in her customary flurry of activity. Part of her effort was devoted to support of the FDP challenge to the seating of the five Mississippi congressmen whose seats were being demanded by FDP candidates. She was active in the Northern support movement for the MFDP challenge, speaking on behalf of the candidates and helping to raise money for their effort. She also threw her energies into a newly formed organization, the Charter Group for a Pledge of Conscience, renewed her work with Parents in Action, and struggled to keep FELD in existence to aid burned-out field workers who needed scholarship help to return to school.

Her affiliation with the Charter Group was perhaps an expression of her commitment to more radical political thought. Participants were well-known left-wing political activists like Annie Stein, Jane McManus, and Annette Rubenstein. The Charter Group was organized to rally white support to end racism. Baker also returned to her work to end de facto school segregation, becoming active once again in the Harlem Parents' Committee. But she remained committed to SNCC—the only organization that stated in its executive committee minutes: "If a member is in jail . . . he could give his proxy to another person."

By 1969, when she gave a speech at the Institute of the Black World in Atlanta, Baker pointed to a new phase of the civil rights movement. It was now "a struggle for a different kind of society which will reject, if necessary, the present system." She spoke about economic inequities, pointing to the inflated defense budget compared to limited funds for the poor. "Now is that the kind of system which you can expect to get in and find real value? . . . In order for us as poor and oppressed people to become a part of a society that is meaningful, the system under which we now exist has to be radically changed. This means that we are going to have to learn to think in *radical* terms." She added: "I use the term radical in its original meaning, *getting down to and understanding the root causes*. It means facing a system that does not lend itself to your needs and devising means by which you change that system." Never relinquishing her main thrust, she said: "But one of the guiding principles has to be that we cannot lead a struggle that involves masses of people without identifying with the people and without getting the people to understand what their potentials are, what their strengths are."[12] This was the theme that she was committed to throughout her life.

CHAPTER ELEVEN

Black Power's Gon' Get
Your Mama!

The black power thing. I think they got caught in their own rheto-ric . . . many of them hadn't developed as much of a rationale . . . as Stokely. . . . I've seen him [develop] it at a level that there was nothing irritating about it for anybody who is willing to have sense enough to deal with the facts. . . . And the rhetoric was far in ad-vance of the organization. . . . How can you have a coalition: the first question [is] with whom can you coalesce? The logical groups . . . would be the impoverished white, the misrepresented . . . or the non-represented . . . the alienated Mexican-Americans. These are the natural allies, in my book. But there is no natural alliance between the . . . poor and Walter Reuther.

"BLACK POWER!" When Willie Ricks, a feisty SNCC staffer, first shouted out the slogan during the James Meredith march in June 1966, it was immediately taken up by Stokely Carmichael. Then Ricks yelled, "What do you want?" and the marchers shouted, "Black Power!" The call reverberated through the crowd and across the nation, and swiftly became the battle cry of the movement.

It seemed to be a long way from the 1960 sit-ins, but Baker accepted the change as part of the struggle. At this time the young people needed to band together as black people, to assess their own strengths and their own needs.

During a long and exhausting session at SNCC's 1966 staff meeting in Kingston Springs, Tennessee, Carmichael was elected chairman.

It was generally agreed that Carmichael represented the new mood of militancy and Black Power was the new goal. Many were disturbed by the way in which the election was conducted. Initially, John Lewis, who had been chair since 1963, was reelected by an overwhelming vote, but through a series of maneuvers that smacked of backroom politics, that vote was voided and a new vote taken. Worth Long had called for a new vote, but it was Forman who succeeded in effecting it. Forman had already resigned as executive secretary, and Ruby Doris Robinson had been chosen to replace him. Forman suggested that both she and Cleveland Robinson, newly elected program chair, and Lewis resign to clear the way for a new vote. They did. The ploy worked and Carmichael was swept in, though this was less an ideological victory than one of attrition, for it was late at night and many of Lewis's supporters had already left the session.

There had been criticism of Lewis for his willingness to cooperate with the establishment, for his adherence to old tactics and stances. He had been reelected partly out of loyalty, partly because some staff members did not like what seemed to be a coup in the making. In the main SNCC people were not much concerned with who held office. Past SNCC elections had mostly been routine affairs, much less important than decisions around programs, salaries, and disciplinary and grievance procedures. This election was out of character and proved to be the opening that led to SNCC's disintegration.

Ella Baker took the proceedings in stride. When we left the meeting site for our motel in nearby Nashville, I was fuming but she was calm. She'd seen similar maneuvering on other occasions. More importantly, she had abiding faith in the young people. SNCC was entering a new phase, more militant, more keyed toward the third world, more revolutionary. However, while the majority of the staff embraced the concept of Black Power, they did not go along with the extreme position of the Atlanta Project, which had over the previous few months developed a position paper on black separatism.

The paper called for establishing SNCC as an all-black organization: "black-staffed, black-controlled and black-financed."[1]

As the cry of "Black Power" swept through the more militant portions of the civil rights movement, the reaction from more staid groups, white liberal organizations, the government, and much of the press was one of fear and outrage. Criticism was swift and sharp. Yet there were some public defenses of the term. In an advertisement in the *New York Times* addressed to the country's leaders, the mass media, white churchmen, and the Negro community a group of black ministers pointed out that "none of those civil rights leaders who have asked for 'black power' have suggested that it means a new form of isolationism or a foolish effort at domination."[2]

Donald Harrington, a white minister of New York's Community Church, delivered a sermon entitled, "What's the Matter with Black Power?" Citing the exercise of Catholic, Jewish, and Polish power, he asked: "Why should not the Negro seek the same social solidarity and resultant power that other groups have successfully sought and wielded for their advancement from time immemorial?" He declared that the answer "lies in the depths of the white psyche, the white, Western soul. . . . Our problem is not with the word, 'power,' but with the word, 'black.'" We should give thanks to Carmichael for "forcing us to reveal those hidden fears and deep hatreds of the inner psyche."[3]

Stokely Carmichael explained the call for Black Power in an article entitled "What We Want." "In Lowndes County . . . black power will mean that if a Negro is elected sheriff, he can end police brutality. If a black man is elected tax assessor, he can collect and channel funds for the building of better roads and schools serving black people—thus advancing the move from political power into the economic arena. In such areas as Lowndes, where black men have a majority, they will attempt to use it to exercise control. This is what they seek: control. Where Negroes lack a majority, black power means proper representation and sharing of control. It means the creation of power bases from which black people can work to change statewide or nationwide patterns of oppression through pressure from strength—instead of weakness. Politically, black power means what it has always meant to SNCC: the coming-together of black people to elect representatives and *to force those representatives to speak to their needs*."[4]

Baker patiently explained to white supporters that this was a step that the young people needed to take—a heartfelt necessity to regroup. They needed this time to stand together and declare their belief that black people must declare themselves a force and rely on their own resources. She firmly maintained that the youngsters must be allowed to make their own decisions, make their own mistakes. She believed that the stance was a temporary one and never abandoned her own allegiance to a unified fight—black and white together.

In seeming contradiction of SNCC's nonviolent stance, staffers took part in target practice at the Kingston Springs meeting. While they adhered to nonviolence as a tactic in demonstrations, many SNCC staff people felt that they would have no qualms about using weapons if necessary. In fact, SNCC people had wielded guns many times. On one occasion Jim Forman was almost blown away when he banged on Chuck McDew's door in Natchez without properly identifying himself. It is an indication of how dangerous the time was—a time so fraught with violence and potential violence that guns seemed appropriate, at least for self-defense. Nevertheless, there is not one recorded instance of an SNCC worker firing a weapon.

The question of nonviolence was debated at length in movement meetings. Some staffers insisted on being armed, and some insisted that they had never been nonviolent. Most local people were armed, a fact that could not be ignored. Most rural people owned shotguns for hunting, and most black people owned shotguns for defense. This may or may not have been a shock to SNCC workers, but it certainly was a relief, giving them some feeling of security and a sense of defiance. Baker, with long experience in dealing with local people in small towns and rural areas, understood this. Then, too, there seemed to be a connection between toting a gun to defend one's family and the developing interest in revolution—a connection that came more from African rebellions than from any Marxist analysis.

Baker endorsed SNCC's decision to work more closely with the developing nations—the so-called third world. She proposed that a part of SNCC's education program be devoted to discussion of events in the former colonial countries. While going along with a revolutionary thrust, she resolutely ignored the question of arms, believing—as most SNCC people did—that this was an individual decision. If an SNCC staffer chose to carry a weapon as he or she traveled the dangerous roads of the Delta or Southwest Georgia, rural Louisiana or Arkansas, it was a personal choice. SNCC staff members, ostensibly committed to nonviolence, nonetheless adhered to a community's practice of maintaining armed patrols to guard their homes, and in Harmony, Mississippi, and elsewhere they took their turns on guard duty. Baker, who always said that she would not be able to turn the other cheek, turned a blind eye to the prevalence of weapons. While she herself would rely on her fists—and her intimidating tendency to talk back—she had no qualms about target practice.

In May, SNCC declared itself to be a human rights organization, advocating human rights not only in the United States but throughout the world. The New York SNCC office shifted from fundraising to international relations, and was reorganized as the International Affairs Commission headed by Forman. Forman cultivated SNCC's relationship with United Nations diplomats from Africa, and SNCC attempted to establish an African American skills bank, with an eye to replacing white technical assistance to African countries. Several staff members went to Africa. (Baker was scheduled to go on the first of these journeys, but she felt that the trip would be too much for her to undertake physically. It was a disappointment because she had dreamed of becoming a medical missionary in Africa since her college days. Instead, she had got caught up in the struggle here. As it happened she left the country only once—on a trip with Jackie to Nassau for a brief vacation.)

In 1967, the controversial Atlanta Project was ejected from SNCC and simultaneously the remaining white SNCC staff members were fired. Relationships with former white staff members were to be on a "contractual" basis.[5] The first white to be put on SNCC staff, Bob Zellner, was also the last to be severed. Zellner then proposed that he and his wife, Dorothy Miller Zellner, set up a project called GROW (Grassroots Organizing Project) to work in white communities with SNCC support. That proposal was accepted, as recorded in official minutes, "in principal [sic] and with resources if they are available."[6]

The following year, at a tense meeting at the African American resort Peg Leg Bates in upstate New York, support for the Zellners' GROW project was withdrawn. SNCC was now officially an all-black organization. Maggie Nolan Donovan, who had worked with the Zellners in Boston Friends of SNCC, and acknowledged that SNCC should become all-black, nevertheless felt bereft at the thought of having to leave the organization that she had been devoted to. "It was deeply wrenching," she said. She had been working with the Zellners, who had been transferred to Boston for a time while Bob returned to school, at Brandeis, to finish his undergraduate work. Maggie said that in the midst of this crisis Miss Baker called and asked if she could stay at her home for the weekend. In a voice choked with emotion, still, thirty years later, Maggie said: "The first thing she did was put her arms around me and stroke my head. No words were spoken on the subject of whites being expelled. After a few moments she got practical. She said that Edward, my boyfriend, was a nice guy and that I should marry him, and then, she said, 'You should learn to cook.' She asked what was for supper and I said that hot dogs were on the menu. She then called Edward in and took us both to the kitchen, where she showed us how to cook hot dogs properly. She gave both emotional support and practical advice, and I felt enormously taken care of. And I did what she said. I married him, and I learned to cook."[7]

Baker, while adhering to her long-held belief in the need for humankind to work together, nevertheless continued to support the young people in their newfound need to withdraw, coalesce, and form bonds among themselves. Though she maintained throughout her life a strong bond with whites, she understood the need that young blacks felt at this time for an expression of their own worthiness. (In 1980, when we were making the documentary film *Fundi: The Story of Ella Baker,* Baker explained in no uncertain terms to her old friend Virginia Durr what black students had been thinking in the late 1960s. Baker and Durr had worked together in the 1940s on black voter registration. Durr was a white Alabama aristocrat from a long-established family, a part of the landed gentry, but she had been an early participant in the civil rights movement. She married an upstanding young man, Clifford Durr, and together they fought for civil rights and civil liberties in the highly segregated atmosphere of Montgomery, Alabama. They had worked with E. D. Nixon, a Montgomery civil rights leader, to secure the release of Rosa Parks, who had been arrested for sitting in the "white" section of a Montgomery city bus. Virginia Durr had long been an active supporter of the rights of black people, she had earned her credentials, but she did not understand the new era. In 1980, she had still not come to grips with the birth of the Black Power movement of the late 1960s. Referring to a 1960s speaking engagement at Tougaloo College, a black college in Mississippi, Durr complained that the black students had adamantly refused to listen to her and her husband. She was absolutely appalled at the militance of the black students, who simply refused to listen to two more white people telling them what to think, what to do, how to act. Baker, in one of her feisty moods, embarked on a heated explanation of what black students had been feeling. She explained that this new generation of black students had no relationship to the previous one, which had seen integration as the goal. The young people whom the Durrs confronted wanted to decide on their own agenda, their own goals, and their own way of achieving them. Durr thought the students rude, but Baker thought them forward-looking. Baker was eloquent in her explication, and Durr, not someone who is easily stopped when she is holding forth, was silenced. The next morning, Virginia commented, "Well, Ella sure shut me up, didn't she?")

The Black Power rhetoric caught on and was taken up across the country, particularly in urban ghettos and on black college campuses. But Black Power was the severing blow to the shaky alliance between SNCC and the other civil rights organizations. In May, SNCC announced that it was withdrawing from the Civil Rights Leadership Conference, which had tried to maintain a united front among the Big Six since its founding. Furthermore, SNCC announced that it would not participate in a White House conference called "To Secure These Rights." The SNCC statement said:

> We believe that the President has called this conference within the United States at a time United States prestige internationally is at a low ebb due to our involvement in the Vietnam Civil War, the Dominican Republic, the Congo, South Africa and other parts of the Third World. We cannot be a party to attempts by the White House to use black Americans to recoup a loss of prestige internationally.
>
> Our organization is opposed to the war in Vietnam and we cannot in good conscience meet with the chief policy maker of the Vietnam war to discuss human rights in this country when he flagrantly violates the human rights of colored people in Vietnam.[8]

Only CORE, which was rapidly changing from a mostly white organization to a black nationalist one, remained as an ally. At the NAACP's annual meeting in July, Roy Wilkins was the first to denounce Black Power, terming it "a reverse Mississippi, reverse Hitler, a reverse Ku Klux Klan."[9] Black Power and Carmichael were roundly denounced by the nation's press and political figures.

Earlier that month a report from the new chair, H. Rap Brown, had set forth a radical plan for organizing in the black community. "We are, without a doubt, vocally the most militant organization in the Civil Rights Movement and the most militant organization taking opposition to the war in Vietnam. . . . We are looked to as the organization inside the United States who is ready to lay the foundation for a revolution." The report goes on to say: "Let it be clear in all our minds that [the] aim of the Student Nonviolent Coordinating Committee is to liberate the oppressed black people in this country from political, economical and social oppression by *any means necessary.*" Discussing empowerment, Brown stated, "We must begin to say that all of the institutions within the black community in this country are to be controlled by black people."[10]

Significantly, in this same speech Brown warned that SNCC would be—and perhaps already was—infiltrated by agents who would attempt to disrupt or destroy the organization.

It was clear that this was the intention of the FBI. On August 21, 1967, a memo from FBI director J. Edgar Hoover ordered security investigations of individual members of SNCC because the organization "has moved from being a civil rights group to a militant revolutionary position." The directive charged that "its leaders have advocated violence and urban guerrilla warfare. Stokely Carmichael, former National Chairman of SNCC, has advocated the overthrow of capitalism." The directive spoke of the necessity of developing informants "at all levels in SNCC and of developing informants who can furnish information concerning other black nationalist groups."[11]

The stepped-up program included such "dirty tricks" as anonymous letters to sow dissension and what the FBI charmingly called "pretext" telephone calls. During the short-lived alliance between SNCC and the Black Panther Party, the FBI formulated many plans to create or exacerbate tensions between the two organizations. According to one COINTELPRO (the U.S. counterintelligence program) memorandum, SNCC had circulated the following statement: "According to zoologists, the main difference between a panther and other large cats is that the panther has the smallest head." The FBI comment on the statement was recorded as: "This is biologically true. Publicity to this effect might help neutralize Black Panther recruiting efforts." To this end the Crime Records Division furnished the statement to "a cooperative news media source" captioned "Panther Pinheads." Fun and games at FBI headquarters.[12]

In an attempt to create panic, there were what the FBI called "pretext" phone calls to Carmichael's mother to say that her son's life was in danger. An FBI report recorded: "It was explained to Mrs. Carmichael the absolute necessity for Carmichael to 'hide out' inasmuch as several BPP members were out to kill him, and it would probably be done sometime this week." The memorandum continued, "Mrs. Carmichael appeared shocked upon hearing the news."[13]

The FBI also carried on an extensive campaign to discredit Carmichael, both with his then-wife, South African singer Miriam Makeba, by sending her anonymous letters saying that he was using her money to fly around the country, not for political meetings but for assignations, and with the black community by publicizing the couple's planned purchase of a $70,000 house. Inventively, it was proposed that invitations to an open house at the new residence be distributed at Resurrection City, a Poor People's Campaign tent city in Washington. It was also suggested by many FBI offices that the rumor that Carmichael was a CIA agent be circulated. Similar campaigns were waged against H. Rap Brown and Forman.

Apparently Baker was not considered dangerous. After carefully monitoring Baker's activities over a twenty-year period, the FBI finally said in 1968: "The subject is not being recommended for the Security Index because in her speeches she has not advocated violence or revolution nor has she ever been a member of the [Communist Party]. Subject's activities reflect that she is interested in obtaining improvement of the Negro by peaceful means only."[14]

Baker, oblivious to the FBI's interest, and undoubtedly unconcerned about it in any case, had been fighting McCarthyism since the mid-1950s, handling correspondence for an organization called Americans for Traditional Liberties. Baker's husband, Bob, was probably instrumental in setting up ATL, whose first address was their home at 452 St. Nicholas Avenue. Bob had organized for the American Labor Party in the 1930s, but, said Baker, "his interest was not as sustained as mine."[15] She continued her work with the National Committee to Abolish HUAC and the Los Angeles Committee for the Defense of the Bill of Rights. She was also affiliated with the Citizens Committee for Constitutional Liberties.

One of several cases that came up at this time was that of Angela Davis, a black militant who was accused of providing weapons to Jonathan Jackson, the brother of George Jackson, an inmate in California's Soledad Prison. Jonathan Jackson entered a courtroom and attempted to take a judge and others hostage to bargain for his brother's release. Jonathan, two prisoners, and the judge were killed in the ensuing shootout. Davis was arrested and spent more than a year in jail before being acquitted. Baker became active in the Davis defense organization and made many speeches on her behalf. Her belief in the fight for civil liberties led her to champion Davis, who was an open member of the Communist Party. Baker had come a long way from her early days in the NAACP when she had participated in the purge of Communists.

At a rally of 150 people, sponsored by the Charlottesville, Virginia, Angela Davis Defense Committee, Baker lashed out against complacency. She said she had come to the university to speak because little was being done about the case in the South. Hitting on one of her favorite themes, she said: "The struggle for rights didn't start yesterday and has to continue until it is won."[16]

In the meantime, Baker was involved with a number of organizations ranging from the National Committee on Interracial Communications—an adjunct of the Research Institute for the Study of Man, a project initiated by Vera Rubin—to the Harlem Inter-Faith Counseling Service. The NCIC was established to provide a venue for dialogue on how to enlarge and enrich the civil rights struggle. At one session, for example, Palmer Weber, an economist and Wall Street analyst, and a Southerner who had been active over the years in the fight for civil rights, provided information on labor and business. Baker pointed out that "business does not function in terms of the interest of people, but in its capacity to earn a profit. . . . This development has sometimes taken place at the cost to the consumer." Another session included a talk by Herbert Hill, labor secretary of the NAACP. These discussions were more intellectual than activist-oriented—not Baker's typical style.

Though active as always, Baker also needed to find a way to support herself. She became a consultant to the executive council of the Episcopal Church at a salary of $250 per week or $50 per day. Her task was to explore ways of heightening awareness of political repression. In her capacity as consultant she traveled to Texas, where she observed some of the same attitudes she had encountered in the 1940s when she visited Albany, New York, during her tenure with the NAACP: "A main reason why I believe these groups [that the Episcopal Church was supporting] should be kept alive is that on the basis of whatever prior knowledge I have on the Texas area, and what I saw of how desperate the needs are, it is obvious that THE MOVEMENT has not come alive in Texas. In my opinion, certainly Houston, like the North Carolina–Virginia Piedmont areas, felt that it was a 'progressive area' and was ahead of such benighted spots as Mississippi and Alabama. So, as a result, sustained efforts for basic change have not been developed. What these young leaders of HOPE, CO-OP and POWER are doing is breaking through its insulation from the realities of 1970."[17]

She also surveyed the status of the legal scene in the South, but pointedly did not limit herself. In a memo to Callender at Episcopal Church headquarters in New York, Baker outlined several cases and spoke of the need to support the Southern Committee Against Repression initiated by the Bradens and the Southern Conference Educational Fund. As to her "personal interest" she wrote: "Although the cases listed in this 'memo' deal with repression against Blacks, and the emphasis has been placed on the South, my interest is not limited by the color line, the Mason-Dixon line, nor any particular ideological line. I am concerned about developing effective forces to counteract the forces of repression."[18]

Baker also worked with an old SNCC colleague, Charles Sherrod, in Southwest Georgia. Sherrod was attempting to set up a self-help community that would function as a self-contained economic unit. Baker did not mince words in her report to Sherrod on the education workshops of the New Communities Charette (as it was called), held at Featherfield Farms, Georgia, during February 1970. They could not "realistically" be regarded as planning sessions, she wrote. What was possible, and what did take place, were multiple explorations of what people thought, hoped for, and dreamed of as the probability of a new system for survival.

True to form, Baker stated that the people who were participating in the project should be the ones who determined its structure. "Since New Communities is based on social values that differ from prevailing ones, it is essential that prospective settlers and supporters be oriented in NCI values. Hence, there is a special and urgent need for extensive and intensive training experiences for the first 100 families that will reside on Featherfield Farms. To meet this need, it was proposed that an additional TRAINING GRANT be requested."

The report was typical of Baker's long-standing approach—even to the emphasis she placed on training. She prefaced her seven-page report with a gentle but pointed letter to Sherrod: "Since you did not get by to pick this up yesterday as you had indicated, I thought it best be sent so that you might have it before your meeting," adding, "Since you and the education chairman, Mrs. Feever, will no doubt both be at the meeting, if there are inaccuracies you can correct them. There are a few other items and/or comments that I will send later which may be of use in the follow-up discussions."[19]

Baker retained her connections to SNCC, of which her work with Sherrod was one, though he had resigned from the SNCC staff and was maintaining SNCC work on his own. She was an adviser at least through 1968 to the New York office. She continued to travel and speak across the country, and remained devoted to FELD, which she felt was so necessary to the sustenance of those young people who had given so much to the 1960s movement. FELD also provided legal assistance to Lowndes County voters, who sought injunctive relief against eviction for having registered to vote, and to Julian Bond, who was denied his seat in the Georgia state legislature after he expressed opposition to the Vietnam war.

FELD also supported the defense of H. Rap Brown, who, according to his attorney William M. Kunstler, appeared "in some fourteen courts in fourteen different parts of the United States" on charges ranging from being a fugitive to the most serious of violating federal gun laws. (He was charged with carrying a rifle on a plane to New Orleans.)[20]

In keeping with Baker's long-held belief in the importance of educating movement workers, FELD conducted in-service training workshops for organizers in Tuskegee, Atlanta, and elsewhere. Though FELD had a board of directors, of which I was a member, the ongoing work was carried out primarily by Baker and attorney Michael Standard, with Baker making the essential decisions about where aid should go. She knew the young people who were requesting aid, she knew the conditions under which they worked, and she knew who needed to get off the battlefield and go back to college. She was also in a position to evaluate the needs of applicants since she was in constant touch with the activists in the field. The board's major input was in fund-raising, though in this area, too, Baker had skills that were often called upon.

The Southern Conference Educational Fund celebrated its thirtieth anniversary in the spring of 1968 with a dinner at New York's Hotel Roosevelt honoring Ella Baker. Robert Zellner, SNCC's first white field secretary, chaired; speakers included Howard Zinn, Rosa Parks, and Stokely Carmichael.

Baker, now in her mid-sixties, continued her organizing activities. She had never abandoned her early affiliation with the NAACP, or with the church. Well into the late 1970s Baker was in demand as a speaker at Women's Day events at churches throughout the country. She continued her association with the organizations that had been concerned with school integration, and more importantly, she stretched her horizons to encompass changing views in the society. Though there had been hints that this was about to emerge, it was not until the early 1970s that Baker's radical impulses came to the fore. In 1973 she joined the Mass Organizing Party, whose prime mover was Arthur Kinoy, the well-known radical lawyer. Kinoy had

Ella Baker speaking at a function of the Southern Conference Educational Fund. (Courtesy of the *Southern Patriot.*)

been one of the main supporters of the MFDP challenge and was,
therefore, a colleague.

During this period Baker became active in the Jeannette Rankin
Brigade, named for the first woman member of Congress, who had
cast the sole vote against U.S. entry into World Wars I and II. The
group took the position that poverty and racism at home were linked
to the Vietnam war abroad. Baker, who attended almost all of the
brigade's planning meetings and was convenor of its executive committee, said that the basic issue was a commitment to social justice

for all. Though she was a prime mover in determining the brigade's policy and plans, she avoided the limelight and kept her eye on what she deemed important: program, goals, and the development of new leadership.

At one point brigade leaders urged Baker to speak before a black group. She demurred in characteristic fashion, saying that she did not want to persuade people who might be influenced solely by her demeanor, her voice, or her diction to rally behind a program that they fundamentally did not understand. Amy Schwerdlow, a brigade founder, said that Baker "gave cogent and forceful expression to the Brigade's concern about the primacy and urgency of the domestic crisis."

On January 15, 1968, more than five thousand women converged on the Capitol. Ultimately a delegation of fifteen was received by the Speaker of the House, John McCormack. They presented their petition calling for an end to the Vietnam war and "an end to violence both at home and abroad." The demonstrators were barred from the steps of the Capitol, so the brigade sued the chief of police, enjoining him from prohibiting gatherings on the Capitol steps. Baker was a party to the suit, and congressional representatives Bella Abzug and Ron Dellums were "intervenor plaintiffs." They won in the Supreme Court in 1971.

Subsequently, the brigade, meant as a temporary organization for the one-day confrontation with Congress, evolved into the Women's Emergency Coalition, an amalgam of many organizations. Baker was active in the WEC and was charged with the task of organizing caravans of women who would travel to selected communities to rouse local women to action. This activity never came off and the WEC quietly died. Cora Weiss, one of the brigade's leaders, said that she keeps two photos of women in her office: Ella Baker and Emma Goldman, both of whom were, for her, "women who made a difference."[21]

Always dividing her attention between local concerns and the problems of the rest of the world, in the early 1970s Baker became active in prison reform and in the campaign to free the Harlem Five.

She participated in the Coalition of Concerned Black Americans and the Independent Black Voters' League, as well as in the women's movement for peace, the Puerto Rican Solidarity Movement, and the Boston Women's Collective. These concerns were examples of her drive—her impulse to help everybody.

The Coalition of Concerned Black Americans, which originally formed around the Angela Davis case, focused on the treatment of African Americans by the criminal justice system. It was financed primarily by the Presbyterian Church. Jewell Gresham, an author and teacher, was executive director and Baker was associate director. According to Gresham, the most significant work of the coalition was the report it compiled on the New York judicial system and its work for prison reform. The coalition also sponsored several public meetings, among which was a Washington pilgrimage, held at the home of Frederick Douglass. There Baker delivered the Black Proclamation, which declared: "The one goal is, after all, liberation from physical, psychological and spiritual destruction. Liberation from the decadent values of 'the American way of life.'" It called for Angela Davis's release on bail, the formation of coalitions to work for the release of all political prisoners, and justice for all black, minority, and poor prisoners, and vowed "to help black men resist being drafted for the war against yellow men."[22]

Gresham spoke of Baker as providing the "democratic edge." By this she meant that Baker urged that every voice be heard. "She was a steadying influence, keeping all of the carpers at bay, providing space for everyone to make their opinions known, but keeping the disrupters out." She had a nurturing tendency. "I am here," she told Gresham, "and so are you. And we matter. We can change things."[23]

Baker was also the catalyst for an organization called We Care, which was founded by five young people from Harlem to provide cultural and recreational activities for Harlem youngsters. The We Care group took youngsters to the Metropolitan Museum of Art to see the exhibit "Harlem on My Mind" and to the United Nations headquarters. Baker used her contacts in Washington to provide housing for fifty and put the group in touch with two groups working with District of Columbia youngsters. Though her confidence in young people was unabated, she carefully spelled out the need to confer with their Washington host as to exact arrival time, numbers, and places they expected to visit. We Care eventually started a film project, with Baker as one of its stars.

Baker carried on her work with young people and with women. She was an active board member of Operation Freedom, the National Sharecroppers Fund, and the Aubrey Williams Foundation, and she lent her name and sometimes her presence to other organizations that she supported ideologically.

SNCC, her beloved organization, was withering away. It had alienated most of its white supporters, it had focused its attention on international issues, and it had, for the most part, abandoned its Southern organizing activities. The disintegration had resulted in part from its short-lived affiliation with the Black Panther Party. It soon became clear that SNCC's aims and those of the BPP were not synonymous. When Jim Forman was threatened at gunpoint by Panther members, SNCC's leaders had second thoughts about the alliance.

SNCC's demise was mainly caused by battle fatigue, however. The young students who had given up sometimes up to five years of their lives, surviving under near-battle conditions, were simply tired out. Certainly the U.S. government's COINTELPRO operation, which was designed to defuse what it deemed to be revolutionary organizations, played some role. Yet, probably the most important factor in SNCC's demise was the students' knowledge that they were not building an organization to exist for its own sake. Baker had inculcated the idea that the real goal was to build new organizations on a local basis, not to create some overarching structure imposed from outside. It left behind some local organizations, such as the Lowndes County Freedom Party. It also left behind a recognition that local people had the ability to exercise power. To this day some SNCC workers remain in place: Sherrod in Southwest Georgia; Robert Mants in Lowndes County, Alabama; David Dennis, Mike Thayer, Hollis Watkins, and Euvester Simpson in Jackson, Mississippi; and many others. But SNCC never enshrined itself. It never thought of itself as an institution. As staff member Courtlandt Cox put it: "The thing that really distinguished SNCC from all the other [civil rights] organizations was that there was not a sense that we were trying to perpetuate ourselves. We were there to do a job."[24]

In 1974, at a Madison Square Garden rally of the Puerto Rican Solidarity Committee, Baker delivered what many regard as her most radical speech, but what was in fact a reiteration of her basic precept: the importance of moving people to action. As she spoke she constantly waved away applause, for she was intent on making her point and had no time for audience appreciation. She electrified the crowd of twenty thousand with an incident from her early childhood. When a young boy on the street called her a nigger, "I hit him," she said. "But then I learned that hitting back at one person was not enough." She went on to her central point: It was crucial to get people to understand that "they as well as you and I cannot be free in America or anywhere else where there is capitalism and imperialism, until we can get people to recognize that they themselves have to make the struggle and the fight for freedom every day in the year, every year until they win it." To her the most important part of her message was the need to expand the fight; get more people involved in solving their own problems and in the fight for freedom, justice, and human dignity.

In 1978 people gathered to celebrate Baker's seventy-fifth birthday at the Carnegie Endowment for Peace in New York City. On this occasion movement activist Randolph Blackwell wrote that he had learned the "real nature of commitment" at 16 years of age, when he had heard her speak at the Big Zion Methodist Church in Greensboro, North Carolina. That evening he realized "what I wanted to do with my life," and the very next day he organized the first NAACP youth council in North Carolina. "I like to believe," he wrote, "that I have not veered from the real commitment made to Ella that evening."[25] Bob Moses spoke of her as the "Fundi," the person in the community who masters a craft with the help of the community and teaches it to other people. He said that this is

Virginia Durr and Ella Baker in serious discussion during the filming of *Fundi: The Story of Ella Baker* in Wetumpka, Alabama, in 1979.

the way it proceeds "without becoming institutionalized." Vincent Harding, who had worked with Baker in the 1960s, and who, among all of Baker's followers, seemed to have the greatest understanding of what she represented, spoke of the changes that had occurred over the past two or more decades, pointing out that if you think that nothing has changed, "then you don't know what was before." He lauded Baker's recognition that people need to adapt to the changed situation in order to move forward. "You move into a struggle with certain kinds of visions and ideas and hopes, you transform the situation and then you can no longer go on with the same kinds of visions and hopes and ideas because you have created a new situation for yourself," Harding said. "And if anybody has taught us how to be flexible and change and recreate our ideas and our thoughts as time has gone on, Ella Baker has done that."

Septima Clark, a coworker and a friend, spoke of the importance of Baker's relationship to the young people of SNCC, who were able to relate better to her than to the staid ministers of SCLC. She said that she was glad that Baker had gotten the young men in SNCC "to see what they needed to do," since the men in SCLC "couldn't see the contribution" that she could make.

Charles McDew, who had known Ella Baker since he was 19 years old, gave what was perhaps the most profound tribute. He told the gathering of her friends and colleagues that she had made him "a caring and compassionate man."[26]

Epilogue

THE CIVIL RIGHTS STRUGGLE has become "a struggle for a different kind of society which will reject, if necessary, the present system," Baker told a conference held at the Institute of the Black World in 1969. Baker rarely wrote her speeches out in full, though she sometimes made notes, but we do have a record of this speech because it was one of the few that was taped. Her talk was wide-ranging, covering her core ideas on the issues that she had dealt with throughout her life, and would continue to address.

She divided her remarks into two parts: the struggle to become a part of society and the struggle to remold that society. She outlined the efforts made in the quest to belong: the emphasis on educating a cultured group to become leaders, and then a long period of fighting through the courts for equal access to public accommodations. "There was an assumption that those who were trained were not trained to be *part* of the community, but to be *leaders* of the community. This carried with it another false assumption—that being a leader meant that you were separate and apart from the masses, and, to a large extent, people were to look up to you, and that your responsibility to the people was to *represent* them. This means that the people were never given a sense of their own values."

Baker went on: "The period that is most important to most of us now is the period when we began to question whether we really wanted 'in.' . . . Even though the sit-in movement started off primarily as a method of getting in, it led to the concept of questioning whether it was worth trying to get in. . . . There were those who saw from the beginning that it was part of the struggle for full dignity as a human being. So out of that came two things that, to me, were very significant. First, there was the concept of the 'trained' finding their identity with the masses. . . . The young people moved out into the community and finally were able to be accepted. . . . They began to discover indigenous leaders. . . . This was a period when we were trying to develop people who would speak for themselves."

Then she asked, What is American society? "Is it the kind of society . . . that permits people to grow and develop according to their capacity, that gives them a sense of value, not only for themselves, but a sense of value for others?"

She concluded with an anecdote. "About twenty-eight years ago I used to go around making speeches, and I would open up my talk by saying that there was a man who had a health problem and he was finally told by the doctor that they could save his sight or save his memory, but they couldn't save both. They asked him which did he want, and he said, 'Save my sight because I would rather see where I am going than remember where I have been.'" But Baker said that in order to see where we are going, "not only must we remember where we've been, but we must *understand* where we have been."[1]

During the 1970s Baker, now living in New York, devoted herself to a number of causes, but her main focus was on the young people of the 1960s movement who came to her for sustenance, advice, and just plain talk. Historians of the movement came to learn whatever they could. Julius Scott was interested in Frank Crosswaith and endeavored to plumb Baker's recollections of the Harlem labor leader. Eugene Walker wanted to know about her relationship with the ministers of SCLC. Others sought to determine how she felt about the women's movement or what her recollections were of the student movement of the 1960s. I was trying to piece together her life. I did not know why. I just felt that it was an important pursuit. And so it was. In a sense, she became my guru, always sitting at my shoulder, giving me a nudge.

I look at all of these thousands of papers, many of them fragments, and I sigh. How to piece together a life that had so many

Ella Baker, Carol Bellamy, and Betty Friedan at International Woman's Day celebrations in New York, 1975. (© Charmian Reading. With permission.)

facets. If one were a novelist, one could fabricate and make it sing, but for an historian, a reporter, a journalist, the life is not so easily reconstructed. During the last ten years of her productive life, Miss Baker basically held court. She made herself available to those who needed her counsel, but she was also there for the organizations that sought her out: the Third World Women's Alliance, the Mass Organizing Party, the Puerto Rican Solidarity Committee.

She was still creating a whirlwind of activity, moving people, stirring them to greater efforts, trying to build a mass movement for change. Her interest in the Mass Organizing Party stemmed from her always present desire to form a grassroots organization that would nurture local leadership and become a base for genuine local participation in politics. But it was deeper than that. She felt that such a party might bring about the transformation of society. In an

Ella Baker at the microphone at International
Woman's Day celebrations in New York, March 8,
1975. (© Charmian Reading. With permission.)

interview in 1977 with two Mississippi SNCC workers, Wesley
Brown and Arverna Adams, Baker explained that the Mass Organizing Party sought to bridge the gap among all of the groups that
were trying to bring about "a society constituted toward meeting
the needs of people." "We won't be free until we've done something
to change the society," she declared. "The only society that can serve
the needs of large masses of poor people is a socialist society."[2]

This belief moved her to become affiliated with the Puerto Rican
Solidarity Committee as a board member and an activist and to join
the Mass Organizing Party as a founding member. She had not often
declared herself as a socialist, but she said in a speech in 1969, "We
are going to have to learn to think in *radical* terms. I use the term
radical in its original meaning: *getting down to and understanding*

Laughing it up at a seventy-seventh birthday party in the home of Lenora Taitt Magubane with Harry Belafonte. (© Leroy Henderson. With permission.)

the root cause. It means facing a system that does not lend itself to your needs and devising means by which you change that system. That is easier said than done."[3]

Baker once said to the author, "[Any] critical thinking that I developed had to be relevant to the experiences of the Depression. I sought answers and the most articulate groups with such answers were the radical political parties. . . . I suppose because I lived in the heart of Harlem, I was much more responsive to the interpretations that went all the way down to the lowest levels of society.

Seventy-seventh birthday gathering. From left: Julie Belafonte, Lenora Taitt Magubane, Ella Baker, Ena Burton, Theresa Ann Walker, Reverend Wyatt Tee Walker, Harry Belafonte. (© Leroy Henderson. With permission.)

[There was] the need for radical change to provide for the masses of people."

In the late 1970s Baker's health began to fail. It was painful to watch her decline, this person who had been named Grand Lady by her grandfather so many years ago. Most of us who knew her well did not easily accept that she was gradually losing hold of her lifeline. But to the end she hung on to her precepts and never wavered in her belief in grassroots activism.

Between 1979 and 1981, when we were making the film, Baker was showing signs of senility. There were times when she would ask the same question several times, and then, as Alzheimer victims often do, she would try to mask her forgetfulness.

Ella Baker and the author at the Washington, D.C., première of *Fundi: The Story of Ella Baker,* in a moment of remembrance of the events of the 1960s. (© Harlee Little, Jr. With permission.)

There were many problems in making the film *Fundi.* Her niece Jackie was unfailingly helpful. Our greatest difficulty was keeping her on the subject. We were always concerned about tiring her and often shortened our shoots.

Miss Ella Baker was living in the past. She could remember much about her grandfather and her mother, and she kept slipping back in time. I didn't realize quite what was happening or how bad it was until I arranged to take her back to Littleton, where she had grown up. In that setting there were tremendous emotional pulls. Jackie had given me Miss Baker's medicines, with instructions about how to administer them. I also helped her to dress each day and acted as general caretaker. My film crew had little idea of Miss Baker's difficulties. Some of them had not known her, some of them thought that she was the same vibrant person they had related to in earlier years, and at least one thought that gentle encouragement and submission to her wishes would be the ideal way of dealing with a tense and exhausting situation. The strains of organizing a film shoot, coupled with my caretaker responsibilities, became a burden that I eventually found to be almost unbearable.

At this time she was still in great demand as a speaker, but getting her to events was a difficult chore. Jackie and I and other friends, like Jewell Gresham, would get her to the plane and to the hotel, to the meeting and on her feet. She was by now a slight figure, not the robust, stocky fighter of former years, but she was still willful and thus difficult. Jackie had put me in charge of the keys to Baker's house in Littleton. Sometimes Miss Baker would get hold of an idea and not let go. This happened one day over possession of the keys, and there ensued a heartwrenching scene during which I refused to give up the keys and she adamantly insisted on having them. It finally ended when I allowed her to unlock the door, but then retook possession of the keys.

I was emotionally wrung out, and exhausted as well, as I had to be vigilant all night to make sure that Miss Baker did not venture downstairs on some dimly remembered task. Early in the morning, often at daybreak, I would awaken to sounds from the kitchen. Scurrying downstairs I would find her wandering around and all the burners on the kitchen stove lit.

Monitoring was stressful. On one occasion, an SNCC worker, Colia Lafayette, came to me to say that she must take Miss Baker to a meal as she had had no lunch. I had filled her lunch plate at Tougaloo College and had seen to it that she had eaten. Miss Baker no longer knew whether she had eaten, or whether she was even hungry.

Yet, in the midst of this I filmed an encounter with Colia's young daughter during which Baker displayed her magic touch with young people. She had an affinity to the young. Frances Johnson reported that in the early 1950s her young son, aged 4, had gone down in the elevator of their apartment house to search for Ella Baker because he liked to talk with her. My own niece, Julee, seemed to be an honored guest at Miss Baker's apartment, as Ella kept supplying her with tuna fish sandwiches and blending a special fruit drink long after I thought she should have been cut off. Then, of course, there was the best scene in the film—her discussion with the young student, my son, who laid out his school problems to her automatically, because she asked. Aunt Ella had a special relationship with her grandniece Carolyn, lavishing grandmotherly love and teachings on her. She would be gratified to know that Carolyn, now a neurologist, had entered the medical profession to which she herself had aspired.

Often filming was difficult as her respiratory troubles might erupt and cause her to wheeze. On one occasion we tried to get her to read from her NAACP resignation letter, but she couldn't manage it. Another sad moment was when she spoke of the murder of Emmett Till, a lynching that moved her deeply. She began to cry, the only time that I ever saw her do that. It was a wonderful scene for the film—except that, recalling other lynchings she had known, she remembered Till hanging from a tree. We couldn't use the scene; she had gotten it wrong. Till's body had been found in a Mississippi river.

It was a joy, however, to see how she rallied when she stood before an audience. At a Jackson, Mississippi, gathering in 1980, William Strickland introduced her as "a national monument, an awesome danger, a profound threat, a shining black beacon," and she rose to speak of the need to continue the struggle. And she was indeed shining—not as brightly as in earlier days, but still shining.

In 1980, she gave her last major address at the Smithsonian's commemoration of the twentieth anniversary of the sit-in movement, surrounded by her many children. Introducing her, Bernice

Ella Baker getting her grandniece, Carolyn Brockington, ready for a stroll. (Courtesy of Jacqueline Brockington.)

Johnson Reagon recalled Baker's reaction to her decision to leave college. She said that Miss Baker had questioned her for about twenty minutes about her plans and then said: "Well, you thought it through." Reagon said, "I felt like I'd passed. . . . If Miss Baker questioned you and then said it looks like you've thought it through you really felt like somebody just slipped a foundation under you."[4]

Baker spoke of one of the guiding principles of her life: "Trying to relate to people and share whatever capacity I have to help them to use [their own] capacities." She said that she had tried "to facilitate those who are involved with struggle and who are struggling not just for themselves."[5] Her credo remained the importance of getting people to understand that "Nobody is going to do for you that which you have the power to do for yourself."

In a speech to a 1964 mass meeting in Hattiesburg, Mississippi, Ella Baker said, "I was never working for an organization; I have always tried to work for a cause. And the cause to me is bigger than

Ella Baker after receiving a doctorate of letters at City College, New York, on May 28, 1985, with grandniece Carolyn Brockington and niece Jacqueline Brockington. (Courtesy of Jacqueline Brockington.)

any organization, bigger than any group of people. It is the cause of humanity. . . . The drive of the *human* spirit for freedom. . . . All of us stand guilty at this moment for having waited so long to lend ourselves to a fight for the freedom, not of Negroes, not of the Negroes of Mississippi, but for the freedom of the American spirit, for the freedom of the human spirit."[6]

In May 1985 she was awarded a doctorate of letters from the City College of New York in recognition of her contributions to the humanities.

Ella Baker died in 1986 on her birthday, December 13, at the age of 83. She had been determined to hang on until she was at least 86, the age at which her mother succumbed.

ON A BLUSTERY, COLD DECEMBER DAY hundreds of friends and associates of Ella Baker gathered at the Abyssinian Baptist Church in
Harlem to invoke her spirit. Anne Braden struck the truest note
when she spoke of Ella Baker's ability to sift through the superficial
to find the real human being. "She didn't deal in labels," Braden
said. "She wanted to know what people thought, but mostly she
wanted them to think." Then she quoted Baker, who said that the
problem in the South was not conservative thought or radical thought,
but *lack* of thought. I spoke of her faith in humanity and said that
she did not distinguish between individuals on the basis of race.
"We were all, no matter our color, her children."[7] Bob Moses then
stood and asked that all of Ella's children come forward. Hundreds
came forward; many were youngsters, but some were her contem-
poraries. We all stood in a semicircle in testimony to the work she
had done to bind us together.

She would have been pleased by the gathering because it brought
together so many disparate elements of the movement that she had
helped forge: integrationists, ministers, socialists, Black Muslims,
black revolutionaries, and ordinary folk.

At the graveside members of SNCC spontaneously began to sing
her favorite hymn: "Guide my feet while I run this race, Guide my
feet while I run this race, Guide my feet while I run this race, So I
won't have to run this race in vain."

"The Black Woman in the
Civil Rights Struggle"

*Speech by Ella Baker, given at the Institute for the Black World,
Atlanta, Georgia, 1969*

I THINK THAT PERHAPS because I have existed much longer than
you and have to some extent maintained some degree of commitment to a goal of full freedom that this is the reason Vincent Harding invited me to come down as an exhibit of what might possibly
be the goal of some of us to strive toward—that is, to continue to
identify with the struggle as long as the struggle is with us.

I was a little bit amazed as to why the selection of a discussion
on the role of black women in the world. I just said to Bernice
Reagon that I have never been one to feel great needs in the direction of setting myself apart as a woman. I've always thought first
and foremost of people as individuals . . . [but] wherever there has
been struggle, black women have been identified with that struggle.
During slavery there was a tremendous amount of resistance in various forms. Some were rather subtle and some were rather shocking.
One of the subtle forms was that of feigning illness . . . One of the
other forms of resistance which was perhaps much more tragic and
has not been told to a great extent is the large number of black
women who gave birth to children and killed them rather than have
them grow up as slaves. There is a story of a woman in Kentucky
who had borne thirteen children and strangled each of them with

her own hands rather than have them grow up as slaves. Now this calls for a certain kind of deep *commitment* and *resentment*. *Commitment* to freedom and deep *resentment* against slavery.

I would like to divide my remaining comments into two parts. First, the aspect that deals with the struggle to get into the society, the struggle to be a part of the American scene. Second, the struggle for a different kind of society. The latter is the more radical struggle. In the previous period, the period of struggling to be accepted, there were certain goals, concepts, and values such as the drive for the "Talented Tenth." That, of course, was the concept that proposed that through the process of education black people would be accepted in the American culture and they would be accorded their rights in proportion to the degree to which they qualified as being persons of learning and culture . . .

[There was] an assumption that those who were trained were not trained to be *part* of the community, but to be *leaders* of the community. This carried with it another false assumption that being a leader meant that you were separate and apart from the masses, and to a large extent people were to look up to you, and that your responsibility to the people was to *represent* them. This means that the people were never given a sense of their own values . . . Later, in the 1960s, a different concept emerged: the concept of the right of the people to participate in the decisions that affected their lives. So part of the struggle was the struggle toward intellectualism [which] so often separated us so far from the masses of people that the gulf was almost too great to be bridged.

The struggle for being a part of the society also led to another major phase of the civil rights struggle. That was the period in which legalism or the approach to battling down the barriers of racial segregation through the courts which was spearheaded by the National Association for the Advancement of Colored People . . . We moved from the question of equal educational opportunity in terms of teachers' salaries into another phase: equality in travel accommodations . . . One of the young persons who was part of the first efforts to test [segregated travel] was Pauli Murray. Pauli Murray and I were part of a committee that was organized to try to go into the South to test Jim Crow in bus travel. But the decision was made that only the men could go . . . I had just finished a tour of duty with the NAACP and had ridden a lot of Jim Crow buses and wanted very much to go, but I guess it was decided that I was too frail to make such a journey.

I think the period that is most important to most of us now is the period when we began to question whether we really wanted in. Even though the sit-in movement started off primarily as a method of getting in, it led to the concept of questioning whether it was worth trying to get in. The first effort was to be able to sit down at the lunch counters. When you look back and think of all the tragedy and suffering that the first sit-iners went through you begin to wonder, Why pay a price like that for the privilege of eating at lunch counters? There were those who saw from the beginning that the struggle was much bigger than getting a hamburger at a lunch counter. There were those who saw from the beginning that it was part of the struggle for full dignity as a human being. So out of that came two things that to me are very significant. First, there was the concept of the trained finding their identity with the masses. Another thing that came out of it at a later period was that of leadership training. As the young people moved out into the community and finally were able to be accepted, they began to discover indigenous leaders . . .

Around 1965 there began to develop a great deal of questioning about what is the role of women in the struggle. Out of it came a concept that black women had to bolster the ego of the male. This implied that the black male had been treated in such a manner as to have been emasculated both by the white society and black women because the female was the head of the household. We began to deal with the question of the need of black women to play the subordinate role. I personally have never thought of this as being valid because it raises the question as to whether the black man is going to try to be a man on the basis of his capacity to deal with issues and situations rather than be a man because he has some people around him who claim him to be a man by taking subordinate roles.

I don't think you could go through the Freedom Movement without finding that the backbone of the support of the Movement were women. When demonstrations took place and when the community acted, usually it was some woman who came to the fore . . .

I think at this stage the big question is, What is the American society? Is it the kind of society that either black women or black men or anyone who is seeing a dignified existence as a human being that permits people to grow and develop according to their capacity, that gives them a sense of value, not only for themselves, but a sense of value for other human beings. Is this the kind of society that is going to permit that? I think there is a great question as to whether it can become that kind of society . . .

In order for us as poor and oppressed people to become a part of a society that is meaningful, the system under which we now exist has to be radically changed. This means that we are going to have to learn to think in *radical* terms. I use the term radical in its original meaning—getting down to and understanding the root cause. It means facing a system that does not lend itself to your needs and devising means by which you change that system. That is easier said than done. But one of the things that has to be faced is, in the process of wanting to change that system, how much have we got to do to find out who we are, where we have come from and where we are going. About twenty-eight years ago I used to go around making speeches, and I would open up my talk by saying that there was a man who had a health problem and he was finally told by the doctor that they could save his sight or save his memory, but they couldn't save both. They asked him which did he want and he said, "Save my sight because I would rather see where I am going than remember where I have been." I am saying as you must say, too, that in order to see where we are going, we not only must remember where we've been, but *we must understand where we have been*. This calls for a great deal of analytical thinking and evaluation of methods that have been used. We have to begin to think in terms of where do we really want to go and how can we get there.

Finally, I think it is also to be said that it is not a job that is going to be done by all the people simultaneously. Some will have to be in cadres, the advanced cadres, and some will have to come later. But one of the guiding principles has to be that we cannot lead a struggle that involves masses of people without getting the people to understand what their potentials are, what their strengths are.

Awards Granted to Ella Baker
for Her Work in Human Rights

June 1975, L.C.B.F.S.A.: "Ella Baker, founder of SNCC, in recognition of your courage and persistence in the struggle for BLACK LIBERATION."

April 1976, African Heritage Studies Association: "For your outstanding contribution to the liberation and development of peoples of African descent in the world."

1976, Lester Blackwell Granger Urban League Award to Ella J. Baker. The Plontford Point Marine Association.

August 4, 1977, First Annual Fannie Lou Hamer Award, National Clients Council, Inc.

March 4, 1978, Woman of the Year Award, National Association of University Women, New York Branch: "For contributions to the civil rights movement."

January 1979, Board of Directors and Staff of Agricultural Teams Inc.: "Ms. Ella Baker, in recognition and appreciation of your dedication and humanitarian service."

November 3, 1981, House of the Lord Annual Women's Committee, Reverend Herbert Daughtry, pastor, "In appreciation for concern, courage and commitment Given in the Struggle for the Liberation of our people."

January 10, 1982, Emmanuel Baptist Church: "In recognition of exemplary service to the community; may God's grace ever embrace you."

January 22, 1982, Bill of Rights Award, American Civil Liberties Union of Georgia: "With appreciation for dedicated service to the cause of civil liberties."

April 2, 1982, Martin Luther King Jr. Humanitarian Award, Black Christian Caucus, Riverside Church of New York: "In recognition of over 50 years of continuous service and leadership in the struggle for human and civil rights, keeping alive the principles for which Dr. King lived and died."

June 9, 1984, Trans-Africa Freedom Award, Washington, D.C.

September 24, 1994, Ella Baker inducted into National Women's Hall of Fame, Seneca Falls, N.Y.

Notes

Ella Baker papers on deposit at Schomburg Center for the Study of Black Culture, the New York Public Library. Joanne Grant interviews and papers in author's possession.

Chapter 1
Roots of Rebellion

1. Deed for this land was not recorded until after seller's death. Recorded in 1888. Warren County register of deeds, Book 53, pp. 130, 323, and 540, Department of Archives and History; Raleigh, N.C.

2. Ibid., p. 625.

3. Ibid., Book 54, p. 848 and Book 55, pp. 682–684.

4. Sue Thrasher and Casey Hayden, Interview with Ella Baker, New York, April 19, 1977, p. 25.

5. Ibid., p. 26.

6. Joanne Grant, Interview with Ella Baker, New York, 1966–1968.

7. Rosemarie Harding, Interview with Ella Baker, New York, 1976.

8. Grant, Interview with Ella Baker, op. cit.

9. Harding, op. cit., p. 21.

10. Ellen Cantarow and Susan Gushee O'Malley, *Moving the Mountain.* Old Westbury, N.Y.: The Feminist Press, 1980, p. 59.

11. Joanne Grant, Interview with Helen Gilchrist, Littleton, N.C., June 28, 1992.

12. Grant, Interview with Ella Baker, op. cit.

13. Ibid.

14. Women's Union State Convention program, Ayden, N.C., 1924, Ella Baker papers.

15. Grant, Interview with Ella Baker, op. cit.

16. Ibid.

17. Thrasher and Hayden, op. cit., p. 21.

18. Grant, Interview with Ella Baker, op. cit.

19. Ibid.

20. Ibid.

Chapter 2
Reveling in New Ideas

1. Joanne Grant, Interview with Ella Baker, New York, 1966–1968.

2. Sue Thrasher and Casey Hayden, Interview with Ella Baker, New York, April 19, 1977, p. 35.

3. Ibid., p. 34.

4. Advertisement, undated, Ella Baker papers.

5. James Weldon Johnson, *Black Manhattan*. New York: Arno Press/ *New York Times,* 1930, p. 161.

6. Ibid., p. 162.

7. Joanne Grant, Interview with Robert Moses, New London, Conn., November 5, 1995.

8. James Weldon Johnson, op. cit., p. 162.

9. Joanne Grant, Interview with Lee Simpson, New York, April 12, 1997.

10. Claude McKay, *Home to Harlem*. New York: Cardinal, 1928, p. 25.

11. Judkins News Service, undated. Father Divine was apparently known for creating words; in an interview with John Britton, Baker commented, "I'm coining phrases like Father Divine," Ella Baker papers.

12. Letter to P. B. Young Jr., Managing Editor of the *Norfolk Journal and Guide,* May 12, 1935, Ella Baker papers.

13. Langston Hughes, *The Big Sea*. New York: Knopf, 1940, p. 247.

14. Mark Naison, *Communists in Harlem during the Depression*. Urbana: University of Illinois Press, 1983, pp. 116 and 124, note 3: "The estimates on Harlem unemployment come from *New York Amsterdam News,* Nov. 1, 1933, and *New York Post,* Mar. 21, 1935."

15. Grant, Interview with Ella Baker, op. cit.

16. John Britton, Interview with Ella Baker, Washington, D.C., June 19, 1968, p. 4, Civil Rights Documentation Project, Moorland-Spingarn Research Center, Howard University.

17. George Schuyler, leaflet, November 1930, p. 1, Ella Baker papers.

18. Ibid.

19. George Schuyler, oral history, Columbia University, New York.

20. Letter to Ella Baker from Josephine Schuyler, 1941, Ella Baker papers.

21. Resolution, Young Negroes' Cooperative League conference, 1931, Ella Baker papers.

22. "Straight Talk," undated, p. 2, Ella Baker papers.

23. George Schuyler, "The Young Negro Co-operative League," *The Crisis,* January 1932, p. 45, Ella Baker papers.

24. Penny-A-Day Synopsis, 1931, Ella Baker papers.

25. Letter from the National Office, Young Negroes' Cooperative League, undated, Ella Baker papers.

26. Letter to I. E. Woodcock from Ella Baker, 1941, Ella Baker papers.

27. Letter to Board of Directors, Harlem's Own Cooperative, incomplete, undated, Ella Baker papers.

28. Flyer, "New Shopping Tips," Harlem's Own Cooperative, October 1932, Ella Baker papers.

29. Flyer, The Problem's Cooperative Association, September 10, 1933, Ella Baker papers.

30. Letter to Youth Committee of One Hundred Members from Ella Baker, January 8, 1936, Ella Baker papers.

31. Letter to Ernestine Rose from Ella Baker, December 22, 1933, Ella Baker papers.

32. Prospectus, "Guide to Consumer Cooperation," Ella Baker, National Archives, Box 18, folders 36–39.

33. Ella Baker and Marvel Cooke, "The Bronx Slave Market," *The Crisis,* November 1935, p. 330.

34. Grant, Interview with Ella Baker, op. cit.

35. Cheryl Lynn Greenberg, "Or Does It Explode?" *Black Harlem in the Great Depression.* New York: Oxford, 1991, pp. 216–217.

36. Naison, op. cit., pp. xvii–xviii.

37. Ibid.

38. Letter from Ernestine Rose to NAACP, June 11, 1940, Ella Baker papers.

39. Letter from J. H. Robinson to Ella Baker, September 25, 1940, Ella Baker papers.

Chapter 3
Putting People in Motion:
The NAACP Years

1. Letter to Walter White from Herbert Marshall, received March 24, 1924, Library of Congress, NAACP papers, Group II, Box A572.

2. NAACP Board Report #6, December 1941, Ella Baker papers.

3. Ibid.

4. Ella Baker, Report of Field Work, July 8, 1942, Schomburg Library, NAACP papers, Group II, Box A.

5. Ella Baker, "Notes on Houston Conference," July 15, 1941, p. 1, Ella Baker papers.

6. Ibid., p. 2.

7. Letter to Lucille Black from Ella Baker, May 4, 1942, Library of Congress, NAACP papers, Group II, Box A572.

8. Memorandum to Executive Staff from Ella Baker, January 14, 1942, Library of Congress, NAACP papers, Group II, Box A572.

9. Memorandum from Ella Baker, September 28, 1944, Library of Congress, NAACP papers, Group II, Box A572.

10. Letter to Roy Wilkins from Ella Baker, March 11, 1942, Library of Congress, NAACP papers, Group II, Box A572.

11. Speech by Ella Baker, NAACP Annual Conference, July 17, 1942, NAACP papers, Mark Fox, ed., Reel 11, frames 201–203, Schomburg Library.

12. Letter to Walter White from Leslie Perry, Washington, D.C. Bureau, May 4, 1943, Library of Congress, NAACP papers, Group II, Box C86.

13. See Louis Ruchames, *Race, Jobs, and Politics: The Story of FEPC.* New York: Columbia University Press, 1953.

14. "A Job for You to Do," September 29, 1943, memorandum from Ella Baker to branches, youth and college councils, September 29, 1943, Ella Baker papers.

15. OPA report, March 3, 1945, Ella Baker papers.

16. Letter to Walter White and NAACP Board of Directors from William Pickens, February 17, 1942, Schomburg Library.

17. Letter to William Pickens from Reverend John Haynes Holmes, February 18, 1942, Schomburg Library.

18. Letter to William Pickens from Thomas L. Griffith Jr., March 19, 1942, Schomburg Library.

19. Letter to William Pickens from Mary White Ovington, April 24, 1942, Ella Baker papers.

20. News report by the Associated Negro Press, Minutes of the NAACP Board, April 22, 1942, Schomburg Library.

21. Memorandum to the Board of Directors from the Committee on Administration, NAACP, June 8, 1942, Schomburg Library.

22. Joanne Grant, Interview with Ella Baker, 1966–1968.

23. Grant, Interview with Ella Baker, 1966–1968.

24. Letter to William Pickens from Walter White, June 15, 1942, Schomburg Library.

Chapter 4
The Travel Was Bum

1. Joanne Grant, Interview with Ella Baker, New York, 1966–1968.

2. Letter to Roy Wilkins from Ella Baker, April 3, 1942, Library of Congress, NAACP papers, Group II, Box A572.

3. Grant, Interview with Ella Baker, op. cit.

4. Memorandum on Difficulties in Securing Dining Car Service on the Sealand Airline Railroad, July 22, 1943, NAACP, Ella Baker papers.

5. NAACP Annual Report, 1942, Schomburg Library.

6. Ella Baker script, used on *NAACP Hour,* radio station WINX, Washington, D.C., Monday, February 8, 1943, Ella Baker papers.

7. Ella Baker script, prepared for delivery on radio station WEVD, April 17, 1945, Ella Baker papers.

8. Patricia Sullivan, *Days of Hope: Race and Democracy in the New Deal Era.* Chapel Hill: University of North Carolina Press, 1996, p. 141.

9. NAACP Minutes of the Board, December 10, 1945, Schomburg Library.

10. Ibid., September 11, 1944, Schomburg Library.

11. Ibid., April 9, 1945, Ella Baker papers.

12. Churchill speech at Westminster College, Fulton, Missouri, March 5, 1946. See D. F. Fleming, *The Cold War and Its Origins, 1917–1950,* vol. 1. Garden City, N.Y.: Doubleday, 1961, pp. 348–357.

13. Report of the Secretary, NAACP Minutes of the Board, April 1946, Ella Baker papers.

14. Letter to Ella Baker from Walter White, April 15, 1943, Ella Baker papers.

15. Letter to Walter White from Ella Baker, April 17, 1943, Ella Baker papers.

16. Letter to Walter White from Ella Baker, April 21, 1943, Ella Baker papers.

17. Letter to Ella Baker from Walter White, April 22, 1943, Ella Baker papers.

18. NAACP Board Minutes, April 12, 1943, Ella Baker papers.

19. Recommendation of the Committee on Branches, July 8, 1943, Ella Baker papers.

20. Ibid.

21. Ibid.

22. Letter to President Roosevelt from Attorney General Francis Biddle, June 15, 1943, in Earl Brown, *Why Race Riots? Lessons from Detroit.* New York, Public Affairs Committee, 1943, p. 23.

23. Earl Brown, *Why Race Riots? Lessons from Detroit.* New York, Public Affairs Committee, 1943, p. 23.

24. Walter White and Thurgood Marshall, "What Caused the Detroit Riots?" July, 1943, p. 31, Library of Congress, NAACP papers, Group II, Box A505.

25. *New York Times,* August 3, 1943.

26. Memorandum from Ella J. Baker to the Committee on Branches, July 6, 1943, Ella Baker papers.

27. Memorandum to Miss Baxter from Ella Baker, April 24, 1945, Library of Congress, NAACP papers, Group II, Box A579.

28. "A Digest of Regional Leadership Training and In-Service Training Program, Conducted by the Branch Department during 1944–46," Ella J. Baker, Director of Branches, July 10, 1946, Ella Baker papers.

29. Memorandum to Executive Staff, January 4, 1944, Library of Congress, NAACP papers, Group II, Box A572.

30. Annual Report, 1947 (with summaries of 1944–1946, no annual reports). Schomburg Library.

31. Letter and memo to Walter White from Ella Baker, March 1, 1941, Library of Congress, NAACP papers, Group II, Box A572.

32. Letter to Walter White from Ella Baker, December 3, 1942, Schomburg Library.

33. Letter to Ella Baker from Walter White in Norfolk, Va., October 27, 1941, Library of Congress, NAACP papers, Group II, Box A572.

34. Digest of the Report of the Department of Branches for the November Meeting of the Board of Directors, 1941, Ella Baker papers.

35. Letter to Lillie Jackson from Walter White, Library of Congress, NAACP papers, Group II, Box C76.

36. Letter to Ella Baker from Roy Wilkins, April 22, 1943, Ella Baker papers.

37. Letter to Ella Baker from LeRoy Carter, October 25, 1945, Ella Baker papers.

38. Letter to Ella Baker from Lillie Jackson, April 19, 1946, Library of Congress, Group II, Box C77.

39. Letter to Walter White from Stanley Issacs, December 27, 1943, Library of Congress, NAACP papers, Group II, Box A627.

40. Telegram, January 2, 1944, Citizens Commission for Adequate Medical Care, Library of Congress, Group II, Box C400.

41. Memorandum to Miss Baker, Mrs. Hurley from Walter White, May 17, 1944, Ella Baker papers.

42. Memorandum to Roy Wilkins from Walter White, May 18, 1944, Ella Baker papers.

43. Memorandum to Walter White from Ella Baker, May 22, 1944, Ella Baker papers.

44. Memorandum to Walter White from Ella Baker, April 14, 1944, Ella Baker papers.

45. Memorandum to Walter White from Ella Baker, June 28, 1944, Ella Baker papers.

46. Memorandum to the Secretary from Ella J. Baker, Julia E. Baxter, Edward R. Dudley, Noah W. Griffin, Ruby H. Hurley, Norma Jensen, Donald Jones, Daisy E. Lampkin, Irvena Meng, Thurgood Marshall, Leslie S. Perry, Coral Sadler, and Roy Wilkins, November 8, 1944, Ella Baker papers.

47. Rosemarie Harding, Interview with Ella Baker, New York, 1976.

48. Arnold Rampersad, *The Art and Imagination of W. E. B. Du Bois.* New York: Schocken Books, 1990, p. 246.

49. Walter White, Memorandum to the Committee on Administration, December 28, 1945, Ella Baker papers.

50. Letter to Walter White from W. E. B. Du Bois, January 3, 1946, Ella Baker papers.

51. Rampersad, op. cit., p. 250.

52. Letter to Walter White from Gloster Current, July 12, 1946, Library of Congress, NAACP papers, Group II, Box A579.

53. "Status of the Department of Branches," letter to Gloster Current from Ella Baker, July 20, 1946, Ella Baker papers.

54. Letter to Walter White from Ella Baker, May 14, 1946, Ella Baker papers.

55. Letter of resignation to Walter White from Ella Baker, May 14, 1946, Ella Baker papers.

56. Ibid., p. 3.

57. Joanne Grant, Interview with Herbert Hill, New York, 1997.

Chapter 5
The Northern Challenge

1. Letter to Branches from Ella Baker, July 16, 1946, Ella Baker papers.

2. Letter to Ella Baker from John LeFlore, June 19, 1946, Ella Baker papers.

3. Letter to Ella Baker from Daniel E. Byrd, June 1, 1946, Ella Baker papers.

4. Letter to Ella Baker from G. F. Porter, June 1, 1946, Ella Baker papers.

5. James Forman, *The Making of Black Revolutionaries*. Washington, D.C.: Open Hand Publishing, 1985, p. 404. Also minutes by Courtlandt Cox and Mendy Samstein, author's possession.

6. Joanne Grant, Interview with Ella Baker, New York, 1966–1968; also Herbert Hill Interview, May 15, 1996.

7. Letter to Edward Lewis from Ella Baker, January 19, 1947, Ella Baker papers.

8. Letter to Lester B. Granger, Executive Secretary, National Urban League, from Ella Baker, July 10, 1947, Ella Baker papers.

9. Joanne Grant, *Fundi: The Story of Ella Baker*. First Run Features, 153 Waverly Place, New York, N.Y., 10011.

10. *Atlanta Daily World,* January 2, 1947, Ella Baker papers.

11. Grant, Interview with Ella Baker, op. cit.

12. Letter to Mr. Green from Ella Baker, February 13, 1948, Ella Baker papers.

13. Letter to Ella Baker from Aurelio Sterling Jr., chairman, November 4, 1947, Ella Baker papers.

14. Memorandum to Russell P. Crawford from Ella Baker, 1952, Ella Baker papers.

15. Letter to Caroline F. Ware from Ella Baker, February 6, 1947, Ella Baker papers.

16. Letter to Ella Baker from Caroline F. Ware, February 9, 1947, Ella Baker papers.

17. Grant, Interview with Ella Baker, op. cit.

18. Joanne Grant, Interview with Percy Sutton (telephone), New York, February 21, 1996.

19. Grant, Interview with Ella Baker, op. cit.

20. Annual Report, New York City Board of Elections, 1953.

21. Memorandum to NAACP Branches from Roy Wilkins, Acting Secretary, March 22, 1950, courtesy of Herbert Hill.

22. Grant, Interview with Ella Baker, op. cit.

23. Joanne Grant, Interview with Anne Braden, January 26, 1997.

24. "That You Might Know," In Friendship report, March 6, 1957, Library of Congress, NAACP papers, Group III, Box A203.

25. Britton, op. cit., p. 13.

26. See Adam Fairclough, *To Redeem the Soul of America: The Southern Christian Leadership Conference and Martin Luther King, Jr.* Athens: University of Georgia Press, 1987, p. 20.

27. David Garrow, *Bearing the Cross: Martin Luther King, Jr., and the Southern Christian Leadership Conference.* New York: William Morrow, 1986, p. 644, note 2.

28. Britton, op. cit., p. 8.

29. Garrow, op. cit., p. 86.

30. Grant, Interview with Ella Baker, op. cit.

Chapter 6
Confronting "De Lawd"

1. "The Crusade for Citizenship," Memorandum from Martin Luther King Jr., February 4, 1958, Ella Baker papers.

2. "In Friendship," newsletter, Atlanta, Ga., undated, Ella Baker papers.

3. Letter to Ralph Abernathy from Ella Baker, March 26, 1958, Ella Baker papers.

4. Letter to Martin Luther King Jr. from Ella Baker, March 26, 1958, Ella Baker papers.

5. Joanne Grant, Interview with Ella Baker, New York, April 2, 1968.

6. Joanne Grant, Interview with Ella Baker, New York, 1966–1968.

7. In one of her letters, dated April 18, 1958, Baker indicated her characteristic tendency to work out personal problems before tackling work-related ones. She apologized for seeming "disconnected," but stated that he had caught her "in the midst of a bit of marital counselling," adding in handwriting "for office efficiency." Ella Baker papers.

8. Letter to Martin Luther King Jr. from Ella Baker, May 19, 1958, Martin Luther King Center, Box 32, folder 36.

9. Minutes of the Administrative Committee, July 3, 1958, pp. 6–7, Ella Baker papers.

10. Grant, Interview with Ella Baker, op. cit.

11. Eugene Walker, Interview with Ella Baker, Durham, N.C., September 4, 1974, p. 20.

12. Joanne Grant, Interview with Juanita Abernathy, Atlanta, Ga., September 26, 1995.

13. Memorandum to the Executive Board from Ella Baker, December 3, 1958, Ella Baker papers.

14. Letter to A. Philip Randolph from Ella Baker, November 10, 1958, Ella Baker papers.

15. Letter to Ella Baker from A. Philip Randolph, November 14, 1958, Ella Baker papers.

16. Joanne Grant, Interview with A. Philip Randolph, New York, 1970.

17. Ibid.

18. Letter to the Reverend John L. Tilley from Ella Baker, March 4, 1959, MLK Center, Box 32, folder 8.

19. Letter to Registered Voters from the Reverend R. C. Thomas, March 14, 1959, Ella Baker papers.

20. Memorandum to the Reverend R. C. Thomas from Ella Baker, March 21, 1959, Ella Baker papers.

21. Ibid.

22. *Pittsburgh Courier*, April 4, 1959, Ella Baker papers.

23. "What Price Freedom?" Press release from SCLC, June 11, 1959, Ella Baker papers.

24. Report to Board of SCLC by Ella Baker, May 15, 1959, Ella Baker papers.

25. Taylor Branch, *Parting the Waters: America in the King Years, 1954–1963*. New York: Simon & Schuster, 1988, pp. 257–258.

26. Emmett Till was murdered for allegedly whistling at a white woman storekeeper. The men who killed him, Roy Bryant and J. W. Milam, were acquitted.

27. Report to the Director of the Executive Board from Ella Baker, May 15, 1959, Ella Baker papers.

28. Letter to Reverend Thomas Kilgore from Ella Baker, May 22, 1959, MLK Center, Box 32, folder 39.

29. Letter to Ella Baker from Thomas Kilgore, May 27, 1959, Ella Baker papers.

30. Memorandum to Martin Luther King Jr. from Ella Baker, December 9, 1958, Ella Baker papers.

31. Ibid.

32. *Pittsburgh Courier,* August 8, 1959, Schomburg Library.

33. Program, "Workshop on Citizenship," Penn Conference Center, Frogmore, S.C., June 20–21, 1959, Ella Baker papers.

34. Memorandum to King, Abernathy from Ella Baker, July 2, 1959, MLK Center, Box 32, Subgroup B, series II.

35. Report to Executive Director of SCLC Board from Ella Baker, May 16–September 29, 1959, Ella Baker papers.

36. Ibid.

37. Memorandum to SCLC Committee on Administration from Ella Baker, "SCLC as a Crusade," October 23, 1959, MLK Center, Box 32, folder 39.

38. Ella Baker, notes on a telephone conversation with I. S. Leevy and Alice Spearman, December 1, 1959, Ella Baker papers.

39. Letter to Ella Baker from Alice N. Spearman, December 1, 1959, Ella Baker papers.

40. Forman, op. cit., p. 161.

41. Joanne Grant, *Fundi,* Interview with Bob Moses, Boston, 1980.

42. Joanne Grant, Interview with Jacqueline Brockington, New York, March 3, 1996.

43. Joanne Grant, *Fundi,* Interview with Janet Jamott, Boston, 1980.

44. Grant, Interview with Ella Baker, op. cit.

45. *Fundi,* op. cit.

46. Joanne Grant, Interview with Andrew Young, Atlanta, April 24, 1994.

47. Grant, Interview with Ella Baker, op. cit.

Chapter 7
Political Mama

1. Call to Southwide Youth Leadership Conference, SCLC, 1960, Ella Baker papers.

2. Flyer, "Where Do We Go From Here?" Martin Luther King and Ella Baker, undated, MLK Center, Box 25.

3. Joanne Grant, Interview with Effie Yeargan, Raleigh, N.C., June 1992.

4. Memorandum to Martin Luther King, Ralph Abernathy from Ella Baker, March 23, 1960, MLK Center, Box 39.

5. Letter to Anne Braden from Ella Baker, March 21, 1960, MLK Center, Box 32.

6. Joanne Grant, Interview with Ella Baker, New York, 1966–1968.

7. Ibid.

8. Ibid.

9. Joanne Grant, Interview with Charles McDew, April 25, 1993, Charlottesville, Va.

10. Student Nonviolent Coordinating Committee statement, MLK Center, Box 25, folder 9, AII.

11. Ella Baker, "Bigger Than a Hamburger," *Southern Patriot,* June 1960.

12. Grant, Interview with Ella Baker, op. cit.

13. John Britton, Interview with Ella Baker, Washington, D.C., June 19, 1968, pp. 65–66. Civil Rights Documentation Project, Moorland-Spingarn Research Center, Howard University.

14. Ibid.

15. Clayborne Carson, Interview with John Lewis, Atlanta, Ga., April 17, 1972, p. 24.

16. Joanne Grant, Interview with Judy Richardson, Washington, D.C., June 13, 1993.

17. Held at Butler Street YMCA, August 4–5, 1960, Ella Baker papers.

18. Letter to contacts from Ella Baker, July 31, 1960, Ella Baker papers. The Bible passage is from Paul's Epistle to the Romans, 13:11–14.

19. Joanne Grant, Interview with Bob Moses, New London, Conn., November 5, 1994.

20. Recommendations passed by the Student Nonviolent Coordinating Committee, October 14–16, 1960, p. 2, Ella Baker papers.

21. Nelson Mandela, *Long Walk to Freedom.* Boston: Little, Brown, 1994, p. 179.

22. *Fundi,* op. cit.

23. Grant, Interview with Charles McDew, op. cit.

24. Grant, Interview with Ella Baker, op. cit.

25. Letter to Anne Braden from Ella Baker, August 16, 1962, Ella Baker papers.

26. Grant, Interview with Ella Baker, op. cit.

27. Britton, op. cit., pp. 58–59.

28. SNCC staff minutes, Louisville, Ky., June 9–11, 1961.

29. Grant, Interview with Charles McDew, op. cit.

30. Ibid.

31. Report of Harry Belafonte Committee to SNCC, August 11, 1961, Ella Baker papers.

32. SNCC staff meeting, October 8–10, 1961, Ella Baker papers.

Chapter 8
On the Way to Freedom Land

1. Author notebook, February 1962.

2. Claude Sitton, "Sheriff Harasses Negroes at Voting Rally in Georgia," *New York Times,* July 27, 1962.

3. *Student Voice,* October 1962, author's possession.

4. Joanne Grant, Interview with Ella Baker, New York, 1966–1968.

5. Report on the Special Project in Human Relations, September 1, 1960–August 31, 1961, National Board YWCA, College and University Division, New York, p. 60.

6. Grant, Interview with Ella Baker, op. cit.

7. SNCC, "Violence Stalks Voter-Registration Workers in Mississippi," *Student Voice,* March 12, 1963, New York.

8. Grant, Interview with Ella Baker, op. cit.

9. Ibid.

10. Joanne Grant, "Negro Students Map Rights Fight in 3-Day Conference in Atlanta," *National Guardian,* May 2, 1963.

11. Minutes, Atlanta meeting, SNCC, March 24, 1962, MLK Center, Box 6, folder 5, series II.

12. Letter to Martin Luther King Jr. from Aubrey Williams, undated, Ella Baker papers.

13. Ella Baker, "Shuttlesworth Says" column, *Pittsburgh Courier,* September 22, 1959, Ella Baker papers.

14. Ella Baker, "Shuttlesworth Says" column, *Pittsburgh Courier,* August 29, 1959, Ella Baker papers.

Chapter 9
Grassroots Politics

1. Joanne Grant, "Mississippi Politics: A Day in the Life of Ella J. Baker," in Toni Cade, ed., *The Black Woman.* New York: New American Library, 1970, p. 56 ff.

2. See Constance Curry, *Silver Rights.* Chapel Hill, N.C.: Algonquin Books, 1995, p. vii.

3. SNCC Executive Committee Minutes, April 18–19, 1964, Joanne Grant papers.

4. SNCC staff minutes, June 11, 1964, p. 30, Joanne Grant papers.

5. The Platform and Principles of the Democratic Party of the State of Mississippi, June 30, 1960, Joanne Grant papers.

6. SNCC press release, April 2, 1964, Ella Baker papers.

7. "Allen's Army," *Newsweek,* February 24, 1964, Ella Baker papers.

8. *Washington Post,* July 26, 1964, Anne Marie Buitrago papers, author's possession.

9. Night letter to Oregon State Democratic Party from Ella Baker, July 2, 1964, Anne Marie Buitrago papers, author's possession.

10. Ella Baker, Speech to Governor's Convention, June 8, 1964, Anne Marie Buitrago papers, author's possession.

11. SNCC WATS report, October 5, 1964, Betty Garman Robinson papers, author's possession.

12. John Ditmer, *Local People: The Struggle for Civil Rights in Mississippi.* Urbana: University of Illinois Press, 1994, p. 292; also see Garrow, op. cit., pp. 347–348; Kenneth O'Reilly, *Racial Matters,* New York, The Free Press, 1989, p. 186.

13. FBI report, Communist Party, United States of America, Negro Question, Communist Influence In Racial Matters, FOIA, Ella Baker, author's possession, July, 1964, 67C. At issue was Rustin's proposal that a national committee be set up to orchestrate the demonstrations at the Atlantic City convention. Baker adamantly opposed the idea, saying that whatever took place at the convention should be controlled by the MFDP delegation.

14. Joanne Grant, Interview with Ella Baker, New York, 1966–1968.

15. *Washington Star,* August 23, 1964.

16. Grant, Interview with Ella Baker, op. cit.

17. Anne Romaine, Interview with Ella Baker, New York, March 25, 1967, Anne Marie Buitrago papers, author's possession.

18. Rowland Evans and Robert Novak, "Inside Report: Rebels without a Cause," *Washington Post,* August 25, 1964.

19. Nelson Lichtenstein, *The Most Dangerous Man in Detroit: Walter Reuther and the Fate of American Labor.* New York: Basic Books, 1995.

20. Ditmer, op. cit., pp. 295–297.

21. Speech by Robert Moses, National Guardian Dinner, fall 1964, author's possession.

22. Grant, Interview with Ella Baker, op. cit.

23. Robert Moses, op. cit.

24. Anne Braden, "The Southern Freedom Movement in Perspective," *Monthly Review,* 17(3):54, 1965.

Chapter 10
In Her Image

1. SNCC WATS report, 1965, Ella Baker papers.

2. SNCC Programs for 1965, February 23, 1965, Ella Baker papers.

3. Ibid.

4. Carson, op. cit., p. 160.

5. Minutes, SNCC Executive Committee, April 12–14, 1965, Holly Springs, Miss., author's possession.

6. Ibid.

7. Justice Department Activity in Dallas County, Ala., February 25, 1965, author's possession.

8. Garrow, op. cit., p. 268.

9. Joanne Grant, Interview with Ella Baker, New York, 1966–1968.

10. Ibid.

11. Joanne Grant, Transcript of Press Conference held at Delta Ministry, Greenville headquarters, February 1, 1966, *Black Protest: History, Documents, and Analyses 1619 to Present*. New York: Fawcett Premier, Ballantine, 1996, p. 502.

12. Ella Baker, "The Black Woman in the Civil Rights Struggle," Speech given at the Institute for the Black World, Atlanta, Ga., 1969, author's possession.

Chapter 11
Black Power's Gon' Get
Your Mama!

1. Carson, op. cit., p. 198.

2. *New York Times,* July 31, 1966.

3. Sermon, the Reverend Donald Harrington, Community Church, New York, 1966, Ella Baker papers.

4. Stokely Carmichael, "What We Want," *New York Review of Books,* September 22, 1966.

5. Summary of SNCC Central Committee Minutes for January–December 1967, p. 13.

6. Ibid.

7. Joanne Grant, Interview with Maggie Nolan Donovan, Boston, April 20, 1996.

8. SNCC statement, released May 24, 1967, author's possession.

9. Manning Marable, *Race, Reform, and Rebellion: Second Black Reconstruction in Black America, 1945–1990*. Jackson: University of Mississippi Press, 1984, p. 95.

10. H. Rap Brown, "Where SNCC Now Is," May 5, 1967, pp. 1–2, MLK Center, Box 6, series I.

11. Memorandum to All Federal Offices from J. Edgar Hoover, Director of FBI, August 21, 1967, Freedom Of Information Act, Ella Baker files, author's possession.

12. Memorandum to W. C. Sullivan from G. C. Moore, COINTELPRO, October 10, 1968, author's possession.

13. COINTELPRO, New York, 100–161140, FOIA, Clayborne Carson papers.

14. Freedom Of Information Act, FBI, New York, January 26, 1968, Ella Baker files, author's possession.

15. Joanne Grant, Interview with Ella Baker, New York, 1966–1968.

16. *Cavalier Daily,* University of Virginia, Ella Baker papers.

17. Memorandum to Herbert Callender from Ella Baker, March 18, 1970, Ella Baker papers.

18. Memorandum to Herbert Callender from Ella Baker, February 3, 1970, Ella Baker papers.

19. Letter to Charles Sherrod and report from Ella Baker, March 17, 1970, Ella Baker papers.

20. William H. Kunstler, "In Defense of Rap Brown," *Let Rap Rap,* SNCC, January 18, 1969, author's possession.

21. Joanne Grant, Telephone interview with Cora Weiss, New York, January 1997.

22. Advertisement, *New York Amsterdam News,* June 3, 1971, Jewell Gresham papers.

23. Joanne Grant, Interview with Jewell Gresham, April 1996.

24. Joanne Grant, Interview with Courtlandt Cox, Washington, D.C., June 13, 1993.

25. Letter to Ella Baker from Randolph Blackwell, December 9, 1978, Ella Baker papers.

26. *Fundi,* op. cit.

Epilogue

1. Ella Baker, "The Black Woman in the Civil Rights Struggle," Speech given at the Institute for the Black World, Atlanta, Ga., 1969, author's possession.

2. Wesley Brown and Arverna Adams, Interview with Ella Baker, New York, 1977.

3. Ella Baker, "The Black Woman in the Civil Rights Struggle," speech, op. cit.

4. *Fundi* outtakes. Author's possession.

5. Ibid.

6. Speech by Ella Baker to Hattiesburg, Mississippi, mass meeting, 1964, transcribed by Catherine Orr from the Smithsonian Institution Archives, author's possession.

7. Audiotape of funeral service, December 1986, author's possession.

Bibliography

Books, Articles, Theses

Anderson, Jervis. *Bayard Rustin: Troubles I've Seen.* New York: Harper-Collins, 1997.

Anderson, Terry. *The Movement and the Sixties.* New York: Oxford University Press, 1995.

Belfrage, Sally. *Freedom Summer.* Charlottesville: University Press of Virginia, 1990.

Braden, Anne. "The Southern Freedom Movement in Perspective," *Monthly Review* 17(3):1–92, 1965.

Branch, Taylor. *Parting the Waters: America in the King Years, 1954–1963.* New York: Simon & Schuster, 1988.

Brown, Earl. *Why Race Riots? Lessons from Detroit.* New York: Public Affairs Commission, 1943.

Cagin, Seth, and Philip Dray. *We Are Not Afraid: The Story of Goodman, Schwerner, and Chaney and the Civil Rights Campaign for Mississippi.* New York: MacMillan, 1988.

Cantarow, Ellen, with Susan Gushee O'Malley and Sharon Hartman Strom. *Moving the Mountain.* Old Westbury, N.Y.: The Feminist Press, 1980.

Carmichael, Stokely, and Charles V. Hamilton. *Black Power: The Politics of Liberation in America.* New York: Random House, 1967.

Carson, Clayborne. *In Struggle: SNCC and the Black Awakening of the 1960s.* Cambridge: Harvard University Press, 1981.

Curry, Constance. *Silver Rights.* Chapel Hill, N.C.: Algonquin Books, 1995.

Dittmer, John. *Local People: The Struggle for Civil Rights in Mississippi.* Urbana: University of Illinois Press, 1994.

Durr, Virginia Foster. *Outside the Magic Circle: The Autobiography of Virginia Foster Durr,* Hollinger F. Barnard, ed. Auburn: University of Alabama, 1985.

Fairclough, Adam. *Race and Democracy: The Civil Rights Struggle in Louisiana, 1915–1972.* Athens: University of Georgia Press, 1995.

————. *To Redeem the Soul of America: The Southern Christian Leadership Conference and Martin Luther King, Jr.* Athens: University of Georgia Press, 1987.

Fleming, D. F. *The Cold War and Its Origins, 1917–1915,* vol. 1. Garden City, N.Y.: Doubleday, 1961.

Forman, James. *The Making of Black Revolutionaries.* Washington, D.C.: Open Hand, 1985.

Garrow, David J. *Bearing the Cross: Martin Luther King, Jr. and the Southern Christian Leadership Conference.* New York: William Morrow, 1986.

Hamilton, Charles V. *Adam Clayton Powell, Jr.: The Political Biography of an American Dilemma.* Toronto: Macmillan, 1991.

Hill, Herbert. "Racism Within Organized Labor: A Report of Five Years of the AFL-CIO, 1955–1960." Speech delivered at annual meeting of the NAACP, 1960.

Holt, Len. *The Summer That Didn't End: The Story of the Mississippi Civil Rights Project 1964, and Its Challenge to America.* London: Heinemann, 1966.

Horne, Gerald. *Black and Red: W. E. B. Du Bois and the Afro-American Response to the Cold War.* Albany: State University of New York Press, 1986.

————. *Black Liberation/Red Scare: Ben Davis and the Communist Party.* Newark, Del.: University of Delaware, 1994.

Howlett, Charles. *Brookwood Labor College and the Struggle for Peace and Justice in America.* London: Edwin Mellon Press, 1974.

Hughes, Langston. *Fight for Freedom: The Story of the NAACP.* New York: W. W. Norton, 1962.

Hunter, Gary Jerome. *Don't Buy Where You Can't Work: Black Urban Boycott Movements during the Depression, 1929–1941.* Ann Arbor: University of Michigan Press, 1977.

Kelley, Robin D. G. *Race Rebels: Culture, Politics, and the Black Working Class.* New York: Free Press, 1994.

King, Mary. *Freedom Song: A Personal Story of the 1960s Civil Rights Movement*. New York: William Morrow, 1987.

Korstad, Robert, and Nelson Lichtenstein. "Opportunities Found and Lost: Labor, Radicals, and the Early Civil Rights Movement," *Journal of American History*, 75(3): 1988.

Lee, Alfred McClung, and Norman Daymond Humphry. *Race Riot*. New York: Wydan Press, 1943.

Lerner, Gerda. *Black Women in White America: A Documentary History*. New York: Pantheon, 1972.

Lewis, David L. *King: A Biography*. Urbana: University of Illinois Press, 1978.

————. *When Harlem Was in Vogue*. New York: Oxford University Press, 1979.

————. *W. E. B. Du Bois: Biography of a Race, 1868–1919*. New York: Holt, 1993.

Lichtenstein, Nelson. *Labor's War at Home*. Cambridge, Mass.: Cambridge University Press, 1982.

————. *The Most Dangerous Man in Detroit: Walter Reuther and the Fate of American Labor*. New York: Basic Books, 1995.

Mandela, Nelson. *Long Walk to Freedom*. Boston: Little, Brown, 1994.

Marable, Manning. *Race, Reform and Rebellion: The Second Reconstruction in Black America, 1945–1990*. Jackson: University of Mississippi Press, 1984.

Martin, Charles H. "The Civil Rights Congress and Southern Black Defendants," *Georgia Historical Quarterly*, 71(1):25–52, 1987.

McKay, Claude. *Home to Harlem*. New York: Cardinal, 1928.

Mills, Kay. *This Little Light of Mine: The Life of Fannie Lou Hamer*. New York: Penguin, 1993.

Murray, Pauli. *The Autobiography of a Black Activist, Feminist, Lawyer, Priest and Poet*. Knoxville: University of Tennessee, 1987.

Naison, Mark. *Communists in Harlem during the Depression*. Urbana: University of Illinois Press, 1983.

Nelson, Bruce. "Class, Race and Democracy in the CIO: The 'New' Labor History Meets the Wages of Whiteness," *International Review of Social History*, 41(3):351–374, 1996.

————. "Organized Labor and the Struggle for Black Equality in Mobile during World War II," *Journal of American History*, 80(3): 952–988, 1993.

O'Reilly, Kenneth. *Racial Matters: The FBI's Secret File on Black America, 1960–1972.* New York: Free Press, 1989.

Paige, Thomas F. *Twenty-Two Years of Freedom.* Norfolk, Va.: Thomas F. Paige, 1885.

Payne, Charles M. *I've Got the Light of Freedom: The Organizing Tradition and the Mississippi Freedom Struggle.* Berkeley: University of California Press, 1995.

Peplow, Michael. *George Schuyler.* Boston: Twayne Publishers, G. K. Hall, 1980.

Powledge, Fred. *Free At Last? The Civil Rights Movement and the People Who Made It.* New York: HarperCollins, 1991.

Rampersad, Arnold. *The Art and Imagination of W. E. B. Du Bois.* New York: Schocken Books, 1990, p. 246.

Robinson, Jo Ann Gibson. *The Montgomery Bus Boycott and the Woman Who Started It.* Knoxville: University of Tennessee Press, 1987.

Schuyler, George. "The Young Negro Cooperative League," *Crisis,* January 1932.

Sitkoff, Howard. *The Struggle for Black Equality.* New York: Hill & Wang, 1993.

Suggs, Henry Louis. *P. B. Young Newspaperman: Race, Politics, and Journalism in the New South.* Charlottesville: University Press of Virginia, 1988.

Sullivan, Patricia. *Days of Hope: Race and Democracy in the New Deal Era.* Chapel Hill: University of North Carolina Press, 1996.

Swerdlow, Amy. *Women Strike for Peace: Traditional Motherhood and Radical Politics in the 1960s.* Chicago: University of Chicago Press, 1993.

Watters, Pat. *Down to Now: Reflections on the Southern Civil Rights Movement.* New York: Random House, 1971.

Weisbrot, Robert. *Freedom Bound: A History of America's Civil Rights Movement.* New York: Norton, 1990.

Youngblood, Susan Bernice. Testing the Current: The Formative Years of Ella J. Baker's Development as an Organizational Leader in the Modern Civil Rights Movement. Master's thesis, University of Virginia, August 1989.

Zinn, Howard. *Albany: A Study of National Responsibility.* Atlanta, Ga.: Southern Regional Council, 1962.

———. *SNCC: The New Abolitionists.* Boston: Beacon Press, 1964.

Archival Sources

Author's papers
Ella Baker papers
Ella Baker FBI files
Library of Congress: NAACP papers
Martin Luther King papers, Mugar Library, Boston University
Martin Luther King Center: Martin Luther King papers, Southern Christian Leadership Conference papers, Student Nonviolent Coordinating Committee papers
National Archives, Washington, D.C.
Norfolk Collection, Norfolk Public Library, Norfolk, Va.
North Carolina Department of Archives and History, Raleigh, N.C.
Shaw University Archives, Raleigh, N.C.
Schomburg Center for Research in Black Culture, New York Public Library
Warren County Public Library, Warrenton, N.C.
Warren County Registrar of Deeds, Warrenton, N.C.

Interviews with Ella Baker

John Britton, Moorland-Spingarn Collection, Howard University, June 19, 1968
Wesley Brown and Arverna Adams, New York, October 1977
Clayborne Carson, New York, May 5, 1972
Rosemarie Harding, New York, 1976
Lenore Bredson Hogan, New York, March 4, 1979
Julius Scott, New York, May 1979
Sue Thrasher and Casey Hayden, New York, April 19, 1977
Eugene Walker, Durham, N.C., September 4, 1974

Interviews by Joanne Grant

Juanita Abernathy, Atlanta, Ga., April 20, 1994
Ella Baker, New York, 1966–1968
Anne Braden, telephone, March 12, 1997
Jacqueline Brockington, New York, May 23, 1995
Courtlandt Cox, Washington, D.C., June 13, 1993
Constance Curry, Atlanta, Ga., April 20, 1994

Dion Diamond, Washington, D.C., June 12, 1993
Ivanhoe Donaldson, Washington, D.C., June 13, 1993
Dr. John Fleming, Raleigh, N.C., June 30, 1992
Helen Gilchrist, Littleton, N.C., June 28, 1992
Lawrence Guyot, Washington, D.C., October 9, 1995
Casey Hayden, Jackson, Miss., June 26, 1994
Vincent Harding, Denver, Colo., 1996
Ludie Hicks, Littleton, N.C., June 28, 1992
Herbert Hill, New York, May 15, 1996
Bertha Hurst, Paterson, N.J., September 10, 1993
James and Esther Jackson, Brooklyn, N.Y., January 31, 1996
Janet Jamott (Moses), Cambridge, Mass., February 1980. *Fundi.*
Francis Johnson, New York, April 12, 1997
Mary King, Washington, D.C., June 12, 1993
Dorie Ladner, Jackson, Miss., June 26, 1994
Joyce Ladner, Washington, D.C., undated interview
Charles McDew, Charlottesville, Va., April 25, 1993
Robert Moses, New London, Conn., November 5, 1995
Estelle Noble, New York, April 12, 1997
Eleanor Holmes Norton, telephone, December 29, 1994
A. Philip Randolph, New York, undated interview
Judy Richardson, Washington, D.C., June 13, 1993
Annie Ross, Elams, N.C., June 28, 1992
Lee Simpson, New York, April 12, 1997
Percy Sutton, New York, telephone, February 21, 1996
Roberta Yancey, New York, 1994
Effie Yeargin, Raleigh, N.C., June 30, 1992
Andrew Young, Atlanta, Ga., April 21, 1994

Fundi: The Story of Ella Baker interviews
Audio recording of Ella Baker funeral service, Anthony Sloan

Index